Language planning and social change

Language planning and social change

ROBERT L. COOPER

Professor of Education and Sociology
The Hebrew University of Jerusalem

The right of the
University of Cambridge
to print and sell
all manner of books
was granted by
Henry VIII in 1534.
The University has printed
and published continuously
since 1584.

CAMBRIDGE UNIVERSITY PRESS

Cambridge

New York   Port Chester   Melbourne   Sydney

Published by the Press Syndicate of the University of Cambridge
The Pitt Building, Trumpington Street, Cambridge CB2 1RP
40 West 20th Street, New York, NY 10011, USA
10 Stamford Road, Oakleigh, Melbourne 3166, Australia

First published 1989

Printed in Great Britain at The Bath Press, Avon

British Library cataloguing in publication data
Cooper, Robert L.
Language planning and social change.
1. Language. Social aspects
I. Title
401′.9

Library of Congress cataloguing in publication data
Cooper, Robert Leon, 1931–
Language planning and social change / Robert L. Cooper.
p.   cm.
Bibliography.
Includes index.
ISBN 0-521-33359-8. – ISBN 0-521-33641-4 (pbk)
1. Language planning.   2. Social change.   I. Title.
P40.5.L.35C67   1989
306.4′49 – dc20   89-9694 CIP

ISBN 0 521 33359 8 hard covers
ISBN 0 521 33641 4 paperback

Contents

For Bill Blum

Preface

When I started to write this book, I had two principal aims. First, I hoped to present a general overview of language planning. I wanted to define the field, relate it to other fields, outline its scope, and offer generalizations which would relate language-planning goals, procedures, and outcomes to one another. Second, I hoped to relate language planning to public policy more generally and to social change. If these goals have been to some degree attained, it is because I was able to rely on the pioneering work of many scholars, in particular Jyotirindra Das Gupta, Charles A. Ferguson, Joshua A. Fishman, Einar Haugen, Björn Jernudd, Heinz Kloss, Jiří Neustupný, Clifford H. Prator, and Joan Rubin. My intellectual debt to them is great. Without their work, this book would not have been possible.

A writer's debts are not only intellectual. To Joshua Fishman I owe a great deal beyond the academic foundations which his work provides. In 1966, he hired me fresh from graduate school to work with him for two years on a major sociolinguistic project, funded by the U.S. Department of Health, Education, and Welfare, and ultimately published as *Bilingualism in the Barrio* (Fishman, Cooper, and Ma 1971). Later, in 1972, he invited me to join him in Jerusalem for two years on a Ford Foundation project, subsequently published as *The Spread of English* (Fishman, Cooper, and Conrad 1977). He introduced me to the sociology of language, language planning, and applied linguistics, and he brought me to Israel, where a two-year stay has lengthened to sixteen. His influence on me, personally and professionally, has been profound.

Another important influence has been Charles A. Ferguson, who hired me in 1968 (at Joshua Fishman's recommendation) to work with his team on the Ford Foundation's Language Survey of Ethiopia, ultimately published as *Language in Ethiopia* (Bender, Bowen, Cooper, and Ferguson 1976). Although our fieldwork lasted only a year, it taught me lessons upon which I still draw. He also sponsored my Social Science Research

Council postdoctoral fellowship in linguistics at Stanford University in 1970. I was fortunate to work with each of these men at the outset of my career, when their guidance and encouragement were especially influential. For their help then and for the stimulation which they continue to provide, I am grateful indeed.

It is a pleasure to acknowledge the assistance of Penny Carter, Numa P. P. Markee, Clifford Prator, Gerard K. Schuring, G. Richard Tucker, and Brian Weinstein, all of whom read the entire manuscript and offered detailed comments, criticisms, and suggestions for revision. I am also grateful for the suggestions offered by M. Lionel Bender, Susan Laemmle, and Peter H. Lowenberg, who read smaller sections of the manuscript. All saved me from errors, obscurities, and infelicities.

Most of this book was written during my sabbatical year and leave of absence from the Hebrew University of Jerusalem during the academic years 1985-1987. I am grateful to my departments, the School of Education and the Department of Sociology, for granting me those leaves. I am also grateful to the Program in Applied Linguistics at the University of California at Los Angeles, which hosted me at various times during this period and provided me ideal working conditions and warm collegiality.

I have revised parts of two of my previously published papers for use in chapter 4. These are Cooper (1979) and Cooper (1985).

Overview

It was September 12, 1974. An old man stood on the steps of his palace. "You can't be serious!" he protested to the soldiers accompanying him, when he saw the green Volkswagen which had been sent to fetch him. "I'm supposed to go like this?" But this was his only protest. The King of Kings, the Elect of God, the ruler of Ethiopia for more than fifty years bent forward and stepped into the back of the car. It took him to a small building where he was to spend the remaining months of his life under house arrest. On the way, he waved to his former subjects (Kapuscinski 1983: 162).

Along the route traversed by the green Volkswagen, an observer could see some arresting juxtapositions: barefoot youngsters leading sheep and goats past tall office buildings, homespun-clad arrivals from the countryside terrified by the traffic, and women carrying on their heads black clay jugs of water drawn from municipal spigots. These contrasts were a reminder of the empire's ongoing modernization and urbanization, changes which the emperor helped to introduce, which he tried to control, and which in the end overwhelmed him.

Haile Sillase's downfall marks the beginning not only of a fascinating story in the annals of language planning but also of a new act in the drama of social change in which the old man had been a significant player. One of the aims of this book is to demonstrate that an understanding of language planning demands an understanding of the social changes which promote it. This book, then, is about language planning and the changing social context in which it is embedded.

The first chapter presents four cases of language planning: the establishment of the Académie française, the revitalization of Hebrew in Palestine, the American feminist campaign for nonsexist language usage, and the Ethiopian mass literacy campaign which followed the emperor's house arrest. These four cases illustrate the broad range of goals to which language planning is directed and they also serve as a test of a definition of language

1

planning. An adequate definition should encompass them. Evaluating a definition without prior examples is a bit like trying to imagine how new clothes will look on you when you first see them on a shelf. Thus this book reverses the usual procedure whereby examples follow the definition, and the definition of language planning is reserved for chapter 2. The third chapter argues that descriptive frameworks can enhance our understanding of language planning, and the fourth chapter offers four such frameworks drawn from the study of the diffusion of innovation, marketing, power, and decision-making. The fifth through the seventh chapters deal respectively with the three major types of language planning: status planning, corpus planning, and acquisition planning. The eighth chapter discusses language planning in terms of various theories of social change, and the ninth chapter offers some concluding observations.

1

Four examples in search of a definition

This chapter provides four defining examples of language planning, found at different times, in different places, and addressed to different problems, both overt and covert. The selection of the four defining examples has undoubtedly been influenced by my own prejudices and personal interests. Nonetheless, these cases form a heterogeneous set which any satisfactory definition of language planning must encompass.

Founding the Académie française[1]

Inasmuch as the work of language academies offers a conspicuous instance of language planning, it is appropriate that one of my defining examples concerns the most eminent of the language academies, the Académie française.[2] The Académie française is not the oldest language academy in the world, nor is it the first to be founded even in France. But of the world's language academies it is the best known and the most consistently respected. Election to membership in this august body, limited to forty at any one time, has long been the supreme tribute to a French writer or scholar. Since its inception in 1634, most of the greatest French writers, with some egregious exceptions such as Molière, have been elected.

The founding of the Academy provides an excellent illustration of the principle that language planning cannot be understood without reference to its social context. When Armand-Jean du Plessis, Cardinal de Richelieu, came to power as first minister to Louis XIII in 1624, France was in danger of disintegration. The country was surrounded by the empires of two Habsburg sovereigns, cousins related to one another many times over through royal intermarriages, who between them dominated Europe. The Holy Roman Emperor ruled Austria and Hungary and controlled more loosely all the German states. His cousin ruled Spain, Portugal, the Netherlands, Franche-Compte, Milan, and the kingdom of the two Sicilies, as well as immense territories in the New World, and he dominated most

3

of Italy, including the papal states. Habsburg hegemony posed a formidable threat to the integrity of France.

But French integrity was threatened from within as well. A succession of religious civil wars in the second half of the sixteenth century had left a well-organized Protestant minority in control of 150 armed strongholds, virtually a state within a state, which challenged the authority of the king. Furthermore, the great nobles acted as satraps in their own territories, levying taxes, raising armies, carrying on private feuds, and intriguing against the king. France was riven not only by religious dissension and by an unruly nobility but also by peasant riots and revolts. Crushed by taxation and rising wheat and cereal prices, reduced to misery, peasants would arm themselves, march to the nearest town, and attack the government tax officers. Scarcely a year went by without an agrarian revolt which had to be forcibly repressed. "Laid waste, sunk from the rank of a continental power, reeling from plague to plague, from famine to famine, [France] was torn into factions . . . . Complete anarchy, confusion, and exhaustion prevailed everywhere" (Burckhardt 1940: 9–10).

To make matters even worse, the king was very young, chronically ill, moody, unhappy, withdrawn, incapable of sustained concentration on affairs of state, and susceptible to the influence of his mother, who was both pro-Spain and stupid. But Louis XIII was far more capable than his mother. He was intelligent, he was conscious of his royal authority, and he wanted to be a great king. Had there not been a brilliant and strong minister to guide him, France might well have been dismembered. But such a minister did arise and Louis had the acuity to realize that with Richelieu's help he could be great and his kingdom glorious.

For eighteen years, until his death in 1642, Richelieu, with the king's support, dominated France. He fought the Protestants and disarmed them. He subdued the great nobles. He united France under the absolute monarchy which he created. For the first time, royal authority extended throughout the realm. Once he had consolidated the king's power at home, he proceeded against France's adversaries abroad, "by diplomacy, by conspiracy, by bribes, by subsidies, and finally by outright war" (Auchincloss 1972: 11). At his death, Richelieu could rightly tell the king that everywhere, at home and abroad, the enemies of France were in full retreat. France became the arbiter of Europe, with Richelieu the architect of her greatness. He created the modern French state.

All his life, Richelieu battled against disorder, "dérèglement," the enemy not only of the state but of God as well. Richelieu believed that God had specially chosen Louis XIII to rule France and that God had chosen Richelieu to guide the king. Since disorder threatened the realm, disorder was the enemy of Richelieu, the king, and God. Disorder was heresy, order a superior moral end. In his struggle to impose order on an anarchic world, Richelieu used every resource at his command. He believed that acts which would be immoral if carried out by private persons for private ends, might be justified when carried out by the state for the benefit of the state. His security apparatus identified dissidents and he pursued them pitilessly. He manipulated state trials. He was prepared to see a few innocents condemned if by so doing he could preserve order. He exercised power relentlessly and ruthlessly. He believed that the state must be strong in order to restrain individuals from folly, from irrational behavior, from disorder.

In his obsession with order and in his view of the state as an instrument of power for the creation and maintenance of order, Richelieu was a product of his times. After eight religious and civil wars, there was a growing body of opinion in France that disorder was dangerous. During these wars, moreover, a number of people began to think of the state as "a distinct apparatus of power" (Elliott 1984: 43), which Richelieu believed should be used to defend the common good against selfish private interests. He shared with contemporary philosophers the belief in humanity's ability to apprehend what is consistent with natural reason. At the same time, he shared the contemporary pessimism about humanity's ability to act according to this knowledge. Thus people must be ruled so that they might not act in defiance of reason or contrary to God, the author of reason. Accordingly, both rationalism and faith justified state supervision of private behavior.

Just as Richelieu valued order in government, he valued order in art. He viewed art not as a peripheral activity but as an essential part of life. As such, art, like everything else, must be controlled, directed, and regulated by the state for the benefit of the state. Like his royal master, Richelieu was conscious that rulers and statesmen are often remembered more for the art that they commissioned than for the political and military victories that they won. While his lavish patronage of artists contributed to his own glory, he was convinced that his own glory was inseparable from that of the state. "Even when he bought a picture, he was doing it for France" (Auchincloss 1972: 204). He wanted the reign of Louis XIII to be comparable in artistic and literary brilliance to the great reigns of antiquity. Richelieu viewed a glorious art and literature not simply as the product and trappings of power but as an essential adjunct of power. The beauty, dignity, and magnificence of art could contribute to the might and grandeur of France.

But art could serve the state more directly by espousing themes which supported state policy. Painting Louis as Titus, with Richelieu in a toga at his side, portraying Richelieu in ecstasy, in communion with the spirit of monarchical France, depicting Louis with open arms offering asylum to oppressed Catalonia (Richelieu subsidized Catalonia's revolt against Philip IV), commemorating the great events of the reign, composing hymns of praise for the king and his first minister, and writing political discourses in support of the latter's foreign policy – artists and writers devoted themselves to the glorification of the regime and to the promotion of its policies.

Richelieu's patronage of the arts was more than a reflection of his taste for personal magnificence, his will to power and control, and his preoccupation with detail. He was a genuine enthusiast of all the arts. He loved music. He kept an eight-piece orchestra to play for him daily, even on military campaigns. He played the lute. He liked ballet. He was a discriminating collector of paintings and antique sculpture. He loved literature. He was a passionate collector of books. He wrote poetry and plays. His prose was outstanding for its clarity, elegance, and vigor. His collections, his commissions, as well as his own artistic productions reveal a highly sophisticated taste.

Although Richelieu interacted with artists of all kinds, it was with writers that he was on closest terms. He deliberately courted them as part of his campaign to influence public opinion in support of his policies. At one time he maintained as many as twenty-three writers. An artist with words, a skilled rhetorician, he had a keen appreciation for the power of language. Writers could be dangerous if arrayed against him. He intended to mobilize their support. His founding of the Académie française was one of his efforts to do so.

That Richelieu found it expedient to influence the world of letters and indeed found it possible to do so was the result of several developments. Perhaps the most important was the establishment of Paris as an aristocratic and cultural center. This was a relatively recent occurrence. The French court used to wander through the country from chateau to chateau. There was no single preeminent center of high culture. By and large, nobles remained on their estates. Similarly, writers and artists stayed in their own localities. All this began to change when Henri IV ascended the throne in the late sixteenth century. He made Paris his administrative center and the permanent home of his court, a policy continued by his son and successor Louis XIII. During both reigns, Paris enjoyed relative security and could thus function as a captial without interference. With the administration, the court, and royal patronage now centered in Paris, the feudal aristocracy began to leave their estates to live at or near the court. A scattered aristocracy was transformed into a single social world, "le monde." In the wake of the aristocracy came the artists and writers who served it or depended on it for patronage. The provinces were stripped of artistic and literary talent, which became concentrated in Paris. The court aristocracy and the artists and writers it attracted and supported, all together a social and artistic elite of a few thousand, produced the great high culture of seventeenth-century France. In this they were encouraged and supported by royal patronage and by the patronage of the kings' first ministers, particularly Richelieu.

The centralization of artistic and literary life in Paris, the relative security afforded by the capital, and patronage by king and court were probably necessary conditions for this flowering of artistic creativity. However, they are not sufficient to explain the direction and emphases of the art of this period, which must be understood if we are to comprehend the founding of the Académie française. Here four interrelated elements are of consequence.

First, the French elite, perhaps the best educated in Europe, had begun to be conditioned by classical authors and to become interested in matters of style. This was owing in part to a tradition of interest in intellectual attainments which began to be established among the aristocracy in the sixteenth century, the expansion of secondary education at the beginning of the seventeenth century, and the success of the Jesuits in employing humanist ideals and methods to satisfy the elite's demand for a superior education. The Jesuits emphasized the classic authors. They emphasized style. Students "would become accustomed to corporate discipline, steeped in the ideals and manners of Roman culture, conditioned to accept rule and regularity by the elaborate rules of their own community and the constant elevation of classical models . . . . They were trained to recognize good taste and harmony in their study of antiquity, and they learned that to innovate was to undermine . . . . They came out steeped in Latin, ready to become lawyers and diplomats, eager material for the expansion of the bureaucracy" (Treasure 1972: 242).

Second, the yearning for peace and the role of law and order, which had grown during the anarchy of the sixteenth century, made the clarity, restraint, discipline, and order of classical models appealing.

Third, French was beginning to be used for functions formerly served by Latin. The vernacularization of Europe has been so complete that it comes as something of a surprise to a modern person to learn how long Latin was used as the language of learning. Schoolchildren were not taught to read in French until the beginning of the seventeenth century. The first major work of scholarship written in French, Descartes' *Discourse de la Méthode*, did not appear until 1637. Richelieu was himself the first French theologian to write in French. It was he who established the conventions of theological exposition in French. And the first treaty to be written in French rather than Latin was as late as 1714 (the Treaty of Rastatt). To equip French for new functions, its vocabulary had to be enlarged and the additions standardized.

Fourth, a movement for the "purification" of French developed under the leadership of the court poet François de Malherbe (1555–1628). Coarse in his personal habits, he was devoted to what he conceived of as the purity of French, as can be seen from the following anecdote. On his deathbed, he chastised his nurse for an incorrect expression. Advised by his confessor to think henceforth only of his Savior, he replied that he intended "to uphold the purity of the French language till he died" (Boulenger 1963: 127).

The purification movement can be explained in part by the collision of the new classical sensibility with the efflorescence of French vocabulary. In the sixteenth century, French writers enlarged the literary vocabulary to meet the new demands being placed upon it. They borrowed from Greek and from Latin. But they also used local terms and idioms which reflected the writers' residence in the provinces. As a consequence, the literary language was "rich even to the point of incoherence" (Lough 1954: 244). With the elevation of classical authors as models, there arose an effort to prune this rich vocabulary of obscure terms, particularly archaic terms, terms from regional dialects, and technical terms. Malherbe wanted the literary language to be comprehensible to the common person, and indeed the reform he instituted did make the literary language comprehensible to a wider circle of readers.

But the purification movement also reflected an effort to establish "le monde," the narrow aristocratic society which had crystalized in Paris, as the supreme arbiter of language, a principle which began with Malherbe and which became accepted by the middle of the seventeenth century, although not without opposition. Good usage became defined as that of the elite, bad usage as that of the mass of the people. Accordingly, not only were obscure terms proscribed from the literary vocabulary but also terms which appeared coarse to refined taste, such as *vomir* (vomit) and *cracher* (spit), as well as terms considered indecent or capable of indecent associations. "For more than a century the language of the common people disappeared from all the higher forms of literature – from tragedy, and all serious types of poetry and prose – and the aristocratic, literary language ... reigned supreme" (Lough 1954: 246). Thus the elite from which France's rulers were drawn was able to invest its language with the aura of high culture and to clothe its authority in this language.

Finally, that characteristically French phenomenon, the *salon*, must be mentioned. Actually, in seventeenth-century France the term was not *salon* but *ruelle*, the space between the wall and the side of a bed, the space in which a lady's guests were seated. In those days, hostesses often sat or reclined on a day bed in their chamber when they received their guests. (There was then no separation of functions for the rooms of a house. The same room could be used for sleeping, dining, and receiving one's friends.) The most famous and influential *ruelle* of the day was that of the Hôtel de Rambouillet, presided over by Catherine de Vivonne, Marquise de Rambouillet (1588–1665).

The marquise, disgusted by the uncouth society at the court of Henri IV, left the court when her daughter Julie was born and retired to her townhouse, a few steps from the palace. Within a few years, the court was coming to her. From 1617 until at least 1648, she was at home to her friends every Thursday. Beautiful, cultivated, witty, and rich, she had a love of boisterous practical jokes, a gift for entertaining, and a talent for friendship. She attracted to her home a glittering crowd of aristocrats and the leading writers of the day. The Hôtel de Rambouillet brought amusing conversation into fashion. Its frequenters were expected to be witty and entertaining. Bravery and magnificence, the aristocratic ideals of the previous century, no longer sufficed to make a nobleman acceptable in this select society. He had to be able to amuse, charm, and please. If the Hôtel elevated conversation to an art, it also promoted among its *habitués* a taste for literature and an interest in matters of language and literary style.

"Poetry and letters were handed about like so many dainties," (Boulenger 1963: 117), authors read aloud their works to an audience that eagerly discussed them, and grammatical and lexical issues were among the more serious topics of conversation. Should *muscadin* (dandy, fop) be spelled and pronounced *muscardin*? Should the conjunction *car* be banned? The Hôtel, supporting the purification movement, encouraged an excision of the coarse, the vulgar, and the plebian from polite speech and from serious literature and elevated polish, clarity, refinement, and discrimination as literary and linguistic ideals.

Among the frequenters of the Hôtel de Rambouillet was Valentin Conrart (1603–1675). A rich man and an enthusiastic book collector, he bought himself an appointment as counsellor-secretary to the king in 1627 and entered literary society. By about 1629, a number of men interested in language and literature had begun to meet at his house on the rue des Vieilles-Etuves on Saturday mornings to enjoy one another's company and conversation. If one of them had written anything, as was often the case, he would read it aloud and the others would offer him their comments. But they were not so much a literary salon as a club. The professional writers among them were glad to meet their colleagues in an atmosphere which was free of the condescension they felt at the Hôtel de Rambouillet. And no doubt all were glad to meet in an atmosphere of masculine solidarity.

There were nine original members of this club, which kept its meetings secret. But its membership increased and it began to be known. One guest, invited to discuss his book, was so stimulated by the discussion that he told one of Richelieu's protégés, who in turn informed his master.

Richelieu saw an opportunity to transform this private club into an institution that could serve the state. He could not have been pleased by Conrart's remark that the Hôtel de Rambouillet was "a select court, less crowded and more refined than that at the Louvre" inasmuch as the existence of a cultural center that was independent of his control must have been intolerable to him (Maland 1970: 96). He could not appropriate the Hôtel de Rambouillet, of which he himself was one of the most brilliant guests, but he could take over Conrart's club. Accordingly, he wrote to the members inviting them to form themselves into an official body under state sponsorship. They greeted his invitation with dismay. Gone for good would be their privacy, their informality, their freedom. But the Cardinal could scarcely be refused. Reluctantly they accepted his offer.

After debating several names, including the Académie des beaux esprits and the Académie de l'éloquence, they agreed to call themselves the Académie française, to limit their membership to 27 (later expanded to 40), and to meet on Mondays, with Conrart as secretary. Their first session was held on March 13, 1634.

At first the Paris Parlement opposed the Academy, suspecting any new institution controlled by Richelieu. But in 1635, they registered its edict of incorporation, after having limited the Academy's authority to the French language and to those books written in French which were submitted to it for its judgment.

It is true that Richelieu had a political purpose in transforming an unofficial club into an official language academy. He wanted to mobilize writers in support of his policies. Consistent with this aim, he exercised tight control over the academy's membership. (A contemporary engraving shows Richelieu as the sun surrounded by the academicians as his satellites.) Thus the political writers among them wrote polemical tracts in support of his war with Spain (begun in 1635); the poets among them wrote odes in his praise and in praise of the king; and he was not above asking individual members to review his speeches and writings. But Richelieu kept such work to a minimum. He intended the Academy's principal function to be the regulation of the French language. He wanted the Academy not only to purify the language but also to equip it for all domains in which an imperial language can serve, including science and scholarship. Richelieu wanted French to replace Latin, as Latin had replaced Greek as a language of high culture and power. The regulatory aims of the Academy were set forth in Article 24 of its statutes, which asserted that its principal function would be "to give explicit rules to our language and to render it pure, eloquent, and capable of treating the arts and sciences." This article also set forth in a few words the work which was to occupy the Academy for the next 300 years: the production of a rhetoric, a grammar, a poetics, and a dictionary.

Work on the poetics and the rhetoric never began in any serious fashion. The work on the grammar, begun soon after the formation of the Academy, was soon abandoned, to be taken up only in the twentieth century, when a slim volume was published. Although work on the dictionary began almost at once, it did not appear until 1694. This first edition (there have been eight in all, the last appearing in the 1930s) had an indifferent success, in part because it left out so many words. True to the spirit of its founders, the Academy explicitly excluded the words scorned by polite society.

In sum, the founding of the Académie française is unintelligible without reference to its social context. It was a product of numerous confluent factors, the most important of which were the new classicism, the new functions being met by French, the centralization of aristocratic and literary life in Paris, the literary salon, weariness with disorder, and Cardinal Richelieu's dominating personality and obsession with order, discipline, regulation, and control. Samuel Johnson said that an academy of the English language would be "un-English." In contrast, the establishment of the Académie française was a quintessential expression of seventeenth-century France.

The promotion of Hebrew in Palestine

Although the ravages of the Roman-Judean wars substantially depleted the Jewish population of Palestine, and although there was a large-scale conversion to Christianity among the remaining Jews during the Byzantine period, a remnant of Jewry survived and lived continuously in Palestine until modern times. Their number was augmented by Jews from communities abroad who returned to Palestine because they sought asylum from wars or from persecution or because they wanted to study, pray, or be buried in what they viewed as their ancestral land, to which the daily prayers of their religion refer. Until the nineteenth century, however, immigration was small and sporadic, and reemigration, owing to poor economic conditions and to poor conditions of public health and personal security, was probably substantial (Bachi 1977: 77).

When local conditions improved somewhat in the mid-nineteenth century, Jewish immigration to Palestine became continuous, with perhaps 25,000 Jews immigrating between 1850 and 1880. This was a substantial number in comparison with the small size of the total population, which is thought to have been around a half-million in 1890. Of these about 40,000 are thought to have been Jews (Bachi 1977: 32, 77).

The developing Jewish population of mid-nineteenth-century Palestine was divided into several communities, each speaking its own language. Jews from Eastern Europe spoke Yiddish. Jews from Balkan countries and other parts of the Ottoman Empire spoke Judezmo or Arabic, and Jews from North Africa and Western Asia spoke Arabic, often a Jewish communal variety (Bachi 1977: 286). The only language which united them all was Hebrew.

Although Hebrew had been abandoned as a language of everyday communication in about the year 200 of the current era, it continued to be used as a written language, not only in prayer and as the medium of sacred texts, but also in the composition of legal, scientific, and philosophical texts. It began to be used as a medium for modern *belles lettres* in the eighteenth century. Until the nineteenth century a large proportion of the Jewish male population in most countries of the Diaspora could read and understand Hebrew, and many could write it as well (Rabin 1973: 42).

While it is true that between its abandonment and its revival as a vernacular it was used principally as a liturgical and literary language, it was occasionally spoken as a lingua franca by Jews who shared no other language. It appears to have been used by Jews in mid-nineteenth-century Palestine as a lingua franca, although in restricted contexts such as the market. It is possible, moreover, that in the Judezmo- and Arabic-speaking Jewish communities in Palestine a gradual transition to Hebrew as an all-purpose lingua franca was taking place (Rabin 1973: 70). Thus as Blanc (1968), Fellman (1973, 1974), Rabin (1973) and others have pointed out, the term Hebrew *revival* is a misnomer. Hebrew is no exception to the rule that once a language has passed out of all use whatsoever, it remains dead. The "revival" of Hebrew refers to its resuscitation as a vernacular, as a spoken language of everyday life.

The movement for the revival of Hebrew began in Palestine and in Eastern Europe in the 1880s, under the influence of European nationalist movements, which viewed the language of a people as inseparable from its nationality. Language served these movements as a symbol around which protoelites could create a nationalist self-consciousness and a respectable focus for nationalist aspirations. In the case of the Jews, there was already a clear sense of separateness from surrounding peoples. The promotion of Hebrew served not to create self-consciousness, which preceded the campaign, but rather to mobilize support for political self-determination. A common language symbolized the unity of those who spoke it (or the unity of the *descendants* of those who spoke it), expressed their uniqueness, highlighted the difference between them and those who ruled them via an alien tongue, and legitimized their self-assertion and their struggle for autonomy. The promotion of Hebrew was a tool in the struggle for social change.

As Rabin (1973: 69) has pointed out, the Hebrew revival movement differed from many of the language movements associated with European nationalism. Whereas many of the latter attempted to extend the range of a vernacular's functions to include those of high literate culture, the task of the Hebrew revival movement was to extend the range of a written language to include everyday, spoken functions. Whereas the peoples mobilized by European nationalist movements would often be united by a common vernacular, the Jews were divided by their vernaculars. But they could be unified through Hebrew.

A series of massacres and repressive measures in Russia following the assassination of Czar Alexander II (1881) started a wave of mass emigration of Jews, a small number of whom came to Palestine, which was then part of the Ottoman Empire. Many of those who came to Palestine in those years were young intellectuals, influenced by European ideas of nationalism and imbued with the desire for a life better and different from the one they had known in Russia.

The young idealists who started coming to Palestine in the 1880s welcomed the idea of using Hebrew as an all-purpose vernacular, an idea first promoted by Eliezer Ben Yehuda, a young Russian Jew who arrived in Palestine in 1881 and an indefatigable promoter of the Hebrew revival. To use the language of their ancestors in the land of its birth would symbolize the continuity of Jewish attachment to that land, an attachment which legitimized attempts to reestablish a national home there. Further, the new settlers' use of Hebrew would distinguish them from the traditional, "old-fashioned" Palestinian Jews, who avoided using Hebrew for secular purposes, a distinction which could legitimate the new settlers' claims for leadership in the struggle for independence.

Between 1881 and 1903, from twenty- to thirty-thousand Jews arrived in Palestine (Bachi 1977: 79). They were quick to adopt Ben Yehuda's idea of using Hebrew as the medium of instruction in the schools of the settlements they founded. A system of Hebrew schools was established, including kindergartens (from 1898) and high schools (from 1906). "Between 1900 and 1910 young couples began to enter into matrimony who had gone through the Hebrew school and whose Hebrew speech was fluent and natural. At that time were born the first children in families who spoke nothing but Hebrew in the home, and those babies grew up in Hebrew without anyone making a special effort to assure this. They were the first people, after a lapse of 1,700 years, who knew no language but Hebrew" (Rabin 1973: 73).

Ben Yehuda was the first person in modern times to speak Hebrew and only Hebrew at home and to bring up his children in Hebrew. But it was not his example which brought Hebrew into the homes of Palestinian Jews. Indeed, in 1901, 20 years after his arrival, only ten Jewish families in Jerusalem were using Hebrew at home (Rabin 1973: 70). There seems to be general agreement that what led to the use of Hebrew at home was its prior promotion as the language of instruction at school.

The idea of reviving Hebrew as the chief language of everyday life among the Jews of late nineteenth- and early twentieth-century Palestine was con-

sistent with their nationalist aspirations. Their ideological commitment
to Hebrew must have been strong, in view of the many difficulties which
they encountered when using it as a vernacular. The terms for everyday
items and activities were missing, requiring an extensive modernization
and elaboration of Hebrew vocabulary. Still, one can argue that the increasing linguistic heterogeneity of the growing Jewish population demanded
a lingua franca and that Hebrew was the "natural" medium for this purpose. It was "natural," at least with the benefit of hindsight, because
most Jewish men and many Jewish women of that time had had a religious
education which made them familiar with literary Hebrew. Any of the
other chief possibilities as lingua franca – Yiddish, Arabic, or Judezmo
– would have had to be learned by a substantial portion of the population.
In contrast, a larger number of Jews knew some Hebrew from the start.
And of course Hebrew did not have the communal associations attached
to Yiddish, Arabic, or Judezmo. Indeed, it symbolized the tradition common to all Jews. Where there was opposition to the use of Hebrew for
secular pupposes, it was found among "old-fashioned" ultra-orthodox persons of Eastern European background. Almost all of these spoke Yiddish
and thus had no need of a lingua franca with one another. If opponents
to Hebrew for secular purposes had been linguistically heterogeneous,
Yiddish would have been their probable choice of lingua franca because,
of the three communal languages, it was Yiddish that claimed the largest
number of speakers. As it was, the opponents to Hebrew were linguistically
homogeneous whereas those not opposed to Hebrew were linguistically
heterogeneous. So the field was left clear for Hebrew.

The idealistic young immigrants of the late nineteenth and early twentieth centuries laid the foundations of the modern Israeli state and ensured
the success of the Hebrew revival. The question can be asked, however,
whether the revival might not have occurred anyway had those immigrants
been less idealistic and less ideologically committed, given the practical
need for a lingua franca. If this is the case, then material incentives for
the revival of Hebrew may have been important even in those days of
nationalist fervor.

Androcentric generics and the feminine mystique[3]

When goddesses are born, they emerge fully formed: Aphrodite from the
sea, Athena from the brow of Zeus. Social movements have no such neat
beginnings. Their antecedents are many. They develop over time. The
modern feminist movement in the United States, which began to impinge
upon that nation's consciousness in the 1960s, is no exception. Its antecedents are many. It did not emerge fully-formed.

One can, of course, point to certain events which in retrospect seem seminal. Such an event was the publication in 1963 of Betty Friedan's *The Feminine Mystique*. Although it said nothing new, it presented a passionately and eloquently stated message. It evoked a tremendous response. Women who read the book were helped to understand that the anxieties, frustrations, despair, and rage which they felt about their personal situation were not a result of personal inadequacy but rather a result of socialization. Women had been taught that their greatest fulfillment lay in the enactment of their roles as wives and mothers, that therefore the appropriate arena for their talents lay in the home, and that this state of affairs was not the result of human arrangements which might be changed but rather that of immutable, biological characteristics. Thus they were taught and thus they taught their children. But if the lesson had been truly learned, Betty Friedan's book would have had little influence. Such was the fate of Mary Wollstonecraft's *A Vindication of the Rights of Woman*, which appeared in 1792. Commonly viewed as a milestone in the history of feminism, it made a sensation. But it was either condemned or ridiculed. Why was Friedan's book so enthusiastically received?

Friedan's book appeared at the right time, *after* substantial social change had already occurred. The mobilization of men into the armed forces during the Second World War plus the creation of new jobs, as the country rearmed, promoted the employment of women on a massive scale. Thus "Rosie the Riveter," the heroine of a popular song of the period, could take satisfaction not only in fulfilling a patriotic duty but also in succeeding in a job which had previously been the exclusive province of men, although the financial rewards and social stimulation that accompany work outside the home may well have been even more compelling motivations.

After the war, the female labor force declined as a percentage of the female population, not returning to its wartime peak until 1960, when about 35 percent of American women were employed outside the home. This statistic increased all through the 1960s and 1970s and indeed continued to rise in the 1980s, so that by 1984, more than half of all American women were working outside the home. Whereas fewer than 17 percent of all American *married* women were in the labor force in 1940, this statistic rose to 25 percent in 1950 and 32 percent in 1960. In 1963, the year Friedan's book appeared, it reached 35 percent. The percentage has continued to climb until in 1984 it reached 53.

When Friedan published her book, there had been no marked improvement in the ratio of women's to men's wages to match the increase in women's participation in the labor force. In 1949, the average female worker earned about 60 percent of the average male worker's salary (Sanborn 1964). By 1963, the year in which the *Feminine Mystique* appeared, the female-male wage ratio was substantially unchanged (U.S. Bureau of the Census 1974: 361).

Why was there so little protest at this state of affairs before the 1960s? Why did the feminist movement, which collapsed after women attained the right to vote in 1920, not revive in the 1940s or 1950s? According to William Chafe (1975), it was not until the 1960s that there were enough protestors with an alternative ideology who could mobilize opposition to traditional views. The traditional view, the feminine mystique, was that woman's primary responsibility and greatest fulfilment lay in her roles as wife and mother. Married women could justify their entry into the job market on the grounds that they were helping their husbands. Indeed, rising prices along with a desire for a higher standard of living frequently demanded two incomes. Once accustomed to the style of life which could be supported by two salaries, it was often difficult to revert to one.

So long as women considered motherhood and wifehood to be their primary roles, they could view their own participation in the workforce as supplementary to their husbands' efforts and their own careers as secondary to those of their husbands. But the massive entry of married women into the workforce began to change traditional role relationships between spouses. Women could claim greater control over family expenditures because they were now contributing to family income. Furthermore, their ability to work outside the home often depended upon their spouses' willingness to assume some domestic and child-care responsibilities. It was, perhaps, inevitable that the shift toward greater equality at home should ultimately lead to a demand for greater equality outside the home.

That this demand became audible and respectable in the 1960s and not regarded as the cry of a lunatic fringe was owing to the Afro-American civil-rights movement, which came to the fore in that decade. The demonstrations, sit-ins, lawsuits, voter-registration drives, and acts of civil disobedience which marked the campaign for full racial equality sparked a wider concern for the remediation of social ills which had long plagued the nation, including those of poverty and sexual discrimination. The protests of Black Americans and their drive for full civil rights led to the mobilization of groups which had formerly been passive. Furthermore, the civil-rights movement served as a model for the movement against the war in Vietnam, a movement which gathered momentum in the late 1960s. The tactics which had been so effective in awakening the nation's conscience with respect to its treatment of Blacks, were taken over by the anti-war protestors.

Women were active in both the civil-rights and the anti-war movements. But many of the young radical males involved in both movements held distinctly anti-feminist views. They expected women to make coffee and to operate mimeograph machines while the men devised grand strategy. When Ruby Robinson, a Black founding member of the Student Non-violent Coordinating Committee (SNCC), protested against the inferior position of women within the movement, in a paper addressed to an SNCC conference in 1964, her young male colleagues ridiculed her point of view (Carden 1974). Their attitude was succinctly expressed in Stokely Carmichael's notorious remark that "the only position of women in SNCC is prone." Just as the nineteenth-century feminist Susan B. Anthony, who began her career as temperance worker, was drawn to feminism by the arrogant response of men to her efforts, so were many modern women drawn to feminism by the anti-feminist stance they encountered in the radical movements of the 1960s.

Many women withdrew from these movements and formed their own "women's lib" groups. Their response demonstrates that it is mistaken to view the women's movement solely through the lens of economic determinism. True, equality in the workplace is a pressing concern. But the goal of the new feminism is broader than the attainment of equal access to employment and equal pay for equal work. Rather, the goal is no less than the liberation of women – and, by implication, men as well – from those socially imposed limitations which restrict their ability to realize their full potential as human beings. If the feminist movement's aims were fully realized, we would see a radical social transformation.

Since gender is a primary component of social identity and a fundamental basis around which social life is organized, the removal of sexual bias is a tall order indeed. Parents, teachers, authors of children's books, toy manufacturers, and writers for the mass media combine to display one set of expectations for boys and another for girls. These expectations encourage male assertiveness and female docility and promote one set of life goals for boys and another for girls. So pervasive are these different social expectations that they become part of the "grounds of everyday life." They are, in other words, taken for granted.

Inasmuch as verbal behavior serves as a primary medium for socialization, it is plausible that our use of language serves to create and reinforce sexual stereotypes. The use of the so-called androcentric generics is a case in point. Androcentric generics are masculine forms which refer to females as well as males. Alexander Pope's "Essay on Man", written in the eighteenth century, provides some fine examples. Consider the following:

> Know then thyself, presume not God to scan;
> The proper study of mankind is man . . .
> Whate'er the passion, knowledge, fame, or pelf,
> Not one will change his neighbor with himself.
> The learn'd is happy Nature to explore,
> The fool is happy that he knows no more;
> The rich is happy in the plenty given,
> The poor contents him with the care of Heaven.

See the blind beggar dance, the cripple sing
The sot a hero, lunatic a king;
The starving chemist in his golden views
Supremely blest, the poet in his Muse . . .
A wit's a feather, and a chief a rod;
An honest man's the noblest work of God.

Can anyone read this without conjuring up images of males? Does not the mind's eye see the chemist and the poet (as well as the sot, the beggar, and the cripple) as males? Do we not see the honest man as a male as well? This is, at any rate, a feminist argument.

But what is the harm in all this? Some feminists argue that such imagery reinforces the notion that males are the standard, the normal, the unmarked, whereas females are the exceptional, the abnormal, the marked. They argue that the terminological exclusion of half of humanity not only undermines the confidence of the excluded but also helps to determine their occupational expectations. According to this argument, terms such as *chairman*, *weatherman*, and *draftsman* suggest that these occupations are inherently masculine.

It is one thing to demonstrate that people tend to envisage males rather than both males and females when encountering androcentric generics. It is quite another to demonstrate that the use of androcentric generics contributes to sexual discrimination. If such generics had never existed, would discrimination be any the less? Might not these generics simply *reflect* existing sexism without necessarily reinforcing it? Be that as it may, the avoidance of sex bias in language became a target of feminist energy.

There were at least three possible motivations for the campaign against sex-bias in language. First, it is possible that some feminists believed that reducing bias in language would serve to reduce discrimination. If there were such believers in the strong form of the Whorfian hypothesis, i.e. that language structure influences nonverbal behavior, they acted to change language structure in order to influence social behavior. A more plausible motivation was that the campaign was a means of consciousness-raising. Calling attention to biased usage reminded both speaker and audience of the discrimination implied by the linguistic form. Finally, some persons may have been offended by sexist language forms in much the same way that racial and ethnic epithets are offensive.

But if such usage was offensive, it was not always so. Witness the following passage from *The Feminine Mystique* (299):

Scientists of human behavior have become increasingly interested in the basic human need to grow, man's will to be all that is in him to be . . . . This 'will to power,' 'self-assertion,' 'dominance,' or 'autonomy,' as it is variously called, does not imply aggression or competitive striving in the usual sense; it is the individual affirming his existence and his potentialities as a being in his own right; it is 'the courage to be an individual.' The premise is that man is happy, self-accepting, healthy, without guilt, only when he is fulfilling himself and becoming what he can be.

In this feminist passage asserting the value of autonomy, individualism, and the realization of each person's potential, androcentric generics abound. Feminists had to learn to object to such usage. But learn they did. Just as in the 1960s militant Blacks sought to substitute *Black* for *Negro*, militant feminists sought to substitute neutral forms for androcentric ones.

What did feminists do to reduce sexist usage, aside from interrupting speakers to suggest substitute terms? They wrote manuals showing us how to avoid such usage. For example, we were enjoined to write *doctors and their spouses* rather than *doctors and their wives*, to replace terms such as *mankind, manpower, to man*, and *chairman* with *humanity, personnel, to staff*, and *chairperson*, and to avoid the sex-indefinite *he* by pluralizing the referent (which requires *they*) or by repeating the referent instead of replacing it with a pronoun. They pressured the professional associations to which they belonged to adopt nonsexist usage in the associations' publication manuals. Journals published by the American Psychological Association, for example, will not consider a manuscript for publication if it violates the APA guidelines for the avoidance of sexist language.

How successful were these efforts? With respect to written usage, they were remarkably successful, according to a study I carried out, with the help of participants in the 1980 Linguistic Institute, at the University of New Mexico (Cooper 1984).[4] We analyzed a corpus of 525,000 words of running text sampled from selected American publications, including daily newspapers and mass-circulation magazines, for the odd-numbered years 1971–1979. This corpus displayed a dramatic decline in the rate of androcentric generics, which fell from 12.3 per 5,000 words in 1971 to 4.3 per 5,000 in 1979, with successive declines registered for each of the surveyed years in between.

The rate for each of the androcentric forms examined, *man, man* in compounds, and *he* and its inflected forms, also fell during this period. The largest decline was in the use of *man*, for which the 1979 rate was only 16 percent of the 1971 rate, and the smallest decline was in the use of *man* in compounds, for which the 1979 rate was 55 percent of the 1971 rate.

Why did the use of *man* in compounds show the smallest decline? This can be explained, perhaps, on the grounds that *man* enters into hundreds of compounds, which cannot all be replaced by the same form. For example, *fireman, fisherman, mailman, mankind, newsman, spokesman, weatherman*, and *workmanlike* can be replaced by *fire fighter, fisher, letter carrier,*

humankind, reporter, spokesperson, weather forecaster, and *skillful* respectively. Just as phonological change may spread gradually across a lexicon,
from morpheme to morpheme (Chen and Wang 1975), perhaps the declin-
ing use of *man* in compounds spreads from compound to compound as
each replacement is accepted as normative.

Another explanation for the smallest decline being found for the use
of *man* in compounds may be that it seems less incongruous to use this
form to refer to occupations or positions dominated by men – and these
represent many of the observed forms – than to use *man* and *he* to refer
to males and females equally.

Our data, of course, are limited to written, not spoken, language. Thus
we have no evidence as to the changes taking place in speech. Another
limitation concerns the representativeness of the corpus. While a variety
of mass-circulation publications was surveyed, no claim is made that the
sample represents all newspapers or all magazines. We cannot claim, therefore, that we would have obtained the same figures had we surveyed a
representative sample of all published mass media. But the sample was
large enough and diverse enough for us to be confident that the feminist
movement has had an observable impact on the written usage of publications addressed to a general audience.

While much feminist energy was invested in the campaign against sex-
biased language, the language-planning campaign was inaugurated as part
of a larger battle for women's liberation. How successful has this war
been? If labor statistics are an indication, the evidence is at best equivocal
(see, for example, Fuchs 1986; Mellor and Stamas 1982; Norwood 1985;
Reskin 1984; Rytina 1982a, 1982b; and the U.S. Bureau of the Census
1982: 386). One cannot claim that there has been *no* improvement in American women's position in the labor force relative to that of men in the
generation that has elapsed since the publication of *The Feminine Mystique.*
The female–male wage difference is smaller and the proportion of women
in the higher-paying occupations is growing. The changes have not been
dramatic, however. Perhaps one generation is insufficient for a more radical
social change.

Has the campaign for nonsexist language usage contributed to whatever
gains have been made? Or would the gains have been the same had no
such campaign been mounted? It is hard to know what criteria would
reflect the influence of the language campaign, as distinguished from other
activities of the women's liberation movement, on behaviors other than
linguistic ones. The women's movement shows us that social movements
have linguistic consequences, whether or not such consequences influence
nonlinguistic behavior. It has, in any event, proven easier to change written
usage than to change the practices and attitudes which subordinate women.
It is easier, in other words to write *chairperson* than to pay a chairwoman

as much as a chairman.[5] It would be pleasant to assert that the change in written usage is contributing to a changed climate of opinion and to pressure for behavioral change. In the absence of convincing evidence, however, such an assertion would reflect little more than a pious hope.

A mass literacy campaign[6]

Haile Sillase's deposition marked the formal accession to power of the Derg, as the Provisional Military Administrative Council was usually called. *Derg* means *committee* in Amharic, the language in which Haile Sillase had ruled, the language which he promoted, and the language in which his successors were to continue to rule and to promote. But in the early days of the revolution, one might have thought that the Emperor's policy of Amharicization had been overturned along with so much else. Within a few months more than 50,000 students were to be sent into the countryside on a rural development campaign, which included teaching the peasants, almost all of whom were illiterate, how to read and write. And instead of teaching them only via Amharic, which had been the policy of the imperial regime, the literacy workers were to use other major languages of the countryside as well. Peasants were to learn to read a language they could speak. What were the antecedents of this policy reversal and what were its consequences?

First the antecedents. At the time of the revolution, the population of Ethiopia was thought to be about 26 to 30 million. As in most sub-Saharan African countries, its population is extremely diverse linguistically. Ethiopians speak between 70 and 80 different indigenous languages, of which Amharic, Oromo, and Tigrinya are the most prominent. As in other African countries, its linguistic diversity is in part a product of imperial conquest, which brought together diverse ethnolinguistic groups within a single political administration. Unlike other African countries, however, its conquerors were not Europeans but Africans.

The Ethiopians who created the modern empire were the heirs of the Aksumite Empire, which reached its peak at about the fourth century C.E., when its emperor adopted Christianity. Located in the northern Ethiopian highlands, Aksum conducted an extensive trade in gum, ivory, incense, spices, and slaves, with markets in Alexandria, Suez, Cairo, Aden, Jiddah, Damascus, and Baghdad (Abir 1980). At its apogee, Aksum's territories extended from Southern Arabia, across the Red Sea, to the upper Nile. The language of this empire was Giiz, a Semitic language which is no longer spoken as a vernacular today, although it remains the language of liturgy and scripture for the Ethiopian Orthodox Church, as well as a medium for the composition of poetry. Giiz is related to the modern Ethio–Semitic languages spoken today, the most prominent of which are Amharic and Tigrinya, the mother tongues of the Amhara and the Tigré peoples respectively. (Tigrinya is not to be confused with Tigré, an Ethio–Semitic language spoken by Muslims in northern Eritrea.)

By the thirteenth century, the locus of imperial power in Ethiopia had moved southward to the Amhara, in the geographical heart of the Ethiopian plateau, although from time to time control passed further north to their cousins the Tigré, mostly Christian people of Tigray Province and Eritrea, who speak Tigrinya. Culturally similar, primarily Orthodox Christian (although there are some Muslims among them), the Amhara and Tigré regard each other as rivals, even though they stand together in viewing themselves as superior to other Ethiopian ethnolinguistic groups, most of whom became part of the empire during the late nineteenth century when the Emperor Minilik II, an Amhara from the southernmost part of the highlands, doubled the size of the empire, extending it to the south and to the east.

The largest of these conquered groups is the Oromo. Some Oromo are Muslim, some are Christian, while others maintain other traditional religious practices. Some are semi-nomadic pastoralists; others are settled agriculturalists. They are divided into numerous clans. But they are united by a single language, whose many dialects are mutually intelligible. Because no census has ever been carried out and because ethnic boundaries are permeable, no definite population figures are available, but the Oromo are thought by many authorities to be the largest single language group in Ethiopia, accounting for perhaps 40 percent of the population. Other authorities believe they are about equal in size to the Amhara, with each group making up about one third of the population. Many Oromos have become Amharicized by adopting the practices of the Ethiopian Orthodox Church, changing their names, and speaking Amharic as their principal language. Some of the great Oromo families are indistinguishable from the Amhara nobility, with whom they have intermarried for generations. Haile Sillase's empress, for example, was an Oromo princess, and he himself had Oromo forebears.

Before the revolution, Amharas, Tigrés, and Oromo worked together at the national level. But they were not on an equal footing. Most of the top positions in the army and in the government were occupied by Amhara and Tigré. Relatively few, in view of their number in the population at large, were held by Oromo, and fewer still by Muslims, who were, and still are, about as numerous as Christians in the empire as a whole. The same disparities were found in school attendance, with the largest share of the places going to Amhara and Tigré and with relatively few going to Oromo and to Muslims. While there were millions of poor Amhara and Tigré peasants, most of the political and financial elite were either Amhara or Tigré.

But even among the peasants, the Oromo had fewer rights than the Amhara and Tigré. Many Amhara and Tigré farmed land communally, with land use determined in part by rights claimed on the basis of inheritance and in part by skill in persuading others to recognize one's rights. Oromo, on the other hand, were often alienated from their land, which had been given either to Amhara soldiers, as a reward for military service, or to absentee Amhara grandees, as a means of insuring their loyalty to the regime. Thus many Oromo who had been independent farmers found themselves sharecroppers on what had been their own land. In the case of the Oromo, class conflict was superimposed on ethnic conflict, inasmuch as their landlords were often Amhara. In contrast, Amhara and Tigré, who live in regions which are relatively homogeneous ethnically, paid taxes to landlords from their own ethnic group.

That this state of affairs should have caused resentment among the Oromo is understandable. They were subject to a corrupt and inefficient administration, to the extent that the central authority exerted control at all, and the benefits they received, such as schools and health care, were relatively sparse. At the time of the revolution, Ethiopia was one of the poorest countries in Africa, itself the poorest of the world's inhabited continents. If the mass of the Amhara and Tigré received little, most Oromo received less.

While the immediate cause of the revolution appears to have been economic dissatisfaction among the small urban middle class and among the lower ranks of the military, brought on by rising oil and food prices on the one hand and the world-wide economic recession on the other, there seems to be little doubt that the basic cause of the revolution was the extreme inequality in the distribution of power and income among the country's ethnic groups. This inequality was enhanced by the exclusive promotion of Amharic during Haile Sillase's reign.

Amharic was the country's official language. It was the sole medium of initial primary-school instruction throughout the country, even in Eritrea in which, until its annexation in 1962, Tigrinya and Arabic had been used as mediums of instruction. Where demand for admission to the first grade exceeded the number of places available, schoolmasters sometimes reduced demand by requiring that entering scholars already know how to read and write Amharic. When such skills were acquired outside modern schools, they were typically acquired via attendance at traditional church schools, to which Muslim parents often refused to send their children. In any case, the requirement that initial schooling be conducted via Amharic made it more difficult for the non-Amhara majority to acquire a modern education.

Christian missionaries were turned into agents of Amharicization. Permitted to open and maintain schools only in non-Christian areas, missionaries were required to teach via Amharic. Since most Amhara are Christian, missionaries had to teach in non-Amhara areas and thus served as agents for the spread of Amharic. The only indigenous languages in which newspapers and books were published were Amharic and Tigrinya. Publication in other Ethiopian languages was proscribed. Missionaries who wanted to distribute bibles in Oromo had to smuggle them into the country. There was a token degree of radio broadcasting in other languages but the lion's share was in Amharic. Government courts of law were conducted in Amharic, even in non-Amhara areas, and even where both judges and litigants spoke a language other than Amharic as their first language.

The Amharicization policy could be justified on several grounds aside from the Amhara view of themselves as offering civilization to the benighted, whose languages, in any case, had no written tradition. With respect to education, it would have been difficult and expensive to train teachers to prepare materials in the many languages of the empire when there were inadequate resources for instruction even in the official language, Amharic. This would have been true even had there been no need to develop literary forms for unwritten languages. Furthermore, the promotion of a single lingua franca could serve as a distinctive, supra-ethnic, unifying factor. Indeed, Amharic is spoken only in Ethiopia, and its script, the indigenous Giiz syllabary, is also unique to Ethiopia. Furthermore, Amharic has a literary tradition. Finally, as the language of most of Ethiopia's rulers since the thirteenth century, it symbolizes a glorious imperial tradition. The problem was that for many, perhaps most, this imperial tradition remained an alien one.

Before the revolution, adult-literacy campaigns were conducted only in Amharic. While Amharic had spread as a second language throughout the towns of the empire and, from the towns, along the roads which joined them, it was probably spoken by no more than half the population as either a first or additional language. Thus the number of adults who could be reached by literacy campaigns was by necessity substantially limited. Of course, even limited to the Amharic-speaking population, literacy workers faced a gargantuan task.

Like the Emperor, the Derg saw the importance of language in social control. Shortly after taking power, the Derg announced a multilingual mass-literacy campaign. Why did the Derg announce the campaign when it did and why did it reverse the imperial language policy?

Answers to the two questions are related, and the basis of the relationship lies with the agents chosen to carry out the campaign: university and high-school students. After an abortive coup in 1960, which marked the beginning of the Emperor's slow collapse, university students emerged as the most vocal and consistent critics of the regime. This was so even though most would eventually work for the government, the major employer of university graduates, and become themselves objects of denunciation among the students who followed them. While there were many Amhara students in opposition – indeed Amhara formed the bulk of the student body – the most radical student leaders tended to be Oromo and Tigré. The persistent demands of the university students were three: land reform, representative government, and ethnic self-determination, by which was meant the right of ethnic groups, such as the Tigré in Eritrea, to govern themselves.

That language served as a symbol of ethnic distinctiveness among university students is clear. Towards the end of the 1960s, Tigréan university students refused to speak Amharic, which they viewed as a colonial language. Thus university-wide student gatherings had to be held in English, the medium of instruction.

When the civil disturbances leading to the Emperor's downfall began in early 1974, students were among the most active and vociferous demonstrators. But they were unable, either by themselves or in alliance with other civilian groups, to govern the country. The only institution with that power was the armed forces. Its representatives, mainly privates, non-commissioned officers, and junior officers, who claimed to speak in the Emperor's name, isolated him from his chief supporters one by one until he was utterly alone and powerless. While the students were not sorry to see the old man removed from power, they were appalled to see his power transferred to a military regime. As the Derg consolidated its power, students, along with other civilian groups, demanded a civilian government.

After the summer holiday, as students began returning for the new academic year, they spoke of mounting renewed demonstrations in support of a "people's democracy," i.e. a civilian regime. The Derg acted promptly. On September 6, nine days before the Emperor's deposition, the Derg closed the country's only university (then the Haile Sillase I University, later Addis Ababa University) and announced that all university students and all students in the last two years of high school were to suspend their studies and engage in rural development work for the next two years. The students were to teach reading and writing, organize the construction of schools and roads, and bring the message of the revolution to the peasants.

Students had, in fact, proposed such a campaign back in April. But now they were furious. What they had proposed in a surge of revolutionary fervor as a strictly voluntary affair was now an obligation. Furthermore, they viewed the campaign, with some justification, as a means of removing them from the political arena. In defiance, some tore up the campaign registration forms. The students' opposition collapsed when the Derg announced that students who did not participate in the campaign could not continue their studies in Ethiopia or abroad or obtain any employment whatsoever. With considerable reluctance they then agreed to participate.

Most observers agree that one of the campaign's primary aims was to give the new regime a respite, if only temporarily, from the vocal opposition of the students. Like that of the imperial regime which it replaced, the central government's control did not extend much beyond the towns, which held perhaps 10 percent of the country's population. Demonstrations and strikes in these urban centers could pose a serious threat. Indeed, civil disturbances had helped to topple the Emperor. It was therefore expedient to send the students into the countryside.

The Derg's motivation for assigning priority to an adult-literacy campaign and for encouraging literacy in languages other than Amharic must be a matter of conjecture. The Derg acted in secrecy. Not all of its members were known. Its composition changed as some members were recalled by their units, reassigned, or executed by their rivals. But some suggestions can be advanced.

First of all, if the rate of literacy could be increased, the regime would be better able to exert control over the population. While Lévi-Strauss (1969) may not have been entirely serious when he claimed that the primary function of literacy is the enslavement of the masses, the notion contains more than a kernel of truth. In any event, literacy could be extended to far more people if the Amharic-only restriction were dropped. Little account was taken of the fact that only in Amharic and Tigrinya were there reading materials – other languages having no written tradition. This would have been a serious bar to the attainment of functional mass literacy, which requires access to useful, everyday written materials if new readers are not to lapse back into illiteracy. They need things to read and they must read what they need. But at the time the campaign was announced, the Derg was operating in a crisis. There was little time for thoughtful analysis and careful preparation.

A more likely explanation for the Derg's commitment to mass literacy, and to the conveyance of literacy in the major languages of the countryside, is that such a proposal would appeal to the radical students, who had long supported ethnic separatism. Teaching literacy in languages other than Amharic was a gesture of support for ethnic self-determination, but a gesture which need not be accompanied by any real grant of power. Indeed, the Derg was unwilling to grant real self-determination, as it demonstrated, almost immediately after taking power, by its vigorous continuation of the war against the Eritrean rebels, who sought political independence, as well as by its later campaigns against other national movements which sought secession from Ethiopia. In fact, the Derg's first chairman, Lieutenant-General Amon Andom, an Eritrean who sought accommodation rather than confrontation with the Eritreans, was purged and killed in 1974 because of his resistance to continuing the imperial policy, which had been adopted by his colleagues in the Derg. ''Victory or death!'' they vowed.

Nevertheless it is likely that many in the Derg were in favor of some respectful gestures in the direction of ethnic sensitivities and thus the idea of teaching literacy in languages other than Amharic may have appealed to them. Observers disagree as to the extent of Oromo influence in the Derg. Some claim that Oromos dominated the Derg. Some claim that the mother of the Derg's dominant figure, Major (later Lieutenant-Colonel) Mengistu Haile Mariam is Oromo. Mengistu's origin, however, is disputed, although there is general agreement that on his mother's side at least he is not Amhara. Others claim that Oromo did not dominate the Derg, although their weight was much greater than it had been in the former central government. Whatever the truth with respect to Oromo influence, Oromos were the major beneficiaries of the revolution, whereas, as a result of the Derg's implementation of land reform, the Amhara–Tigré elite were the major losers.

The Derg's proclamation of land reform on March 4, 1975, a few months after the first students were sent out into the countryside, swung the students, or at least the more radical of them, from resentful participation to enthusiastic promotion, and it changed completely the direction of the campaign. Peasants were given the right to farm the land they were presently working, up to a limit of 10 hectares (about 25 acres). No farmer could have a tenant or employ a worker. Thus onerous rents were removed and farmers' incomes rose. Since a greater percentage of Oromo farmers had been tenants than had Amahara or Tigré farmers, the former benefited more. And, of course, the power held by the great Amhara and Tigré landholders was destroyed along with its economic base. The Derg's proclamation was the first step in dismantling the feudal land-tenure system, a primary demand of generations of students.

Between the inauguration of the literacy campaign on December 21, 1974 and the announcement of land reform, the students had in fact done little. Inasmuch as the campaign was announced only in September, there had scarcely been time to organize it, to say nothing of preparing materials. Now the students were charged with organizing the peasants into rural associations and engaged themselves in this wholeheartedly. Largely owing to their efforts, thousands of associations were registered. The Ministry of Land Reform announced that, by the end of the summer of 1976, about 18,000 associations, with a total membership of about 4.5 million, had been launched.

In spite of their initial enthusiasm for land reform, most students soon became disenchanted with the new regime and often tried to set the peasants against the government. The students wanted to establish communes, and they wanted the peasants to have a democratic voice in the central government. In their enthusiasm, students caused dissension and unrest in the countryside. They fomented pitched battles between peasants and landlords and sometimes between peasants and local police. The government began to withdraw students from the countryside. Other students, politically disillusioned, fled to Kenya or Sudan. Others simply left the campaign because of hard living conditions in the rural camps. By early 1976, little more than one year after the campaign began, the number of students who had been sent into the countryside, more than 50,000, had dwindled to 18,000. Nonetheless, without the students' help, the peasant associations would not have been set up so readily nor would the peasants have become so radicalized.

Needless to say, amidst this revolutionary fervor, the literacy campaign received short shrift. While the new regime continued to pay lip service to the equality of the country's ethnic groups and religions, and while it made some cosmetic changes such as recognizing Muslim holidays, increasing radio broadcast time in Oromo, and permitting publication in Oromo, and while the Ministry of Education briefly considered the possibility of using local languages as the vehicle of instruction in elementary school, the Emperor's policy of Amharicization has essentially been continued. While the rhetoric of the state's rulers has changed, the state's problems have remained. Or rather they have been exacerbated. The tendency towards fragmentation, normally found after the demise of an old regime, is found today. Not only were the new rulers faced with the old problem of separatist rebellions by Tigrés in Eritrea and Somalis in the Ogaden, but they were soon faced with new rebellions among Tigrés in Tigray Province and Afars in the Danakil and by the rekindling of Oromo rebelliousness in Balé Province. While the new and rekindled revolts were led by former landowners who exploited ethnicity in order to mobilize resistance to the new regime, it is possible that the greater tolerance shown to ethnic languages had increased ethnic self-consciousness.

The regime's ultimate adherence to a policy of Amharicization is consistent with its denial of ethnic self-determination and with its attempt to exert central control over the multilingual empire created by its predecessors. In spite of the substantial changes which have swept over Ethiopia – particularly land reform and the radicalization of peasants – much remains the same. If Haile Sillase could view the present scene, he could, perhaps, be forgiven an ironic smile.

2

Definitions: a baker's dozen

If the establishment of the Académie française, the promotion of Hebrew in Palestine, the American feminist movement's campaign against sex-bias in language, and the Ethiopian mass literacy campaign exemplify language planning, then language planning is directed toward a variety of ends and encompasses a variety of means. What characteristics do these examples, and by extension all instances of language planning, share? There is no single, universally accepted definition of language planning. Indeed, there is even disagreement as to what term should be used to denote the activity.

Language planning is not the first term to appear in the literature. Perhaps the first term to appear in the literature was *language engineering* (Miller 1950). This has been used far more often than *glottopolitics* (Hall 1951), *language development* (Noss 1967), or *language regulation* (Gorman 1973). *Language policy* sometimes appears as a synonym for *language planning* but more often it refers to the goals of language planning. Jernudd and Neustupný (1986) have proposed the term *language management* but it is too soon to know if this will catch on. Of all the terms in use today, *language planning* is the most popular. It is found in the titles of a newsletter (*Language Planning Newsletter*), a journal (*Language Problems and Language Planning*), at least five collections of articles (Rubin and Jernudd 1971a; Rubin and Shuy 1973; Fishman 1974a; Rubin, Jernudd, Das Gupta, Fishman, and Ferguson 1977; and Cobarrubias and Fishman 1983), and a major bibliography on the topic (Rubin and Jernudd 1977).

Haugen (1965: 188) tells us that Uriel Weinreich used the term *language planning* for a 1957 seminar at Columbia University, but it was Haugen himself (1959) who introduced the term to the literature. In that article he defined language planning as "the activity of preparing a normative orthography, grammar, and dictionary for the guidance of writers and speakers in a non-homogeneous speech community" (8). He later came to view these activities as *outcomes* of language planning, a part of the implementation of decisions made by language planners, rather than language planning as a whole (Haugen 1966: 52).

Here are twelve definitions of language planning which appeared after the publication of Haugen's 1959 article:

1. "As I define it, the term LP includes the normative work of language academies and committees, all forms of what is commonly known as language cultivation (Ger. *Sprachpflege*, Dan. *sprogrøgt*, Swed. *språkvård*), and all proposals for language reform or standardization" (Haugen 1969: 701).

2. "[Language planning] occurs when one tries to apply the amalgamated knowledge of language to change the language behavior of a group of people" (Thorburn 1971: 254).

3. "Language planning is *deliberate* language change; that is, changes in the systems of language code or speaking or both that are planned by organizations that are established for such purposes or given a mandate to fulfill such purposes. As such, language planning is focused on problem-solving and is characterized by the formulation and evaluation of alternatives for solving language problems to find the best (or optimal, most efficient) decision" (Rubin and Jernudd 1971b: xvi).

4. "We do not define planning as an idealistic and exclusively linguistic activity but as a political and administrative activity for solving language problems in society" (Jernudd and Das Gupta 1971: 211).

5. "The term language planning is most appropriately used in my view to refer to coordinated measures taken to select, codify and, in some cases, to elaborate orthographic, grammatical, lexical, or semantic features of a language and to disseminate the corpus agreed upon" (Gorman 1973: 73).

6. "Language planning refers to a set of deliberate activities systematically designed to organize and develop the language resources of the community in an ordered schedule of time" (Das Gupta 1973: 157).

7. "The term *language planning* refers to the organized pursuit of solutions to language problems, typically at the national level" (Fishman 1974b: 79).

8. "Language planning is the methodical activity of regulating and improving existing languages or creating new common regional, national or international languages" (Tauli 1974: 56).

9. "The [language planning] terms reviewed refer to an activity which *attempts* to solve a language problem, usually on a national scale, and which focuses on either language form or language use or both" (Karam 1974: 105).

10. "[Language planning may be defined as] a government authorised,

long term sustained and conscious effort to alter a language itself
or to change a language's functions in a society for the purpose of
solving communication problems" (Weinstein 1980: 55).

11. Language planning refers to systematic, theory-based, rational, and
organized societal attention to language problems (restatement of
Neustupný 1983: 2).

12. "Language policy-making involves decisions concerning the teaching and use of language, and their careful formulation by those empowered to do so, for the guidance of others" (Prator cited by Markee
1986: 8).

We can discuss these definitions according to their treatment of each
of the underlined terms in the following question: Who plans what for
whom and how?

Who

Some definitions restrict language planning to activities undertaken by
governments, government-authorized agencies, or other authoritative
bodies, i.e., organizations with a public mandate for language regulation
(definitions 3, 4, 10, 12). Such definitions would exclude the activities
undertaken on behalf of nonsexist usage (at least *before* government agencies took up this cause), which appears to have emerged more or less
spontaneously at a grass-roots level. They would also exclude the language-
planning efforts of individuals such as Ben Yehuda in Palestine (Fellman
1974), Samuel Johnson in England (Bate 1975, Sledd and Kolb 1955),
and those enumerated by Haugen (1966: 58): Aasen in Norway, Korais
in Greece, Štur in Slovakia, Mistral in Provence, Dobrovsky in Bohemia,
Aavik in Estonia, and Jablonskis in Lithuania. It would seem, therefore,
that to restrict language planning to the work of authoritative institutions
is to be too restrictive.

What

On what do language planners focus their attention? Thorburn's definition
(2) states the focus quite generally, as "language behavior." The other
definitions are more specific, however. These mention or imply one or
both of the two language-planning foci distinguished by Kloss (1969),
corpus planning and *status planning*.

Corpus planning

Corpus planning refers to activities such as coining new terms, reforming
spelling, and adopting a new script. It refers, in short, to the creation
of new forms, the modification of old ones, or the selection from alternative
forms in a spoken or written code. The language cultivation, reform, and
standardization mentioned in Haugen's definition (1) and the selection,

codification, and elaboration of linguistic features, specified in Gorman's (5) represent instances of corpus planning. Two of the defining examples presented in Chapter 1 exemplify corpus planning: the establishment of the Académie française and the feminist campaign against sexist usage.

Status planning

In line with his interest in the language rights of minorities, Kloss viewed the object of status planning to be recognition by a national government of the importance or position of one language in relation to others. However, the term has since been extended to refer to the allocation of languages or language varieties to given functions, e.g. medium of instruction, official language, vehicle of mass communication. Gorman (1973: 73) defines language allocation as "authoritative decisions to maintain, extend, or restrict the range of uses (functional range) of a language in particular settings." Thus the promotion of Hebrew as the language of instruction in Palestine and the decision to use various languages in addition to Amharic as media for initial literacy in the Ethiopian mass literacy campaign are examples of language allocation, and many would call them examples of status planning.

Rubin (1983: 340), however, suggests that while the allocation of language use among a set of languages or language varieties is related to the relative importance of the language varieties involved, "it is misleading and awkward to include all cases of language allocation under the term 'status planning'; rather, status planning should be put under language allocation." She is quite right if the term status planning is to refer to its original referent, language importance. But the extension of Kloss' term to allocation of use now seems quite well established. Ferguson (1983: 35), for example, writes, in connection with types of language planning: "You can plan changes in the functions or the use of different varieties within the speech community, and you can plan changes in the structure of the language or language variety itself. These are, of course, the familiar categories of language planners that have been mentioned in this volume [Cobarrubias and Fishman 1983], essentially what we call 'status planning' and 'corpus planning', or other similar names."

Thus in our definitions we see references to "changes in the systems of ... speaking" (3), changes in a language's functions (10), "language use" (9), "use of language" (12), and organization of a community's language resources (6), all of which imply or refer to what Gorman (1973) and Rubin (1983) call language allocation but which I, following the more general usage, refer to as status planning.

As Fishman (1983: 382) has pointed out, the distinction between corpus planning and status planning is clearer in theory than in practice. Three of our defining cases, the promotion of Hebrew in Palestine, the Ethiopian mass literacy campaign, and the establishment of the Académie française, exemplify the interdependence between corpus and status planning. The decision to use Hebrew as a medium of instruction required extensive elaboration of Hebrew vocabulary in order to provide terms for modern school subjects. The decision to use hitherto unwritten Ethiopian languages as media for initial literacy, a status planning decision, required decisions as to what script would be used to represent the unwritten languages, what spelling conventions would be employed, and, in cases of variability in vocabulary or grammar, what forms would be chosen, all corpus planning decisions. Richelieu's decision to found an official language academy, while an effort to regulate the forms of the French language – corpus planning – may also be viewed as an effort to promote the use of French for functions which hitherto had been occupied by Latin, an instance of status planning. Additional illustrations of the relationship between status and corpus planning will be seen in subsequent chapters.

Acquisition planning

Prator's definition (12), which mentions *language teaching* as an object of policy making, suggests a third focus of language planning, namely *acquisition planning*. This additional category seems to me useful for at least two reasons. First, considerable planning is directed toward *language spread*, i.e. an increase in the users or the uses of a language or language variety, but not all planning for language spread can be subsumed under the rubric of status planning. When planning is directed towards increasing a language's uses, it falls within the rubric of status planning. But when it is directed toward increasing the number of users – speakers, writers, listeners, or readers – then a separate analytic category for the focus of language planning seems to me to be justified.

Second, the changes in function and form sought by status and corpus planning affect, and are affected by, the number of a language's users. New users may be attracted by the new uses to which a language is put. For example, when a language begins to spread as a lingua franca, like Hebrew in Palestine and Kiswahili in East Africa, it becomes more useful and thus attracts even more speakers. New users may influence the language through language contact, just as the structure of modern Hebrew and Kiswahili have been influenced by their large number of nonnative speakers. And new users may introduce new uses, as in the cases of Hebrew and Kiswahili which are now employed for all functions of a modern state. Since function, form, and acquisition are related to one another, planners of any one should consider the others.

Thus a third focus, *acquisition planning*, needs to be added to the status planning – corpus planning distinction. There is, however, reluctance on

the part of some observers to view language acquisition as an object of
language planning, stemming, perhaps, from a desire to distinguish language planning from applied linguistics, of which language teaching is
a primary concern. In fact it is doubtful, as I argue below, that language
planning can be distinguished entirely from applied linguistics.

Language planning as problem-solving

Five of the twelve definitions are framed in terms of efforts to solve language
or communication problems (3, 4, 7, 9, 11). Haugen (1966: 52) states
the view implied by such definitions when he writes that "LP is called
for wherever there are language problems. If a linguistic situation for any
reason is felt to be unsatisfactory, there is room for a program of LP."
While it is true that language planning is directed to the solution of language
problems, we must distinguish between ostensible and actual, overt and
covert goals. In all four of our defining examples, we see that modifications
in language or in the use of language were sought in order to attain nonlinguistic ends. In each case, efforts to modify language structure or language use constituted one battle in a war. The Ethiopian mass-literacy
campaign, with its use of vernacular languages, was intended to pacify
the students and to remove them from the political arena. The campaign
against sexist language usage was waged in the war for the attainment
or the improvement of women's rights. The promotion of Hebrew as an
all-purpose vernacular was part of a nationalist battle for an autonomous
Jewish homeland. And the establishment of the French Academy promoted
the power of the ruling elite by mobilizing writers and scholars in support
of the regime and by imparting to the language of the elite an aroma
of sanctity: legitimizing its language helped to legitimize its rule. It is
not surprising that after the French Revolution the Academy was sup-
pressed (temporarily as it turned out) as a creature of the *ancien régime*.
The revolutionaries recognized the Academy's covert goals.

   None of this denies the existence of communicative problems. We have
also seen these in our defining examples: the inaccessibility of the literary
language, accompanied by the instability of literary and technical terms,
in seventeenth-century France; the Jews' need for an intercommunal lingua
franca and medium of instruction in nineteenth-century Palestine; the
interpretation of English generic terms as masculine; and mass illiteracy
in Ethiopia. But if the solution to these overt communicative problems
had not promoted the attainment of nonlinguistic goals, it is doubtful
that the language-planning activities described in the first chapter would
have been undertaken. Indeed, it is hard to think of an instance in which
language planning has been carried out solely for the sake of improving
communication, where problems of communication are the only problems

to be solved, or where the facilitation of communication is the only interest to be promoted. Language planning is typically carried out for the attainment of nonlinguistic ends such as consumer protection, scientific exchange, national integration, political control, economic development, the creation of new elites or the maintenance of old ones, the pacification or cooption of minority groups, and mass mobilization of national or political movements. In any war, one uses all the ammunition at hand. If the modification of a language, or its use, or the promotion of its acquisition is perceived as ammunition, such ammunition is likely to be fired.

I agree with Karam (1974: 108) that "regardless of the type of language planning, in nearly all cases the language problem to be solved is not a problem in isolation within the region or nation but is directly associated with the political, economic, scientific, social, cultural, and/or religious situation." But I would go further and assert that the latter considerations – political, economic, scientific, etc. – serve as the primary motivation for language planning. Thus those definitions which are framed in terms of the solution of *language* or communication problems obscure a fundamental point about language planning, namely that it is typically, perhaps always, directed ultimately towards nonlinguistic ends. Definitions of language planning as the solution of language problems are not wrong, but they are misleading. They deflect attention from the underlying motivation for language planning. Inasmuch as language planning is directed ultimately toward the attainment of nonlinguistic ends, it is preferable, in my opinion, to define language planning not as efforts to solve language problems but rather as efforts to influence language behavior.

For whom

Some of the definitions above do not refer at all to the people whose behavior is to be influenced (1, 3, 5, 12). Thorburn's definition (2) refers only to "a group of people." Although the article from which this definition is drawn restricts its discussion to language planning at the national level, he implies that language planning occurs at lower levels as well. Tauli's definition (8) refers to "new common regional, national, and international languages," and other definitions refer to community (6), society (4, 10, 11), and nation (7, 9). Thus all but one of the definitions which mention the targets of planning (the exception being Thorburn's) indicate or imply that language planning is typically carried out for large aggregates.

It seems to me to be a mistake to confine a definition of language planning to aggregates at the national level or to the societal level if *nation* or *society* is understood as synonymous with *nation-state*. Such a restriction would exclude activities which are international in scope, such as the Roman Catholic Church's effort to substitute local languages for Latin in the mass, efforts on behalf of international auxiliary languages such as Esperanto, and standardization of terminology by international organizations which regulate trade or which promote scholarship. Such a restriction would also exclude activities undertaken by and on behalf of groups which are not politically autonomous, such as the promotion of Hebrew in nineteenth-century Palestine, the modernization of liturgical texts by various Christian denominations in the United States, and the modernization and graphization of languages spoken by minorities within a state, as, for example, efforts undertaken by missionaries on behalf of various unwritten languages.

Language planning, in my view, is directed not only towards aggregates at the level of the society or state and not only at larger aggregates which cut across national boundaries but also at smaller aggregates – ethnic, religious, occupational, and so on. But how small can such aggregates be, and still be the objects of language planning? Must we confine the object of our definition to groups so large that their members cannot interact with all other members of the group but only with a subset of the members? If we confine language planning to such "open networks" we would have to exclude small groups such as schools, classrooms, neighborhood and village associations, trade union branches, "women's lib" consciousness-raising circles, local professional and occupational organizations, religious congregations, and branches of fraternal associations. But the communicative behavior of such small groups is often the object of explicit attention.

My synagogue in Jerusalem provides one such example. The congregation consists of about 100 families, about equally divided between immigrants, mainly from the United States, and native-born Israelis. Virtually all the native-born Israeli adults can readily understand spoken English. In contrast, some of the immigrants, particularly the older ones, have difficulty understanding Hebrew. The latter complain that they cannot follow the commentary on the weekly portion of the Torah, delivered every Sabbath morning by a different member of the congregation, and the announcements, made by the congregation's president, at the conclusion of the Sabbath morning services.

When the congregation was younger, some of the older immigrants asked that the commentary and announcements be delivered in English instead of Hebrew. From the point of view of communicative efficiency, their request was reasonable. More of the congregation would have understood a version in English than in Hebrew.

But there were other considerations. Most members were eager to establish the synagogue as an *Israeli* congregation, not as an expatriate American one. Thus they did not want to follow the expatriate tradition of using languages other than Hebrew for the commentary and announcements.

Furthermore, they wanted to develop an indigenous Israeli service which would be at the same time faithful to traditional Jewish forms. The Congregation's name, *Mevakshei Derech* or Seekers of the Way, reflects this desire. Hebrew, as the principal daily language of the Jewish population in Israel, the unquestioned language of its public discourse, is at once the bearer of Jewish religious tradition and the symbol par excellence of the Israeli state. Thus Hebrew symbolizes both tradition and change. English, in contrast, is a reminder both of the secular and of the Diaspora. Delivering the commentary and announcements in English would be inconsistent with the congregation's desire to develop as an Israeli institution and to attract native-born Israelis to it.

Thus the congregation early established the policy that the commentary and announcements would be delivered in Hebrew. As a result, the announcements are repeated in English, to accommodate those whose Hebrew comprehension is poor. At the conclusion of the services, after the congregation has left the prayer hall, an English summary of the commentary is delivered to those who request it. Should a commentator forget to prepare a summary in English, or should the president neglect to translate the announcements in Hebrew, some of the older Anglophone members are sure to complain.

Does my congregation's explicit decision differ in anything but scope from, say, a newly independent nation's choice of an official language or a Ministry of Education's determination as to what foreign languages must be taught? We see some of the same considerations at work in language-planning decisions at a microsociological level as at a macrosociological level. In the case of my congregation, we see the same conflicts as we do at a national level: between sentimental and instrumental motivations, between ideology and communicative efficiency, and between the needs of competing sectors of the population.

But if we include my congregation's decision as an instance of language planning, what is to prevent us from including even smaller-scale decisions? Should we, for example, include the decision by bilingual parents as to what language or languages they should speak at home with their children? That many parents debate this issue can be seen by the existence of at least one handbook, Harding and Riley (1987), which offers information and advice to parents about what language policy to adopt at home. The decisions parents make on this matter are important inasmuch as individual family policies cumulate in language maintenance or language shift. But the macrosociological importance of such family decisions does not justify including them as a subject of study by students of language planning. The justification, it seems to me, is the same as that for including the decisions of institutions such as churches and schools, namely that the same processes which operate in macrolevel planning also operate in microlevel planning. It must be admitted, however, that most scholars of language planning are reluctant to include decisions by small-scale social units such as individual schools, workplaces, churches, and families as instances of language planning, a reluctance reflected in our definitions. Indeed, some scholars may view the inclusion of such decisions as trivializing the field (Brian Weinstein, personal communication). It seems to me, however, that to exclude such small-scale instances from the study of language planning is to impoverish the field.

I have already mentioned that Prator's definition (12) refers to *language teaching* as an object of language policy-making. (Prator prefers the term *language policy-making* to *language planning*.) His distinction, between language teaching and language use might be expected, inasmuch as he was the first field director of the five-nation Survey of Language Use and Language Teaching in Eastern Africa, whose funding, by the Ford Foundation in the late 1960s and early 1970s, was justified in part by its potential contribution to national development via language planning.[7] For Prator, language policy-making with respect to language teaching includes not only national decisions as to what languages will be taught to whom but also those subsidiary, lower-level decisions which must be taken in order to implement the higher-level decisions. As Markee (1986) comments, ''a teacher's decision to use a particular text-book is just as much a policy-decision as a Ministry of Education's prescription that English will be taught for X number of hours a week in all secondary schools.''

Prator's view of language planning as a sequence of decisions of smaller and smaller scope is attractive for two reasons. First, at least some of the same principles and factors which constrain planning at the highest levels may be presumed to operate at lower levels as well. Second, his view provides a bridge from macrolevel decisions to microlevel implementation.

It should not be concluded, however, that there is a one-way sequence from macrolevel to microlevel decision-making, whereby the decisions made at lower levels are decisions only with respect to implementation of policies set at higher levels. Policy set initially at lower levels can move upwards as well. The feminist campaign is an instance of language planning which began at grassroots levels and was then subsequently adopted at high levels of authority. In my view, language planning activities move upwards as well as downwards. Microlevel, face-to-face interactional circles can both implement decisions initiated from above and initiate language planning which snowballs to the societal or governmental level. In short, I believe it an error to define language planning in terms of macrosociological activities alone.

Alternatively, one might define the target groups of language planning as communication networks. A communication network is a set of verbal

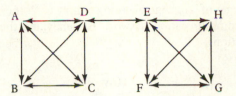

Figure 1. Two interaction networks

interactional links among persons, each network set off from others by
sparsity of interaction. In Figure 1, in which the arrows between pairs
of persons (A and B, B and C, etc.) indicate verbal interaction, whether
oral or written, between them, we can see two communication networks,
ABCD and EFGH. Though these two networks are connected because
D and E interact with one another, there is more communication within
networks than between them. Communication networks can be subdivided
into smaller networks or aggregated into larger ones, corresponding to
different bases of association, such as family, village, ethnic group, trade
union, market, nation, and differing with respect to their structural and
functional properties. Among the properties which might be of interest
to the student of language planning are (a) the size of the subset, (b)
the linguistic heterogeneity or homogeneity of the persons in the subset,
(c) the frequency of interaction among persons in the subset, and (d) the
functions of the contact among members of the subset.

There are several advantages of viewing the language-planning target
population as a communication network. First, we are not restricted to
a particular level of analysis, micro or macro. Second, we are in a better
position to trace the diffusion of innovation or the resistance to innovation
with which language planning is typically concerned. Networks are linked
to one another. An innovation introduced to one may spread to others.
Diffusion may be retarded or facilitated by the structural or functional
properties of the target network and subnetworks. A third advantage is
that viewing the target group of language planning as a communication
network would make the study of language planning consistent with the
study of language spread, as I have defined the latter, namely in terms
of diffusion through a communication network (Cooper 1982(a): 6). Inasmuch as language spread is a frequent target of language planning, viewing
the two phenomena within a common framework would be useful.

The problem with defining targets as communication networks is that
language planners are unlikely to view the target so abstractly. Planners
are more likely to aim their efforts at named entities, this nation, that
ethnic group, that occupational group, and so forth. To say, then, that
language planning *operates* through communication networks is not to say

that it is *directed* towards communication networks. Thus I am inclined to define the target of language planning simply as "others" and to reserve the notion of communication network for analyzing the diffusion of the planned innovation.

How

Should we confine language planning to an activity which approaches a management ideal, whereby needs are rationally determined, goals explicitly stated, means carefully tailored to these ends, and results systematically monitored to permit the adjustment of means and ends to one another? That some authorities believe so may be inferred from Das Gupta's definition (6), which refers to "systematically designed activities" and to "an ordered schedule of time," and from Tauli's definition (8), which refers to "methodical activity." But the view of language planning as a rational activity is best seen in Neustupný's definition (11). Because his view has become so influential (see, for example, the discussion by Jernudd 1983 and Rubin 1985), it is worth setting forth in some detail.

Neustupný views language planning as a special type of what he terms *language correction*, which refers to all planned and unplanned, conscious and unconscious language modification, whether by an individual or an organization. A speaker corrects a slip of the tongue. A speaker clarifies an utterance which he or she perceives has not been understood. A speaker simplifies his or her speech when addressing a learner with imperfect control of the language. In these examples, language correction takes place as a normal part of the speaking process. The speaker perceives a problem, seeks a way to solve it, and then implements the solution. Language correction, then, implies the existence of a communicative problem which requires a solution.

Not all communication problems, of course, are momentary or confined to a single pair of speakers. When the problem confronts a group and when the group or its representatives attempt to solve it, we have what Neustupný calls *language treatment*, which he defines as all organized forms of societal attention to language problems. Just as language treatment is a subset of language correction, language planning is a subset of language treatment. Neustupný defines language planning as that language treatment which is systematic, based on theory, and rational.

The merit of Neustupný's scheme is that it integrates language planning with ordinary communication processes, with grammatical linguistics, and with micro- and macrolinguistic approaches to behavior. Neustupný views all communication problems as located in actual discourse. If grammatical linguistics attempts to account for the generation of utterances, it must also account for the correction of utterances. The difference between micro-

and macrolinguistic approaches is one of scope: the latter represents a summation of the former. Thus language treatment deals with problems encountered by numerous speakers – problems encountered, in short, by a group.

The advantage of Neustupný's formulation is obvious, especially if one views language planning as the pursuit of solutions to language problems. That I am reluctant to view language planning principally as communication problem-solving should by now be clear. But that reservation aside, Neustupný's definition of language planning as a systematic, rational, theory-driven activity suffers from the fact that one must look long and hard to find an example. Certainly none of my four defining cases exemplifies such an activity. If these cases illustrate language planning, then language planning can be a messy affair – ad hoc, haphazard, and emotionally driven. As for being based on theory, we have yet to move beyond descriptive frameworks for the study of language planning. We have as yet no generally accepted language planning theory, if by theory we mean a set of logically interrelated, empirically testable propositions. In this connection, Ferguson's (1967: 653) comments about the language-planning efforts of the fourteenth-century Russian Orthodox bishop of Perm, St. Stefan, are worth quoting:

> In all these decisions the good saint acted without benefit of a sociolinguistic theory or frame of reference, and without any recorded body of previous sociolinguistic experience which he could consult. One must admire St. Stefan's clearcut decisions and successful implementations of them but equally one must bewail the fact that a present-day agent of culture change faced with language problems in a non-literate society still has no sociolinguistic theory and very little in the way of recorded and analyzed case histories to give guidance. We have not progressed much beyond St. Stefan's competence of five centuries ago.

We have indeed progressed since Ferguson's article of 1967 in accumulating a body of case studies and sociolinguistic frames of reference. Indeed, Ferguson has contributed considerably to both. But we have not progressed notably in developing a theory to guide language planning, whether in a non-literate or literate society. Thus if we confine language planning to theory-based treatments, we may need to wait some time to find many examples.

But what's wrong with *aiming* at a management ideal? Surely systematic, rational, theory-based planning would be better than the messy variety which normally obtains. True enough. And if the study of language planning is *prescriptive*, i.e. the determination of what kinds of activity will optimize the desired outcomes at a given cost, then a conception of language planning as systematic, theory-driven, and rational is appropriate. But if the study of language planning is *descriptive*, i.e. the study of what actually happens, then the conception of language planning as a management ideal is inappropriate. An ideal world would probably have no need for language planning.

Language planning in relation to other spheres of inquiry

Language planning is both an activity, the domain of language-planning practitioners, and a topic of scholarly interest, a sphere of inquiry. Scholars of language planning seek to understand its formulation, implementation, and outcome, as these relate to one another and to its social setting.

To what extent does this task represent an independent field of inquiry? If a field is distinguished by its own research methods, then language planning is not an independent field. The research techniques which language-planning scholars employ, such as interviews, questionnaires, rating scales, tests, secondary analyses of census data, content analyses, structural analyses of texts, quasi-experiments, and unobtrusive observations, are employed by other social sciences as well. Scholars have not developed research techniques peculiar to the study of language planning.

If a field is distinguished by a unique central focus, different from that of any other field, then again language planning cannot be considered an independent field, inasmuch as its central focus is closely related to the concerns of its two parent disciplines, applied linguistics and the sociology of language. Indeed, language planning is claimed as a subfield by both. For example, the editors of *Applied Linguistics* write that "the journal welcomes contributions in such areas of current inquiry as first and second language learning and teaching, bilingualism and bilingual education, discourse analysis, translation, language testing, language teaching methodology, language planning, the study of interlanguages, stylistics, and lexicography" (Allen, Spolsky, and Widdowson 1980).

With respect to the sociology of language, Fishman's (1985) review of the field employs language planning as a topical concentration. He found that, of the 466 books and articles abstracted by *Language and Language Behavior Abstracts* and *Sociological Abstracts* in 1980–2 and coded as "sociolinguistics" in either source and "linguistic" in the latter, the topic with the largest number of items (26) was language planning.

That language planning overlaps with both applied linguistics and the sociology of language is not surprising. It developed simultaneously with the rise of scholarly interest in both these fields, which can be dated from the Second World War, but particularly the decade of the 1960s when unprecedented and continuous postwar American prosperity gave rise to a liberal political agenda and the associated confidence that investment in social-science research would advance the solution of pressing social problems, in America and abroad. Some of these problems were seen to have language components. Domestically, for example, efforts to integrate refugees and to improve the economic position of ethnolinguistic minorities led to a consideration of language or communication problems as a barrier to progress.

Abroad, the emergence of newly independent states presented a host of development problems, many of which included a language component. Most of these states were linguistically diverse and had to consider the allocation of languages to various functions and to develop indigenous languages to meet some of these functions. Domestic and foreign language-related issues of public policy were of great interest to sociologists of language and to students of applied linguistics, who obtained government and foundation grants to mount research on these topics and who were consulted in turn by some of the public and private agencies which attempt to solve language-related problems.

Many of the same scholars contributed greatly to the development of both applied linguistics and the sociology of language as fields of inquiry. They interacted with one another in seminars, conferences, and summer institutes devoted to topics of mutual interest; they collaborated on joint research; they published books and articles together; and they served as consultants to one another's graduate students. Indeed, if we look at the founders of language planning as a scholarly topic we see many scholars who are at one and the same time among the founders of both modern applied linguistics and the sociology of language as spheres of inquiry. Prominent among these are Charles A. Ferguson and Joshua A. Fishman. Let us look, then, at Ferguson's definition of applied linguistics and Fishman's definition of the sociology of language.

Applied linguistics

Ferguson (1971: 135) defines applied linguistics as "the application of any of the insights, methods, or findings of linguistic science to practical language problems." The article in which this definition appears deals with applications to problems of second-language acquisition. (Indeed, in Great Britain, the terms "applied linguistics" and "second-language teaching" are almost synonymous.) But at the conclusion of this article he notes that "at the present time the application of linguistics to questions of orthographies for unwritten languages, translation of technical documents, and government language policies in multilingual countries probably employ more man-hours of linguists than applications in the area of foreign language teaching" (147).

As defined by Ferguson, applied linguistics looks a lot like the language planning defined by Fishman (7): both view the activity as the solving of language problems. The primary difference between the two definitions is that Ferguson restricts applied linguistics to the application of *linguistic* science to these problems. Linguistic science here refers to the language sciences generally, including fields such as the psychology of language, the sociology of language, and mathematical linguistics. However, as Ferguson would be the first to agree, the solution of language problems usually requires more than the application of "the insights, methods, or findings of linguistic science," even at its most inclusive. And in practice, whether language problem solvers or language behavior modifiers view themselves as applied linguists or as language planners or, far more likely, as teachers, school administrators, missionaries, politicians, or cardinals, they are likely to compound their potions and elixirs from whatever powders and herbs they can find, whether from a cabinet labelled "language sciences," "miscellaneous social sciences," or "traditional remedies."

As spheres of inquiry, both applied linguistics and language planning are concerned with the relationship between means and ends, i.e. the relationship between the means adopted to solve problems or influence behavior and the extent to which the problem is solved or the behavior influenced. But language planning as a sphere of inquiry is broader, in my view, in that it is also concerned with the *process* of planning. It seeks to determine who defines the problem to be solved or the behavior to be changed, what interests are at stake, how decisions are reached with respect to goals and means, and what relationships exist among the formulation of goals, the specification of means, and the outcomes of implementation, on the one hand, and between each of these and the social context in which planning is embedded, on the other.

The sociology of language

"The sociology of language," according to Fishman (1971: 217), "examines the interaction between these two aspects of human behavior: use of language and the social organization of behavior. Briefly put, the sociology of language focuses upon the entire gamut of topics related to the social organization of language behavior, including not only language usage *per se* but also language attitudes, overt behaviors toward language and toward language users." Inasmuch as language planning is an example par excellence of "overt behavior toward language" and inasmuch as it attempts to influence "language usage" and is itself influenced by "language attitudes," the study of language planning is well within the purview of the sociology of language. Indeed, as we have seen, Fishman (1985) considers language planning a subtopic of the sociology of language. He has called language planning the "applied sociology of language" (1971: 173).

But are there any aspects of language planning as a sphere of inquiry which do *not* fall within the disciplinary boundaries of the sociology of language? Yes. But these aspects have scarcely been studied. As I show in the next two chapters, the application of "the insights, methods, and findings" of disciplines *other* than the language sciences, are potentially useful in our effort to understand the processes and outcomes of language planning.

A thirteenth definition

Having examined the relative merits and demerits of earlier definitions of language planning, I now offer my own: *Language planning refers to deliberate efforts to influence the behavior of others with respect to the acquisition, structure, or functional allocation of their language codes.* This definition neither restricts the planners to authoritative agencies, nor restricts the type of the target group, nor specifies an ideal form of planning. Further, it is couched in behavioral rather than problem-solving terms. Finally, it employs the term *influence* rather than *change* inasmuch as the former includes the maintenance or preservation of current behavior, a plausible goal of language planning, as well as the change of current behavior.

3

The uses of frameworks

Language-planning scholars face four tasks: (1) to describe, (2) predict, and (3) explain language-planning processes and outcomes in particular instances, and (4) to derive valid generalizations about these processes and outcomes. Accordingly, there are four criteria against which our success in carrying out these tasks can be judged: (1) descriptive adequacy, (2) predictive adequacy, (3) explanatory adequacy, and (4) theoretical adequacy, each criterion related to a different task. In the present chapter I argue that descriptive frameworks or accounting schemes help us not only to carry out these tasks but also to evaluate our success in doing so. In the next chapter, I present descriptive frameworks suggested by several disciplines or subdisciplines and apply them to language planning.

Descriptive adequacy

Descriptive adequacy refers to our success in representing what happened in a given instance. The scholar, confronted with this not inconsiderable task, faces two problems. (1) What should be described? (2) On what basis should the description be evaluated?

The first problem arises from the vast range of behaviors which *could* be described. What *should* be described? To what should we pay attention? With respect to my description of the founding of the Académie française, for example, what should I have included that I left out? What should I have excluded that I put in? Was it necessary to refer to events which took place in the century before the Academy's founding? Was it necessary to refer to Cardinal Richelieu's taste in art? Should I have described the composition of the first Academy? Should I have written less or more (and if more, what?) about Mme. de Rambouillet? It seems to me, at the outset, that a descriptively adequate account of any given case of language planning ought to tell us, at a minimum, what *actors* attempted to influence what *behaviors*, of which *people*, for what *ends*, by what *means*,

46

and with what *results*. While other investigators might add or subtract categories, a set of rubrics such as these helps us to select and organize our observations from among the indefinitely large number of observations which could be made.

A framework or accounting scheme helps not only the investigator but also the readers, who can use it to assess the adequacy of the description. This brings us to the second major problem associated with descriptive adequacy: how is descriptive adequacy to be assessed or evaluated? There are three criteria against which descriptive adequacy can be assessed:

Comprehensiveness refers to the extent to which each of the rubrics in the framework or accounting scheme has been covered. With respect to my defining examples, for instance, the reader will probably agree with me that they vary in the extent to which any given rubric is treated. I think that *actors*, for example, are covered best in my description of the founding of the Académie française and covered least well in my description of the feminist campaign.

Whereas comprehensiveness refers to the *extent* of coverage, *comprehensibility* refers to the *coherence* of the coverage, the extent to which a forest emerges rather than a welter of trees. The critic can compare the description to the framework not only to check the extent to which each rubric has been treated but also to assess the extent to which the investigator has connected the rubrics to form a coherent whole. Has the investigator discussed *means* in terms of *ends*, for example, or *results* in terms of *means* and *ends*?

Comprehensiveness and comprehensibility do not, alas, insure the validity of a description any more than a painting which is complete (comprehensive) and fully recognizable as a human figure (comprehensible) provides a truthful representation of the subject, particularly when the subject is unattractive and disagreeable and has not paid the painter in advance. While truth is beauty, beauty is not necessarily truth.

But how is truthfulness in description to be judged? Probably the best solution is to ask a person who is familiar with the events to evaluate the validity of the description. For example, political scientists familiar with the early stages of the Ethiopian revolution could be asked to evaluate the truthfulness of my description of the Ethiopian mass-literacy campaign. To the extent that a descriptive framework can help an evaluator organize his or her own impression of events, against which the description can be compared, an accounting scheme can aid evaluation of a description's truthfulness, as well as aid an evaluation of its comprehensiveness and comprehensibility. A descriptive framework or accounting scheme, then, acts as a template which the investigator can use to impose order on his or her data and which the critic can use to evaluate the description.

Predictive adequacy

Predictive adequacy refers to our ability to forecast events. In terms of the framework suggested above, forecasts could, in principle, be made about what *actors* will attempt to influence what *behaviors* of which *people* by what *means* and with what *results*. Mackey (1983: 202–3), for example, comparing Canadian and U.S. language policies, suggests that we may see a growth of ethnolinguistic pluralism in the United States, "where many well-organized ethnic groups have lobbied for more bilingual education, more bilingual government jobs, and more ethnic immigration. But what will these ethnic groups ask for next? . . . The Constitution of the United States reserves enough power to the states to make possible, *if the voters so decide*, the creation of a Spanish state, a French state, or another ethnic polity. This possibility may be important for some ethnic groups, and I hope that I am not being in any way subversive in pointing this out." Prof. Mackey's suggestion that ethnic lobbying may lead the U.S. to greater ethnolinguistic pluralism "and even political multinationalism" is a prediction of sorts, inasmuch as he states in effect that such a likelihood is greater than zero.

Predictions need not be made on such a grand scale, of course. As we will see in the next chapter, one view of policy making requires decision makers to evaluate the consequences of alternative courses of action in order to arrive at the best possible decision. Evaluating the consequences of competing policies involves, of course, predicting the net benefits of each alternative. In none of my defining examples do we find evidence of explicit, systematic evaluation of competing alternatives. Still, some sort of weighing is likely to have taken place, if only implicitly. With respect to the Ethiopian mass-literacy campaign, for example, the decision makers are likely to have believed that it would be easier to mobilize the students on behalf of the new regime if a gesture were made toward ethnic self-determinism, in the guise of teaching people to read in their own first language, than if the old imperial policy of favoring Amharic were followed. The predicted benefits – mobilizing student support and neutralizing student opposition – were likely to have been valued more highly by the new rulers than the potential cost – encouragement of ethnic separatism – which, though threatening, was a less immediate danger than student rebelliousness. Indeed, comparison of projected net benefits – predictions, in short – are implicit in any choice among alternatives, whether made by revolutionary army officers, feminists, national activists, or cardinals. Students of language planning, however, can try to make *explicit* predictions concerning alternative language policies, whether as scholars or as policy advisers and advocates.

The value of a descriptive framework for predicting net benefits is that the framework serves as a checklist or reminder to the analyst to consider all information relevant to the prediction. While a framework such as the one suggested above is probably too gross to remind the analyst of the main variables which ought to be considered, it could be refined, with each rubric broken down into contrasting types and subtypes. In any case, a descriptive framework or accounting scheme can help language planners and students of language planning make sounder predictions by reminding them of the variables which ought to be taken into consideration when forecasting.

Can an accounting scheme help the critic evaluate the adequacy of a prediction? Or is the only good test of predictive adequacy the correspondence between the predicted and the actual outcome?. There are two problems with empirical correspondence as an exclusive test. First, sometimes we must wait a long time before we can confirm the adequacy of prediction. With respect to Prof. Mackey's prediction, for example, a wait of one generation would not be unreasonable to determine whether the prediction has come true.

Second, language-planning decisions are made under conditions of great uncertainty. Rational predictions can be made on the basis of all readily available, relevant information and still be wrong. What is predicted does not in fact occur: the public does not accept an academy-approved terminology; students do not learn a language better via a highly-touted method; parents refuse to send their children to a new bilingual-education program. Inasmuch as no analyst has perfect knowledge of all relevant information and inasmuch as no decision maker has perfect control over those future events which may affect the outcome, accurate predictions are more desired than found. Nonetheless, if the analyst spells out the basis of his or her prediction, the critic can at least evaluate the soundness with which the prediction was *formulated*. The use of a descriptive framework, prepared by the critic, would serve as a means of checking whether or not the analyst had based his or her predictions on those variables which the critic believes to be relevant. To the extent that the critic has access to the same data base, the critic can also evaluate the soundness of the values and weights which the analyst assigns to each of the variables in the framework.

Explanatory adequacy

We sometimes make successful predictions without knowing why they succeed. Why, for example, are American teachers, principals, and school-district supervisors correct in predicting that working-class Hispanic children who enter their classrooms will perform, on the average, less successfully on tests of academic achievement than will "mainstream" children?

Is the poorer performance of Hispanic children from working-class backgrounds attributable to test bias, to the self-fulfilling prophecies of teachers, to mismatches between the rules of speaking or other behavioral routines learned at home and those assumed or required at school, to interference from Spanish, to poorer teacher preparation, to lower per-student expenditures, to peer-group values antithetic to "mainstream" norms, to inadequate nutrition, to lack of assistance at home, or to some combination of these factors? It is unlikely that there is any single cause of the massive academic failure of working-class Hispanic children. But if several factors are responsible, what are their relative weights? Do the causes and their weights change from community to community? While the predictions of poor performance will be borne out in community after community, the factors underlying the poor performance may not be clear at all. Thus the language planner who seeks to explain the success or lack of success of given bilingual education programs, instituted to improve the achievement of these children, faces a difficult task indeed.

Explanatory adequacy, then, refers to our ability to "account for" a particular outcome. Ideally, we hope to identify the causal or determining factors and their relative importance in the case at hand. There are at least three levels of explanation, which I call here correlative, observational, and experimental.

Correlative explanation refers to the extent to which independent variables, taken together, are associated with variation in the dependent variable or criterion of interest. A study by Fishman, Cooper, and Rosenbaum (1977) illustrates correlative explanation. From secondary sources we gathered statistics with respect to about 100 countries, in which English was not the mother-tongue, concerning both the status of English and economic, educational, demographic, and other variables. We wanted to determine which variables are related to the use of English as an additional language around the world. We hypothesized that the variables isolated by Brosnahan (1963) with respect to the spread of Arabic, Greek, and Latin as mother tongues – military imposition, duration of authority, linguistic diversity, and material advantages – would also be related to the spread of English as an additional language. We also hypothesized that five additional factors would be related to this expansion – urbanization, economic development, educational development, religious composition, and political bloc affiliation. We obtained information for variables representing these nine factors and correlated them with one another and with various criterion variables representing the status of English. These zero-order correlation coefficients (correlations between pairs of variables) were then entered into a multiple regression analysis, which tells us how much additional variation in a criterion variable is associated with the addition of each new independent variable.

As a concrete example, let us take the use of English as a medium of instruction in secondary schools in countries in which English was not the mother tongue. The single best predictor of this criterion was former Anglophone colonial status (r = .62). In other words, countries which had formerly been British or American colonies tended to use English as a medium of instruction in secondary schools more often than countries which had never been ruled by Britain or America. When we added to this variable the percentage of the population *not* characterized as adherents of universal religions or religions associated with high cultures (e.g. Buddhism, Christianity, Confucianism, Islam), we increased the correlation of .62 (between the criterion and former Anglophone colonial status only) to .75, accounting for even more variation in the use of English as a medium of instruction in secondary school. By adding two more independent variables, percentage of exports sent to the United States and linguistic heterogeneity, we were able to bring the correlation to .82, thus "accounting for" more than half of the variation in our criterion variable.

To what extent can we claim to have isolated causal mechanisms? The influence of former Anglophone colonial status, representing the residue of military imposition of the language, seems clear enough. But what about the other variables?

The relationship between the percentage of the population adhering to local, traditional beliefs and the criterion can be explained on the grounds that countries with relatively high percentages tend to be relatively less developed economically. For many such countries, the training of local teachers has not kept pace with the demand for their services and thus reliance on expatriate staff becomes necessary. Expatriates, of course, are more likely to be able to teach in English than in the local languages. Furthermore, the development of textbooks and other educational materials in local languages is an expensive proposition. Religious particularity, therefore, is likely to be related to the criterion because this independent variable reflects economic and educational underdevelopment.

The percentage of exports to the United States was selected to represent economic incentives to learn English. It is reasonable that the higher the incentive to learn English, the more acceptable or desirable are English-medium schools.

The relationship of linguistic diversity to the criterion can be explained in part by the practical difficulties involved in providing secondary-school education in many mother tongues, and to the political difficulties involved in selecting only one or two among many indigenous languages to serve as a medium of instruction. It is often more acceptable politically to use a "neutral," nonindigenous language as medium. Although the correlation between linguistic heterogeneity and the criterion is the second highest of the four independent variables (r = .58), it contributes the least to our explanation of variance. This is because former Anglophone colonies and countries with high traditional-belief percentages are also likely to be linguistically diverse. These aspects of linguistic diversity, therefore, have already been "taken into account" by the time this variable enters the analysis. In fact, it adds about 5 percent to the explanation of variance, compared to the 7 percent and 17 percent of the two previous variables. We see, therefore, not only which variables are related to the criterion and the degree to which each is related individually, but also what the relative importance of each variable is when combined to "explain" criterion variance.

Correlation, of course, is not causation. In the present case, however, it is reasonable to assume that the factors represented by our independent variables promoted the establishment and maintenance of English-medium secondary schools.

To say that the use of English as a medium of instruction in secondary schools is a function of the combination of particular variables is a summarizing statement, based on the effect of innumerable human interactions and motivations. School boards, or other authoritative agencies, determine media of instruction not on the grounds of abstractions such as linguistic diversity or international trade balances but because such abstractions are realized through the pressures exerted by parents, pupils, teachers, administrators, voters, politicians, and budgets. We must not forget that it is human behavior which is reflected, if only palely and imperfectly, by our summary statistics.

The second level of explanation is *observational*. Here we attempt to explain an outcome of interest by careful observation on ongoing behavior. Why, for example, does the average American bilingual education program, instituted to improve the academic achievement of poor, ethnolinguistic minorities, seem to have had little success in reducing the drop-out rate of Hispanic pupils, or in raising their academic performance? Important clues may be found in a study by Fillmore, Ammon, McLaughlin, and Ammon (1985), who suggest that poor teaching practices found in many bilingual (as well as monolingual) classrooms and the often minimal amount of teaching via the mother tongue found in programs labeled as "bilingual" may be responsible in part. Bilingual programs which employ good teaching practices and use the mother tongue for more than a token proportion of the curriculum may well be successful.

Fillmore and her associates carried out elaborate observations of third- and fifth-grade classrooms, seventeen in all, some "bilingual", others English-only, some serving Cantonese-speaking children, others serving Hispanic children. The authors wanted to determine the influence of instructional practices and patterns of language use on the development of those English-language skills which are needed for effective participation in schools.

They observed classroom interaction between pupils and teachers and among the pupils themselves for an entire school year.

Among their findings was the surprising fact that there was little use of the children's first language in the so-called bilingual classes. The average use was only 8 percent (compared to the use of English and silence). The investigators found that the development of English oral comprehension was not affected by the same instructional practices as those which affected the development of English oral production. Further, they found that the practices which influenced second-language development at low levels of initial proficiency differed from those which influenced development at higher levels of initial proficiency. They also discovered that the instructional practices which influenced language development depended on the cultural background of the children. And they found that the role played by the teachers depended on the number of students with poor English proficiency and on the availability of English speakers with whom these children could interact.

Among their specific conclusions are the following: While all learners profited from opportunities to interact with peers who spoke English, the Hispanic pupils benefited especially. Chinese pupils profited from interactional opportunities with English-speaking peers only after having reached an intermediate level of English proficiency. Chinese learners benefited from structured, relatively quiet learning environments more than did Hispanic children, whereas Hispanic children were more sensitive to the quality of teaching (e.g. the appropriateness of the level of the learning tasks and materials) and to the quality of the instructional language that serves as input (e.g. language whose structure is transparent) than were the Chinese students, who seemed more willing to compensate for poor teaching. Thus the researchers found no straightforward relationship between classroom variables and language learning. Different approaches worked best with the tw cultural groups.

All in all, the study by Fillmore *et al.* is encouraging because it suggests "that although extremely complex, there are clear guidelines that [can be offered to] educators on the design of educational programs that will facilitate language and academic development in [limited-English speaking] students" (345). We see here an excellent example of explanation at an observational level.

While the findings of Fillmore *et al.* are reasonable, indeed persuasive, they are necessarily *ex post facto*. That is to say, the factors they suggested as conducive to learning or as impeding learning were identified during the course of the investigation. If similar observations were now made in other classrooms, would the same factors be found to be related to successful (or unsuccessful) learning and would they be related to the same extent as in the original study? The difficulty in obtaining similar results in replicated studies lies not only in the considerable difficulty found in carrying out equivalent measurements with equivalent samples but also in the uncertainty of having identified the principal determinants of variation. For example, let us imagine that all the classrooms observed by Fillmore *et al.* were quite similar with respect to noise level. If this had been the case, the research team would not have identified, as it did, noise level as an important condition influencing learning. If, in a subsequent replication, the classrooms did vary in noise, the relative importance of the other variables might differ considerably from that found in the original study. But even if we were confident that we had identified all important relevant variables (thus meriting a special place in hell for excessive pride), we generally cannot control them in the settings of everyday life.

If we can, however, keep all variables constant except one, in order to chart its influence on the criterion of interest, we reach explanation at the *experimental* level. Complete control, however, is rarely possible in the social sciences. Even the use of control groups only reduces but does not eliminate the influence of uncontrolled or uncontrollable factors. Quasi-experiments, in which we can control *some* of the relevant variables, are probably the best we can do in the social sciences, at least with respect to those kinds of behavior which are of interest to students of language planning.

Consider, for example, the "St. Lambert experiment" (Lambert and Tucker 1972), which started as a result of pressure from English-Canadian parents in the Province of Quebec. They were concerned with the ineffectiveness of traditional methods of teaching their children French as a second language. In response to the growing Quebecois political movement to strengthen the status of French, these parents feared that their children might be ill-prepared to use French upon leaving school. The parents thought that they might improve their children's French by enrolling them in kindergarten and elementary-school classes in which French would be the primary language of instruction. At the same time, they were uncertain about the outcomes of such a "home-school language switch." Accordingly, with the help and encouragement of Wallace Lambert, Richard Tucker, and other scholars at McGill University, the parents decided to begin an experimental program, within an English-language, Protestant elementary school in St. Lambert, a middle-class suburb of Montreal.

All the children in the experimental program came from English-speaking homes. Enrollment was voluntary. Two classes of children were followed from kindergarten through elementary school. Lambert and Tucker (1972), who monitored the impact of this program on the children's linguistic, cognitive, and attitudinal development, report the results for the program's first six years (through grade four of the second experimental group). These children's education was conducted exclusively in French during kindergarten and the first grade. From grades two through four, instruction was primarily in French, except for two half-hour daily periods of English-language arts.

The investigators were interested in the children's achievement in comparison not only to that of conventionally schooled French-speaking children following a standard program in French, but also to that of conventionally trained English-speaking children following a standard program in English. Accordingly, the achievements of three "control" classes, two from English-speaking homes, following a conventional English–Canadian academic program, and one from French-speaking homes, following a conventional French–Canadian academic program were described as well. One of the English control classes was a comparison first-grade class of students attending the same school in St. Lambert as the experimental classes. (In the first cohort, the children from this school were randomly assigned to the experimental and control classes. For both classes, children were drawn from families who requested the experimental class.) The other English control class was chosen from another middle-class suburb of Montreal. The parents of the English control and experimental classes appeared to be comparable in terms of attitudes towards and contact with French Canadians. "If given the opportunity, the large majority of the English control parents would likely have placed their children in the experimental program" (203), which was limited to two classes only. The French control class was chosen from a French Catholic school in St. Lambert. All the children in the control classes had attended kindergarten. Control and experimental classes were equivalent in social-class background and in measured academic aptitude.

The investigators found that at the end of the fourth grade, the experimental classes were doing just as well in home-language skills as their peers in the English control classes. The experimental classes' achievement in mathematics as well as their measured intelligence was as high as that of the control classes. The French-language proficiency of the experimental classes, while distinguishable in some skills from that of the French controls, was still strikingly higher than that of the English controls. All in all, the comparisons with the control classes demonstrated that the experimental program resulted in excellent command of the second language with no accompanying deficits in home-language skills or in non-language subjects.

We have, then, in this quasi-experimental study, an answer to the question of what would be the result of teaching these Anglophone children via French. Here the results were beneficial. Can the beneficial results be reasonably attributed to conditions *other* than the experimental program itself, such as especially gifted teachers in the experimental program or especially strenuous efforts on the part of parents of children in the experimental program? Although it appears unlikely, we cannot know for sure, which of course is almost always the case for the quasi-experiments which are possible in the social sciences.

But assuming that Lambert and Tucker's conclusions are sound, why not teach all ethnolinguistic minority children via the language of the majority? The children enrolled in the St. Lambert experimental classes differed in two important respects from most ethnolinguistic minority children. First, the experimental children's home language is regarded as valuable by the larger community. There are many opportunities for its practice outside the home and neighborhood. It is supported by institutions outside the school. Second, the experimental children's parents were middle-class, well-educated persons, mainly life-long residents of the community. Absent were the disadvantages associated with poverty, dislocation, and powerlessness. That initial schooling in French is beneficial for English–Canadian children from the middle class in Montreal does not mean that initial schooling in English will be beneficial to poor, Hispanic children from a barrio in Los Angeles. On the other hand, as the work of Fillmore *et al.* has shown, initial schooling in the home language will not necessarily be effective for the latter if teaching techniques and the conditions surrounding learning are poor.

In these three examples of explanatory studies, we see efforts to determine cause and effect through statistical "accounting," observation, and quasi-experiment. In the first two examples, numerous independent variables were related to each of various outcomes of interest. In the third example, the outcomes of interest were related to only one variable, type of schooling, experimental or traditional. Here, however, many other variables, such as parental attitudes, socioeconomic status, and academic aptitude, were considered in an effort to equate the experimental and control groups. Just as a descriptive framework or accounting scheme serves as a reminder as to which variables should be examined in descriptive or predictive studies, so a descriptive framework serves as a reminder as to which variables should be "controlled" in quasi-experimental studies.

Theoretical adequacy

Without a theory of language planning, we have no principled means of determining what variables should be included in descriptive, predictive, and explanatory studies of given cases. Each investigator must make this determination on a more or less ad-hoc basis. But ad-hoc studies serve as a preliminary step in the formulation of theories.

A theory is a conceptual scheme which organizes a relatively small number of propositions which, taken together, explain a relatively wide range of human behavior. As an example, let us take speech-accommodation theory as elaborated by Giles and his colleagues (see, for example, Beebe and Giles 1984; Giles and Smith 1979; Giles 1980, 1984). This theory attempts (1) to explain the motivations underlying speakers' linguistic convergence towards or divergence away from the speech patterns of their interlocutors and (2) to predict the social consequences arising from convergence or divergence.

A recent formulation of the theory (Giles, Mulac, Bradac, and Johnson 1987) lists six propositions which assert the conditions under which people will attempt to converge or to diverge, the determinants of the magnitude of the convergence or divergence, and the circumstances under which convergence will be positively evaluated and divergence negatively evaluated by the speaker's interlocutor. These propositions were formulated *after* numerous studies in speech accommodation had been carried out. Observed regularities in the relationships among linguistic modifications of speech, the social characteristics of speakers, speech settings, and interlocutors, and evaluation of speech modification suggested propositions which could then be organized into a coherent conceptual scheme. As propositions are tested against new data, consistent confirmations will lead to acceptance, consistent disconfirmations to rejection or reformulation. The success of the overall conceptual scheme can be judged not only according to the degree to which individual propositions are accepted or rejected but also according to the extent to which it leads to the formulation of additional propositions which widen the range of behaviors which are explained.

Thus the initial construction of a theory *follows* the discovery of behavioral regularities, which in turn depends upon the formulation of descriptive classifications.

At every stage of the scientific enterprise, therefore, descriptive frameworks or accounting schemes can be useful. They can help us to determine what is worth describing, predicting, and explaining in individual cases. Generalizations can be built up from individual cases by observing consistencies in the relationships among descriptive classifications. Such generalizations can be organized into theories designed to explain not simply a given individual case but *all* individual cases represented by the phenomenon of interest. The validity of the theory can then be tested against new data, gathered in terms of the descriptive classifications on which the theory is built. Disconfirmations may suggest new descriptive classifications, which, if productive, can be incorporated into a revised theory.

In language planning we are still at the stage of discovering behavioral regularities. Before we can discover regularities, we must first decide which variables it will be most useful to describe. Descriptive frameworks can help us to make such decisions.

4

Some descriptive frameworks

Descriptive frameworks are molds wherein behavior may be poured to cool and harden for analysis. The same behavior, poured into different molds, takes on different shapes. Thus a political scientist's, sociologist's, and curriculum specialist's account of the Ethiopian mass-literacy campaign will differ substantially one from the other. Each analyst, interested in different aspects of the same behavior, employs that framework which facilitates concentration on the features of interest.

While behavior may be divisible for purposes of analysis, it is nonetheless unitary. Just as different independent variables may be combined via multiple regression analysis to "account for" variation in a given outcome, so can the insights obtained from different disciplines be combined to account for a particular phenomenon overall. Inasmuch as there is yet no generally accepted framework for the study of language planning, it may be useful to look at frameworks suggested by other disciplines or subdisciplines not only to understand language planning better but also to forward the development of a framework particularly suited for language planning. Accordingly, we turn to frameworks suggested for the diffusion of innovation, marketing, politics, and decision making and apply them to language planning. Thus I will consider language planning as, in turn, (1) the management of innovation, (2) an instance of marketing, (3) a tool in the acquisition and maintenance of power, and (4) an instance of decision making. Finally I present a second version of the framework for the study of language planning suggested in the previous chapter, modified and elaborated on the basis of the four frameworks presented here.

Language planning as the management of innovation

Whether or not changes in language behavior are planned or unplanned, they are outcomes of diffusion. Innovations introduced by some speakers or writers are adopted by others. There is an immense literature on the diffusion of innovation. Most of this is in sociology (general sociology, rural sociology, and medical sociology), although a substantial number of innovation studies are found in anthropology, marketing, education, mass communications, and public health. Most studies have focused upon the diffusion of material or physical products or practices as, for example, consumer goods such as personal computers and videorecorders; agricultural practices such as the use of chemical fertilizers and drip irrigation; medical procedures such as the use of anesthetics and the prescription of given drugs; agricultural products such as maize, coffee, and the sweet potato; and so forth.

Communicative innovations (by which I mean changes in language use, language structure, or language acquisition), which of course are nonmaterial, have been largely ignored by students of diffusion. In Rogers (1983), the standard text on the subject, there is no entry for language in the index. Of the approximately 2,750 publications in the Diffusion Documents Center at the Institute for Communication Research, Stanford University (see Rogers, Williams, and West 1977 for a bibliography of the collection), only two items concern the spread of communicative innovations, both drawn from the 1949 volume of *American Speech*, one a single word, "shivaree" (Davis and McDavid 1949), the other a collection of lexical items used by oilworkers (Boone 1949).

That students of diffusion have largely ignored the enormous literature on change in language structure can probably be explained by the fact that until relatively recently, most students of language change have focused upon linguistic properties as sources and mediators of change. Linguistic change, in other words, was explained in terms of the internal structure of the language rather than in terms of the social structure in which the language operates. There is now, of course, a growing literature concerning the social contexts in which change occurs, not only in language structure but also in language use (see, for example, Fischer 1958, Fishman 1964, Gumperz 1958, Labov 1966, Irvine 1978, Kroch 1978, Scotton 1972, Trudgill 1972, Weinreich 1963), although such studies have not yet found their way into the literature on the diffusion of innovation. However, most students of communicative change have ignored the equally vast literature on the diffusion of innovation. One exception is Afendras (1969), who proposed that mathematical models of diffusion, based on density of communication, be used to describe the diffusion of linguistic items and to predict the relative influence which one language will have on another. Another exception is the collection of articles which views language spread as an instance of diffusion (Cooper 1982b).

Students of the diffusion in innovation try to explain differences in the speed and extent of acceptance of an innovation on the basis of characteristics of the innovation, its adopters, and its social setting. We can apply a diffusionist approach to the study of language planning by trying to answer the following summarizing question: who adopts what, when, where, why, and how? (Cooper 1979).

Who

When we think about the characteristics which distinguish adopters from nonadopters of a planned communicative innovation or which distinguish early adopters from late adopters, we typically envisage the actual or potential adopters as individual speakers, writers, listeners, or readers. Individuals, after all, adopt or reject given phonological variants, terms, syntactic structures, and spelling conventions for given communicative contexts, and they learn new languages and writing systems and sometimes abandon others. But corporate bodies can also choose one communicative alternative over another and such bodies often serve as the target of language planners. By corporate body I mean any public or private agency that exists independently of the individuals who compose it and that can act or be acted upon as an entity in its own right.

A good example of language planning directed primarily at corporate bodies is the plain-language movement, which is directed toward improving the comprehensibility of documents such as consumer contracts and warranties, government forms, regulations, and instructions, and legislation. This movement, which arose in the United States as part of the consumer movement and which has spread internationally, aims at agencies such as banks, insurance companies, consumer-goods manufacturers, and government organizations, all of which produce documents with which the public tries to cope.

Sometimes language planners aim at corporate bodies in order to influence individuals. Such a two-step sequence was seen when feminists worked to change the editorial policies of professional organizations. Once an organization like the American Psychological Association announces that its journals will not publish articles employing sexist usage, those who hope to publish in such journals must take care that papers submitted to them conform to the association's guidelines for nonsexist usage. Thus the plain-language movement differs from the feminist campaign in that while both aim at corporate bodies, the latter does so in order to influence the communicative behavior of individuals whereas the former does not.

This discussion leads us to distinguish between *primary* and *intermediary* targets of language planning. Banks, insurance companies, consumer-product manufacturers, government agencies and so forth are primary targets of the plain-language movement. Individuals, it is true, would benefit from the simplified and clarified documents produced by such bodies but it is the language behavior of the corporate bodies rather than that of the individuals affected by these bodies which constitutes the primary object of language planning. For the feminist campaign, publications and professional associations are intermediary targets which can in turn influence individuals, whose language behavior is the primary target.

Whether potential adopters of a planned communicative innovation are corporate bodies or individuals, few studies have been undertaken to determine which characteristics distinguish adopters from nonadopters or quick adopters from slow adopters. Among these studies is one by Fainberg (1983), whose results suggest that new terms approved by the Academy of the Hebrew Language are more likely to be known by women than by men, regardless of age or educational level. Two studies by Hofman suggest that background variables such as language history and claimed language proficiency are helpful in predicting the extent to which terms approved by the Academy of the Hebrew Language are used by chemists (1974a) and by psychologists (1974b), with attitudinal variables also serving as useful predictors for the latter group. Hofman found that psychologists who viewed language as a symbol of national solidarity and prestige tended to produce a greater proportion of Academy-approved terms than did those who viewed language in a more instrumental light. Findings from studies such as these can help language planners direct their campaigns to those most receptive to them (and among these, to opinion-leaders especially), and conversely, they can help language planners identify those segments of the population for whom their promotional strategies have been relatively unsuccessful.

Adopts

Adoption refers to the degree to which the planned communicative innovation has been accepted. Rogers and Shoemaker (1971) propose five stages of acceptance of an innovation: awareness (knowledge that the innovation exists), interest (gaining knowledge about the innovation), evaluation (gaining a favorable or unfavorable attitude toward the innovation), small-scale trial, and decision to adopt or reject the innovation. Rogers (1983) proposes a somewhat different set of stages: knowledge that the innovation exists, persuasion (gaining a favorable or unfavorable attitude towards the innovation), decision to adopt or reject the innovation, implementation (putting the innovation to use), and confirmation (seeks reinforcement of a previously-made decision to adopt the innovation). I propose the following types of adoption with respect to language planning:

1. *Awareness.* Potential adopters can identify the innovation or the *absence* of the innovation. Until the rise of the Women's Liberation Movement, for example, few of us paid attention to sex bias in language. It was

part of the grounds of everyday life. The feminist movement heightened awareness of such bias.

2. *Evaluation.* Potential adopters form a favorable or unfavorable attitude toward the personal usefulness of the innovation. Here, an essentially means-end approach (McGuire 1969) is adopted, whereby potential adopters' attitude towards a planned innovation depends on (a) the extent to which they believe that knowledge or use of the innovation will help them attain valued goals and (b) the degree of subjective importance of the goals to which the innovation is relevant.

3. *Proficiency.* The adopter can use the planned innovation appropriately. Knowledge implies the ability to use the innovation with the right person at the right time and at the right place, as defined by norms of communicative appropriateness.

4. *Usage.* Whereas knowledge refers to the ability to use the innovation, the fourth and last form of adoption refers to the actual frequency with which the innovation is used. One can describe usage in terms of absolute as well as relative frequencies, i.e. how often the innovation is used for a given purpose in a given context as well as how frequently it is used compared to other alternatives available to the adopter.

These four indices of adoption normally represent stages, with awareness preceding evaluation, evaluation preceding knowledge, and knowledge preceding usage. But is this necessarily so? Perhaps some proceed simultaneously. For example, proficiency probably grows as a function of usage. Perhaps there are even reversals in what would appear to be the usual order, so that people use an innovation (a new language, for example) for a given purpose before they know it well enough to use it adequately for that purpose. For example, I began giving university lectures in Hebrew long before I was fluent in Hebrew, a circumstance which forced me, prior to each lecture, to look up and write down a substantial number of the terms I would need.

While language planners are interested in knowledge and usage as the outcomes of ultimate interest, they may want to encourage awareness and positive evaluations in order to promote the higher levels of adoption, just as manufacturers employ advertising campaigns to increase public recognition of new products. I consider such campaigns below, in my discussion of marketing as a framework for the study of language planning. In fact, language-planning campaigns abound. Israel provides several examples. Posters with the (Hebrew) injunction "Hebrew [person] speak Hebrew" appeared in Palestine in the early part of the twentieth century, long before the establishment of the state. The Academy of the Hebrew Language publishes and distributes lists of approved terms for various specialized fields. For many years the Israeli radio broadcast a one-minute skit, twice daily, in which one speaker criticized another for using a given expression (in many cases used by everyone in everyday speech) and then supplied a normative alternative (in many cases used only in writing or only on the most formal public occasions if at all), sometimes justifying the preferred variation by citing its appearance in the Bible. While it can be argued that these examples reflect instructional as well as promotional goals, the desire to sharpen awareness and to shape the public's attitude appears to be a primary aim of such campaigns. Whether language planners engage in promotional campaigns or not, it is likely that they can improve the effectiveness of their activities by sharpening their own awareness about what type of behavior – awareness, evaluation, knowledge, or usage – they are trying to influence.

What

What does the adopter adopt? Both language planners and students of the diffusion of communicative innovation can approach this question from two points of view: form and function.

Form refers to the structure of the innovation. With respect to planning language acquisition, the structural characteristics of most concern are perhaps (1) the extent to which the target language is similar to languages already known by the potential adopter and (2) the extent to which the target language has few stylistic varieties. It seems reasonable to assume that, all things being equal (which, of course, is rarely the case), potential adopters will be able to adopt a language more quickly the more they can rely on what they already know. There is presumably less to learn when a new language is structurally similar to a language already known and when it is relatively unelaborated or undifferentiated. One reason commonly offered for the rapid spread of Kiswahili, for example, is that it advanced initially among speakers of other related Bantu languages. And one explanation suggested for the spread of Malay rather than Javanese as a lingua franca in Indonesia (where the number of native speakers of Javanese is far greater than that of Malay) is that Javanese is composed of several sociostylistic dialects which are lexically quite distinct. If one is to communicate like a Javanese, one needs to learn not only these different sets of lexical alternatives but also the socially complex rules for their appropriate use. Whether or not elaboration really discouraged the spread of Javanese (after all, people could have learned only the base dialect, and in any case they need not have communicated like the Javanese), one can argue that the fewer the lexical, syntactic, or stylistic alternatives that must be learned, the easier and thus the quicker the learning will be.

If structural similarity and homogeneity are important characteristics with respect to language acquisition, their relevance can presumably be explained on the grounds that they are related to the simplicity or complexity of the innovation to be acquired. Certainly, complexity is one of the characteristics examined by investigators of the diffusion of innovation generally. The problem with simplicity or complexity as a characteristic of the communicative innovation is that it is sometimes hard to know in advance what will be simple to learn. This is especially true with respect to the planning of phonological, lexical, or syntactic innovation.

On what grounds do we judge that something will be easy to learn? It is commonly thought, for example, that short words are preferable to long ones when coining new terms, on the assumption that shorter words are easier to learn than longer ones. Fainberg (1983), however, found that for the twenty-five Hebrew neologisms she studied, there was no relationship between the length of the term and the number of respondents who knew or used it. Instead, she found that acceptance of a neologism was related to the number of other words that were based on the same root. Neologisms formed from roots on which relatively few, or relatively many, other words were built tended to be accepted less than innovations formed from roots on which an intermediate number of other words (four or five) were built. She suggested that neologisms based on roots with relatively few words are less conspicuous and therefore less readily learned, whereas neologisms based on roots with relatively more words may tend to become confused with their cognates. While this explanation may be correct, it is clearly *ex post facto* with respect to simplicity. In any case, her study is a pioneering effort to investigate the structural properties of successful neologisms. If language planners are to construct or choose items which have maximum opportunity for acceptance, they would do well to conduct such research themselves and to heed its results.

Function refers to the purpose for which the innovation is planned. It is in the domain of codification and standardization (see Chapter 6) that language planners are most apt to miss the importance of specifying the context in which the innovation is to be used. The Israeli radio program described earlier, which insisted on the normative variation as the only permissible alternative, ignored the fact that such variants, when used at all, are often restricted to a very limited range of contexts. The pervasiveness of such a monolithic view of Hebrew, seen in this program – and, until recently, in the schools – has been one reason why even highly educated native Hebrew speakers feel insecure in their usage (Rabin 1983). A recent curriculum reform, however, undertaken by the Israeli Ministry of Education, seeks to repair and prevent this damage by encouraging the recognition that different spoken and written styles are appropriate for different purposes (Regev 1983).

In sum, what is planned can be specified in terms of structural and functional properties. While differences in these properties are presumably related to differences in the rate and extent of spread, our ability to identify the relevant properties is at this stage limited indeed.

When

Katz, Levin, and Hamilton (1963) point out that, strictly speaking, it is time of adoption rather than adoption itself which is the dependent variable of interest to researchers in the diffusion of innovation. If time of adoption can be determined, then the characteristics of early and late adopters can be compared and diffusion curves, showing the number of adopters as a function of time, can be drawn. Many diffusion studies report S-shaped curves (Warner 1974), i.e. the percentage of potential adopters that accepts an innovation rises slowly at first, then gathers speed, and then slackens off until it reaches a ceiling, with the proportion that has adopted the innovation remaining stable thereafter.

It is likely that the spread of lingua francas in particular exhibits an S-shaped curve. The more people who learn the language, the more useful it becomes as a lingua franca, encouraging a rapid increase in the number of people who know it (Lieberson 1982). The increase then slacks off either as the proportion of additional speakers requiring a lingua franca approaches zero or as the language encroaches upon the boundaries of another lingua franca. I know of no empirical test of this hypothesis, however.

While data on the time of adoption are crucial for the study of the spread of communicative innovations, they are rarely gathered. This seems to be the case for studies of diffusion generally (Katz et al., 1963), probably because of difficulty in obtaining the data. Longitudinal studies are expensive. Furthermore, the time that can be devoted to a single longitudinal study often represents a very small segment of the period in which the communicative innovation spreads. To secure data gathered over longer periods than can usually be covered by a single longitudinal study, one can sometimes examine age cohorts for successive censuses, as Lieberson (1970) has done with Canadian census data. For example, the proportion of the 20 to 29-year-olds who reported knowing a given language in one census can be compared to the proportion of 30 to 39-year-olds who reported knowing it in the census carried out ten years later and with the proportion of 40 to 49-year-olds who reported knowing it in the census carried out ten years after that, and so on. This procedure would permit the drawing of time-based diffusion curves, but the curves would be based on assumptions that are often difficult to justify, e.g. that the demographic composition of the age cohorts has not been substantially altered by immigration or emigration and that neither the language questions in successive censuses nor respondents' willingness to answer them honestly have changed. Another problem with basing diffusion curves on successive censuses is that the interval between censuses is likely to be so long that only a few time-points on the diffusion curve can be plotted. Also, censuses rarely ask more than one language question and that question is often not the question in which we are most interested. Thus successive censuses may ask about languages that the respondent knows, whereas we may be interested in the language(s) the respondent first knew or the languages the respondent currently uses for given purposes. And, of course, censuses do not deal with knowledge or use of individual linguistic items – given phonemes, morphemes, or syntactic structures. In spite of these caveats, the data from language censuses can be profitably analyzed, as Lieberson's (1970) analysis of Canadian data testifies.

If neither longitudinal surveys nor successive censuses are used, we can ask respondents, in a single survey, when they adopted the innovation. This is difficult to remember, however, particularly in the case of linguistic innovations, which would have had to be explicitly recognized by the respondent at the time of adoption. Further, an individual adopter's acquisition is often gradual. In the case of a language, for example, at what point can it be said that the adopter has learned it?

Because of such logistical and methodological difficulties, we typically employ surveys conducted at only one point in time and determine (through observation, Labovian interviews, tests, etc.) the extent to which respondents have adopted the innovation in question. We can then relate extent of adoption with characteristics of respondents, including age. This permits us to trace the progress of the innovation through "apparent time," i.e. across generations.

Although determining the time of adoption is an important problem in the study of the diffusion of innovation generally and the study of communicative innovations in particular, language planners cannot ignore the time-dependent nature of change in language use, language structure, and language acquisition. Plans often specify the date at which a given change is to be accomplished. If interim dates are specified for which successive proportions of the target population are to have accepted the innovation, then the success of the plan's implementation can be monitored, and the data obtained can be used if necessary to revise either the interim or the final goals, or the manner of their implementation. Such interim evaluations, which should be routine in any organized planning, are particularly important in language planning inasmuch as we usually do not know how much time is necessary, under given conditions, to accomplish given language-planning ends. Changes occur not only in response to planning but also in response to factors over which the planners may have no control. But even if planners did not have to take such factors into account, they often have little information as to how much time is required for a given communicative innovation to be accepted for a given purpose under given conditions. Thus periodic interim evaluations can help planners not only to monitor and revise their plans but also to gain experience as to the amount of time that is required to accomplish given ends. Such information will be useful, of course, not only to language planners but also to all students of the diffusion of innovation.

Where

The question of where the innovation is adopted refers not to the location of the adopter but rather to the socially defined location of the interactions through which the innovation spreads. Thus location here is defined not in physical or geographical space but in social space.

Fishman's (1972a) work on language maintenance and language shift has emphasized the societal domain as a crucial locus for the study of societal bilingualism. A domain, according to Fishman, represents a constellation of social situations, each defined by the intersection of role-relationship, locale, and time. The situations comprising a domain are all constrained by the same set of behavioral norms. Participant observation as well as experimental studies have demonstrated the usefulness of this approach.

A study of Puerto Rican bilingual children who attended a Catholic elementary school in Jersey City, across the Hudson River from New York City, provides an example (Edelman, Cooper, and Fishman 1968). The aim of the study was to assess the usage of and fluency in Spanish relative to English in each of four hypothesized domains – education, religion, neighborhood, and home. Accordingly, in individual interviews, the children were asked to report the degree to which they used Spanish relative to English with various bilingual interlocutors in school, at church, in the neighborhood, and at home. They were also asked to name, within 45-second periods, as many objects as could be found in each of four settings – school, church, neighborhood, and kitchen. The children named objects for all four domains in one language and then named objects for all four domains in the other, with half the children beginning in Spanish and the other half in English. The children reported that their Spanish usage relative to their English usage was greatest at home and lowest at school. Similarly, their word-naming scores showed greatest proficiency in Spanish relative to English for the domain of home and lowest relative proficiency for the domain of school. Global, uncontextualized measures, e.g. a general word-naming task, without reference to specific areas, would have masked such differences in usage and in fluency associated with different domains of social interaction.

Societal domain, then, may be a useful construct for both language planners and students of the diffusion of communicative innovations. In what role-relationships (e.g. customer–salesclerk, student–teacher, citizen–government functionary, enlisted soldier–officer), in what locales (e.g. shop, school, government office, parade ground), and at what times is the innovation encountered and accepted? Gumperz (1958), for example, suggested that innovations in the subdialects spoken in a North Indian village spread via friendship networks. It was not simple frequency of interaction that determined who adopted an innovation but rather the relationship between innovators and adopters or between earlier and later adopters. Thus verbal interactions between employers and employees, while very frequent, did not appear to lead one to adopt the speech patterns of the other, whereas informal interactions among friends did seem to lead to such adoptions.

From one point of view, social interactions form the channels through which an innovation flows. From what persons and in what social contexts does the potential adopter hear about or encounter the innovation? What persons influence, deliberately or not, the potential adopter's evaluation of the innovation? From what persons and in what social contexts does the potential adopter learn the innovation, and with whom and in what contexts does he or she use it? We want to specify the characteristics of those persons who influence the potential adopter to change and we want to specify the characteristics of the interactions between agents of change and potential adopters. Once the potential adopter has accepted the innovation, who are the persons that he or she will influence in turn?

The notion of societal domain can help us to group together the inumerable interactions through which communicative innovations spread. These clusters can then be contrasted and compared with respect to their permeability to change. If we can learn to what extent different rates of acceptance are associated with different types of social interaction, language planners will be helped in setting and implementing their goals and students of the diffusion of innovation will increase their understanding of the channels through which innovations advance.

Why

What incentives induce planners and agents of change to promote the innovation? What incentives induce potential adopters to adopt it? If we employ the means-end approach to attitude, mentioned earlier in connection with evaluation by potential adopters, we would want to know the importance of the goals or interests served by the innovation as well as the relevance of the innovation to the goals. With respect to promoters of change, we may need to distinguish two types of covert goals – those goals served by the planning agency and the planners' personal goals.

For example, national goals of political integration might be served by language standardization, but the planners' personal goals might be served if their own variety were used as the model of standardization or if they became the sole guardians of the standardized variety. Similarly, language has often served as a rallying point for the formation of national consciousness, but those who promote the language also promote themselves as a protoelite who will come to power with the political apparatus they create through mass mobilization (Fishman 1972b).

We can perhaps understand the reasons for the facilitating value of the innovation if we can examine the behavioral changes that occur after adoption. Foster (1971), discussing the development of literacy in relation to political and economic development, asks what really happens to people once they become literate. Demand for literacy in sub-Saharan Africa, according to Foster, appears to follow the creation of conditions under which literacy has immediate cash benefits. In rural areas, the introduction of profitable cash crops, the improvement of transportation, and access to credit stimulate a swing from a subsistence to a cash-crop economy. Once such a movement is under way, people begin to see that literacy is worthwhile. It enables farmers to calculate crop yields and returns and to read material designed to help improve productivity. The development of an exchange economy creates, in the towns, modern jobs for which literacy is a prerequisite. According to Foster, the development of literacy does not itself generate the movement to an exchange economy, but once that movement has begun, literacy can help promote further growth.

The same kinds of questions asked about the development of literacy can be asked about the spread of any communicative innovation. What are the behavioral consequences of having adopted it? Conversely, what are the behavioral consequences of not having done so?

How

In the words of Rogers (1983: 17), "the essence of the diffusion process is the information exchange by which one individual communicates a new idea to one or several others. At its most elementary form, the process involves: (1) an innovation, (2) an individual or other unit of adoption that has knowledge of, or experience with using, the innovation, (3) another individual or unit that does not yet have knowledge of the innovation, and (4) a communication channel connecting the two units. A *communication channel* is the means by which messages get from one individual to another. The nature of the information exchange relationship between the pair of individuals determines the conditions under which a source will or will not transmit the innovation to the receiver, and the effect of the transfer."

This paradigm, the classic one for the diffusion of innovation, emphasizes the flow of information and persuasion and the channels of this flow. Thus the work of Katz (1957) on personal communication has stimulated research on the two-step flow of communication in which mass-media messages are followed by word-of-mouth communication (Pool 1973). Rural sociologists have posited a two-step flow from county agent to influential farmer to other farmers in the diffusion of new farm practices (Katz *et al.* 1963). Students of mass communications have typically found that mass-media channels are more important for imparting knowledge about an innovation and that interpersonal channels are more important in persuading the potential adopter to accept the innovation (Rao 1971). It is likely that "the heart of the diffusion process is the modeling and imitation by potential adopters of their network partners who have adopted previously" (Rogers 1983: 18).

The relevance of information and persuasion seems clear for innovations which must be accepted or rejected consciously, e.g. hybrid corn, chemical fertilizer, birth control practices, a brand of toothpaste. Is language such an innovation? Undoubtedly, there are contexts in which a communicative innovation spreads because of the conscious decision of people to adopt it, particularly when adopters must enroll in classes or engage a tutor in order to do so. However, communicative innovations often spread without conscious attention on the part of adopters, particularly in the case of linguistic items. Here the "information exhange" and the "modeling and imitation of potential adopters" are likely to be unconscious.

We can modify the classic paradigm of diffusion in order to accommodate the unconscious transmission or adoption of communicative (as well as other) innovations, as follows: the diffusion process consists of (1) an innovation, (2) individual *A*, who is a potential source of influence with respect to the innovation, and (3) individual *B*, who has not yet adopted the innovation. The social conditions under which *B* encounters *A* determine the likelihood that *A* will influence *B* to adopt the innovation.

In this scheme, *A* is a potential source of influence concerning *B*'s awareness, evaluation, knowledge, or usage. The encounter between *A* and *B* can be through the mass media, as when *B* hears *A* on the radio, or through personal contact, including formal instruction. *A* can intend to communicate with *B* (or to the audience of which *B* is a member), or *A*'s communication with *B* may be incidental or unintentional, as when *A* communicates with *C* in *B*'s presence. Further, *A* need not necessarily use the communicative innovation in *B*'s presence but may merely talk about it, as when a parent or teacher encourages a child to study a given language. In this model, *B* may encounter many different *A*'s, and encounters with different *A*'s may lead to different levels of adoption.

Some individuals or some roles, teachers for example, may be more important than others as sources of influence, depending in part upon the nature and frequency of their interactions with the potential adopter. It is, of course, one of the primary goals of diffusion research to determine the characteristics of those interactions which are related to differences in time and degree of adoption, and these we have discussed under the rubric "where."

The A's in our paradigm, who act as the direct agents of change do not, of course, operate in a social vacuum but are themselves influenced by those social processes which contribute to social change. Language planning, like all social planning, is both a product of and a contributor to these processes. Thus an explanation of the process of diffusion should not only include the interactions and relationships between potential adopters and direct agents of change, but also the processes which influence these interactions and relationships.

Let us take the spread of English in Israel as an example. One factor that contributes to Israelis' incentive to learn English is the importance of foreign trade to the economy. English is most likely to be needed by Israelis for international trade because, as Lieberson (1982) points out, English-speaking nations constitute the most significant world market as measured by the value of their imports and English can be used with "third parties," i.e. those who have learned English as an additional language. Moreover, the use of English by the manufacturing, banking, agricultural, and trading concerns which are directly involved in world trade creates the need for English in some of the companies and agencies which serve them. Thus the use of English in international trade has a multiplier effect.

The economic incentives for Israelis to learn English can be seen from a survey of help-wanted advertisements in the Israeli Hebrew press (Cooper and Seckbach 1977). English was mentioned as a requirement in about 10 percent of all jobs listed and in 17 percent of all jobs listed in nonclassified advertisements. One of the categories most often requiring English was that of white-collar worker (26 percent). Thus it is not only the university-trained worker who needs English in Israel. (A similar search of want ads in American newspapers would reveal the relatively trivial economic importance attached to foreign-language knowledge in the United States.)

Now it is likely that changes in such factors as the attractiveness of Israeli exports, the volume of international trade, and the amount of the gross national product will play a part of creating and sustaining a demand for English. Social planning contributes to such factors but, of course, cannot control them. Social planning also contributes to the opportunity to learn English insofar as it determines the proportion of the national budget devoted to education.

Language planning also affects the demand for English. On the one hand, promotion of Hebrew as the national language has minimized the need for any other internal lingua franca, at least within the Jewish population. (English is sometimes used as lingua franca between Jews and Palestinians, but here too Hebrew is the usual choice.) Moreover, the elaboration and modernization of Hebrew has made it easier to translate technical material into Hebrew and has thus reduced the need for technicians to read technical material in English. On the other hand, compulsory instruction in English from the fourth or fifth grade through high school and the setting of English as a required subject on the high school matriculation examination have both provided opportunity and created incentive to learn English.

In sum

In the process of diffusion suggested here, language planning, other social planning, and social, political, and economic change all influence one another as well as the direct agents of change who, in turn, influence potential adopters of a communicative innovation. Not all processes, including language planning, influence all direct agents. Similarly, different direct agents can influence different levels of adoption, some contributing to adoption at one level only and others contributing to adoption at several levels. Further, the different levels of adoption may mutually reinforce one another. Finally, changes in levels of adoption may affect the social processes which impinge upon the direct agents of change. Thus the diffusion process is a dynamic one, whereby social processes both affect and are affected by the adoption of communicative innovation.

Language planning as marketing

At first glance, the notion of language planning as a set of marketing strategies for behavioral change may seem strange. We are not accustomed to viewing language use, structure, or acquisition as "products" whose acceptance can be promoted. While some language planners may not view their activities as analogous to those performed by the product managers of a toothpaste, detergent, or automobile, there is much to recommend the analogy.

The marketing problem is typically viewed as "developing the right *product* backed by the right *promotion* and put in the right *place* at the right *price*" (Kotler and Zaltman 1971). McCarthy (1968: 31–33) calls these rubrics "the four P's."

Product

Like all marketers, language planners must recognize, identify, or design products which the potential consumer will find attractive. When a language academy undertakes the preparation of a list of new technical terms, for example, its planners would find it useful to know what characteristics of terms are most likely to lead to a term's acceptance. Similarly, when workers for the Summer Institute of Linguistics translate the Gospels into an unwritten language with considerable dialect diversity, they would find it useful to know which of the dialects potential readers will find most acceptable as a literary standard.

Perhaps the first to suggest that effective marketing principles can be applied to non-business organizations were Kotler and Levy (1969), who propose at least three principles relevant to the design of an attractive product. These are principles which they claim are effective for business organizations. These principles are (1) define the product generically; (2) define the target group of consumers; and (3) analyze consumer behavior.

According to Kotler and Levy, business organizations recognize the value of defining their products broadly, emphasizing the basic customer need which the product meets. Thus the generic product for a soap company is cleaning, whereas for a cosmetics company it is beauty or romance. Kotler and Levy argue that non-business organizations should also define their products broadly. For a church this might be human fellowship; for a foundation seeking funds for medical research this might be relief from fear or guilt, or it might be maintenance or enhancement of self-esteem. For language planning, the product definition would vary with the object of planning. For a language academy it might be national pride rather than the product of dictionaries or the standardization of terminology, whereas for a mass-literacy campaign it might be the enhancement of economic opportunity rather than reading and writing. The feminist campaign against sexist language defined its product in terms of social justice – either social justice for all, on the grounds that the liberation of women will liberate men, or social justice for women. These are attractive products inasmuch as most would agree that they are in favor of social justice.

Kotler and Levy point out that a generic definition of the product results in a wide market. Because each organization has limited resources it must limit its product offering to clearly defined groups. While an automobile's generic product might be transportation, it does not produce bicycles, steamships, or planes. It produces cars, but even here, it does not produce every conceivable type. Similarly, Kotler and Levy point out, a school system might define its product generically as the social and intellectual development of young persons, but it restricts the ages of its pupils as well as the subjects and the extracurricular activities which it offers to them.

With respect to the feminist campaign, there appears to have been a restriction both in the product and in the audience to whom it was marketed. If the generic product was social justice for women, then the avoidance of sexist language is one of several "buyable" products that advance this cause. Others might be support for legislation promoting equal rights for women, support for the candidacy of politicians sympathetic to feminist aims, and the initiation of legal proceedings against employers perceived as harassing women or discriminating against them. Even with respect to the avoidance of sexist language there appears to have been a restriction of the product inasmuch as most attention was focused on androcentric generics. There seem to have been four target audiences. These were (1) those feminists who had not yet changed their usage; (2) university lecturers and similar academics whose conversations and lectures were sometimes stopped cold by someone's pointing out an instance of sex-biased usage; (3) professional organizations, such as the American Psychological Association, which were pressured into changing their publications' style manuals, and (4) editors of mass-circulation publications whose sexist usage was pointed out via letters and face-to-face interaction.

To take another example, the plain-language movement, at least in the United States, appears to have directed itself primarily at improving the readability of insurance contracts, consumer-goods warranties, and government regulations addressed to the public. By no means were all texts with which consumers and citizens must grapple targeted. The movement targeted those types of text most salient to consumer protection.

Products are defined and audiences targeted on the basis of consumer needs. Kotler and Levy assert that these needs are not obvious without formal research and analysis. Thus marketers should not rely on impressionistic evidence. Sociologists of language and social psychologists conduct research relevant to the motivations of potential adopters of language-planning decisions, particularly research on language attitudes. While planning agencies may occasionally consider such research findings when evaluating alternative choices, they rarely commission or carry out such work themselves. The particular languages used in the Ethiopian mass-literacy campaign, for example, were chosen on the basis of information published by the Language Survey of Ethiopia, one of five East African language surveys sponsored by the Ford Foundation during the late 1960s and early 1970s. Among other data provided by the Language Survey of Ethiopia were estimates of the number of mother-tongue speakers of each of approximately seventy-five indigenous languages (Bender, Bowen, Cooper, and Ferguson 1976). The literacy materials were written in the most populous languages. The authorities appeared to have assumed that potential readers would prefer to be taught via their own mother tongue, but this assumption may not have been sound. In view of the official status of Amharic, the paucity of reading matter in other indigenous languages save for Tigrinya, and widespread knowledge of Amharic as a second language, many potential readers who spoke mother tongues other than Amharic might well have preferred initial instruction via Amharic. With respect to all of our defining examples, we see little if any effort to determine the motivation of the different target groups to accept the planned innovation. Planners relied on intuition.

Promotion

Promotion of a communicative innovation refers to efforts to induce potential users to adopt it, whether adoption is viewed as awareness, positive evaluation, proficiency, or usage. Relatively few language-planning decisions can be implemented by fiat. In most cases, planners need to consider how they will persuade potential adopters to accept the innovation. Assume, for example, a language academy which produces and publishes a list of approved terms for a technical field, say chemistry. Assume further that until publication of the list, there was considerable variation in usage which, in fact, prompted the academy's efforts at standardization. Will chemists now abandon their previous usages and adopt the new terms without any effort by the academy or by their national association of chemists to get them to do so? Perhaps. But it is unreasonable simply to assume so. Usually some effort is required to persuade the target population to adopt the innovation planned for it.

What techniques of persuasion have language planners used? They have used all of the devices which are available to the promoter of any commodity, product, service, or idea. The province of Catalonia, for example, in 1982–1983, used billboards, radio and television skits, stick-on labels, balloons, cartoons in newspapers and magazines, and short movies, and it sponsored debates, lectures and panel discussions, in order to encourage bilingual interactions between Castilian and Catalan speakers, so that each would use his or her own language with the other (Boix 1985). The Office de la Langue française, established to implement the francization policy of the Province of Quebec, put signs in public places exhorting Quebecois to use correct French and to be proud of their identity: "Parler bien, c'est se respecter" (Weinstein 1983: 52). The skits promoting normative usage, broadcast by the Israeli radio, have already been mentioned. Just as manufacturers of consumer goods offer prizes to arouse or maintain interest ("In 25 words or less explain why you prefer Royal Highland whisky and win a fabulous trip to Scotland for two!"), so do language planners sometimes award prizes or grants to stimulate awareness, interest, proficiency, or usage. Macnamara (1971: 81) reported that the Cumann na Sagart, an Irish clerical group, promoted the use of Irish by awarding prizes to the towns in English-speaking districts which used Irish the most. To promote the use of Welsh, the Welsh Arts Council awarded grants to promising Welsh writers, offered scholarships to enable writers to obtain sabbaticals for more intensive effort, ran competitions, and made grants to the British Broadcasting Authority in Wales to broadcast programs in Welsh (Lewis 1982: 252). Promoters of literacy in Lelemi, spoken by the Buem people in the Volta Region of Ghana, gave T-shirts to literates who led at least five other literates, potential volunteer teachers, through a teacher-training primer (Ring 1985). On the front of the shirt was the outline of a book with a torch inside, with the words (written in Lelemi) "Lelemi Reading" above it and "Let's keep it burning" written below.

In the first decades after independence, the Union Government of India's program for the promotion of Hindi included cash prizes for authors of Hindi books and for writers who prepared Hindi materials for the newly literate. Sometimes the government bought outright the works of some Hindi writers for government publication and distribution (Das Gupta 1970: 173–4).

The feminist campaign against sexist usage employed two major promotional tools. One tool was publicity: letters to the editor, op-ed pieces, and news releases as, for example, about revised liturgical texts which refer to the Deity in a sex-indefinite fashion. The second tool, and probably the more important one, was the face-to-face intervention of feminists, who pointed out to speakers, on the spot, occurrences of sexist language and supplied alternative forms. This behavior is of particular interest in view of an early article by Lazarsfeld and Merton (1949), who explained why mass media are unlikely to be successful very often in propaganda campaigns. Three elements must all be present, they claimed, for mass-media propaganda campaigns to succeed. One of these is what they called *supplementation*, a kind of step-down communication process whereby a message presented by the media is passed on and discussed in more familiar surroundings. The feminist campaign against sexist usage was not a media campaign primarily. Its main vehicle was face-to-face communication. And perhaps face-to-face communicaton is a sufficient condition for the success of a campaign. At any rate, to the extent that the feminist campaign employed the media for promotion, we see a three-step rather than a two-step sequence. Face-to-face communication led to mobilized opinion. Mobilized persons then sought avenues of expression and promotion via the media. Messages transmitted by the media about nonsexist language usage were then discussed in step-down fashion.

The other constraints which operate on mass-media propaganda campaigns, according to Lazarsfeld and Merton, are *monopolization of the media* and *canalization*. Monopolization of the media is usually required to prevent the appearance of counter-propaganda. Thus antismoking campaigns compete with cigarette advertisements, the American Heart Association competes with the American Cancer Society in soliciting funds, and the proponents of birth control compete with proponents of the right to life. Counter-propaganda is sometimes implicit, as in the case of the Israeli mass media, which daily employ non-normative lexical, phonological, and grammatical alternatives. (While the state radio program which advises the public on correct Hebrew usage tells its audience, don't say X, say Y, speakers on other radio programs may well use X.)

But counter-propaganda can also be explicit, as in the case of the feminist campaign, which is often ridiculed by editorials, op-ed pieces, and cartoons. More damaging, perhaps, is the argument of many feminists that the campaign is harmful to the ultimate cause of women's liberation, on the grounds that it deflects attention to a peripheral issue. Furthermore, the Women's Liberation Movement is in competition with many other campaigns for social justice, a competition which reduces the salience of the feminist campaign.

Canalization refers to the reshaping of existing attitudes. It is easier to reshape existing attitudes than to induce a major attitudinal reorientation. For example, it is easier to persuade consumers to buy a particular brand of shoe polish if one does not first have to convince them to wear shoes. In the case of the Israeli radio's normative campaign, most Israelis have yet to be persuaded to wear shoes, so to speak. They are unwilling to replace the language of everyday life with normative alternatives. They are unwilling, in other words, to appear ridiculous. To persuade them to use, in ordinary conversation, the particular variants promoted by the program, one must first change their view of such alternatives. But to persuade people to believe in the unbelievable – in this case the appropriateness of inappropriate language – is a tall order. While Israelis are still shoeless, most feminists are fully shod. The campaign may already have convinced most feminists to avoid sexist usage. Their favorable attitudes towards the women's liberation movement may already have been canalized towards the change in language usage advocated by the campaign. If those who have not changed their usage are hostile or indifferent to the movement or believe that the campaign against sexist usage is an irrelevancy or worse, it will be hard to change their behavior.

While language planners can use all of the promotional devices available to any marketer, they may sometimes enjoy other possibilities as well. When the language-planning agency is an agent of the state, it can employ the coercive power of the state to enforce language-planning decisions. Quebec's Charter of the French Language (1977), for example, forbids punishing a worker for using French. When the H & R Block Company dismissed a Francophone employee because she could not speak English well, she complained to the labor department. A labor relations court required the company to rehire the employee and to restore her back pay (Weinstein 1983: 53).

Whether or not it is proper to view state coercion as a type of promotion, it should be stressed that the coercive power of the state rests, in the long run, on the consent of the governed, even in totalitarian states. Evasion, avoidance, or nonenforcement of a policy generally result when there is widespread resistance to it among the public. While the Irish Constitution proclaims Irish, abandoned by the masses by the mid-nineteenth century, as the country's national and first official language, and while the major political parties support the restoration of Irish, and while knowledge of Irish is required for some important examinations and for appointment to various positions in the civil service and in the courts, English remains the language of everyday life. While Arabic is a required subject in many Jewish primary schools in Israel, resistance to learning it is endemic; few Jewish pupils learn it well enough to be able to use it for any purpose outside the school. Demonstrations in Soviet Georgia forced the USSR to maintain Georgian as an official language of the Republic (Weinstein 1983: 142). African secondary students in Soweto rioted in June 1976 in response to the South African government's decree that half their instruction be via Afrikaans, viewed by the students as a language of oppression. These riots forced the government to back down from its language policy.

Shortly before the introduction of mixed-sex dormitories and the abolition of a rule forbidding women to spend the night in a man's room at a well-known American college, an officer of the college is said to have seen a young man and young woman leaving the former's room before breakfast. Without batting an eyelash, the officer is supposed to have said "Good morning, gentlemen." An unpopular rule was becoming unenforceable. Just as student resistance can defeat or blunt the impact of a college regulation, so can public resistance defeat or blunt the impact of a language policy, even when backed by the power of the state. In most cases, even state-backed language-planning agencies, like all marketers, must consider ways and means to create a climate of opinion favorable to the adoption of the planned innovation.

Place

Place refers to the provision of adequate channels of distribution and response. A person motivated to buy a product must know where to find it. Imagine a promotion campaign for a new product (not merely a new brand). Where can one buy it? Promotion of a consumer product is futile if there are no outlets in which the consumer can buy it. Similarly, promotion of an idea in the service of a social cause will fail if adopters of the idea don't know how to put the new possibilities into practice, e.g. safe driving, safe sex, or a support for the homeless. Feminists did more than inveigh against sexist usage. They provided style manuals which demonstrated ways to avoid the use of androcentric generics. We were not simply told to avoid sin. We were told how to be virtuous.

Price

The price of a consumer good or service is an important determinant of its appeal. The marketer has to try to lower the price in relation to the benefit or raise the benefit in relation to the price. Sometimes tangible costs are involved in the adoption of a communicative innovation. For example, millions of adults worldwide study English as a foreign language in night school. Economic incentives are a powerful stimulus to this learning. Many of these students believe that knowledge of English will improve their earning capacity. Presumably, they view the projected financial rewards as greater than the present costs of tuition fees, time, energy, or income foregone while learning. When banks and insurance companies, to take another example, voluntarily simplify the language of their consumer contracts, they must pay for the services of experts to revise the forms as well as for printing and distributing the new forms, and for training staff to use them. Presumably, the managers of these firms view these costs as smaller than the rewards entailed in improved consumer satisfaction. With respect to the feminist campaign, there are no money costs involved, apart from the purchase of a style manual, but there are energy costs and psychic costs. It requires a conscious effort to learn these new ways of speaking and writing and to unlearn or resist the habits of a lifetime. Furthermore, one must be prepared to withstand a certain amount of chaffing if, as is often the case, ridicule is attached to the adoption of something new. There are, however, costs of *persisting* in one's old behavior. As mentioned above, one can not publish papers in certain journals if one uses sex-indefinite *he*, for instance, or *the man in the street*. Worse, perhaps, one may appear retrograde, illiberal, or insensitive if one does so.

Language planning as the pursuit and maintenance of power

Like language planning, politics refers both to an activity and to a field of study. As philosophical inquiry, politics can be traced at least as far back as Aristotle's *Politics*. But contemporary political science emerged only in the nineteenth century alongside modern sociology. Indeed, St. Simon and Comte (1822) argued that politics would become "social physics," whose purpose was to discover laws of progress and which Comte later elaborated as "sociology" (Latham 1980).

Modern political science has no single, universally agreed upon focus. Some view political science as the study of state or political institutions, others as the study of particular processes. Of the latter, the two most prominent central themes are decision making and power (Easton 1968). Decision making, which in the context of politics refers to the steps whereby public policy is formulated and implemented, provides a framework to be presented in the next section. In the present section, I offer a framework suggested by the study of power.

Power is the ability to influence the behavior of others. Since power is ubiquitous in human relationships, it is by no means studied only by political scientists. It is treated by all the social sciences in varying degrees. But to political science, power is central: "The study of politics is the study of influence and the influential" (Lasswell 1936: 3). Since language planning attempts to influence behavior, the categories employed by political scientists are relevant to students of language planning, an assertion supported by the interest in language planning displayed by some political scientists (see, especially, Das Gupta 1970, Mazrui 1975, O'Barr and O'Barr 1976, Weinstein 1983).

If politics is the study of influence and the influential, who are the influential? According to Lasswell, they are "those who get the most of what there is to get. . . . Those who get the most are *elite*; the rest are *mass*" (1936: 3). In his view, politics determines "who gets what, when, how", a famous short-hand definition which can serve as one framework for the study of language planning.

Who benefits

That scarcity exists in all societies stems from a collision between the finite capacity of human production with the infinite capacity of human desire. Scarcity inevitably creates conflict. When competing interests can not readily negotiate their differences, special institutions and processes impose a settlement (Easton 1968). These institutions are political ones. They allocate scarce resources (values) among an insatiable public, a society in which the less powerful seek a more equitable distribution of values and the more powerful seek to expand their privileges. Those members of society who are the most powerful exert the most influence over the distributive process. Thus in language planning as in politics, it is useful to ask who benefits from any given arrangement.

It is not always easy to answer this question. Who benefited, for example, from the feminist campaign against sexist usage? Feminists might argue that *everyone* benefits, men as well as women, when sexist usage is reduced. A reduction in sexist usage, according to this view, reduces sexual stereotyping and thus expands the opportunities for both sexes to realize their true potential. A more jaundiced viewer might argue that the antisexist language campaign benefited mainly the existing elite. According to this view, the campaign drained popular discontent, or at least feminist discontent, into harmless channels, without changing the fundamental social, economic, and political arrangements that promote sexual inequality. The substitution of one pronoun for another has no more affect on these arrangements than the Sun Dance on the earth's fertility. Both exercises leave existing social structures intact.

To claim that the campaign against sexist language usage benefited elites is not to claim that the elite initiated them. Still, this campaign was a middle-class movement. It was not launched by the disadvantaged or by those who speak for the disadvantaged. Once launched, the movement was adopted and promoted by legislatures and administrations which could win popularity by changes which were essentially cosmetic. The elite, in other words, could appear responsive to the populace and create an illusion of progress without embarking on fundamental alterations of a system, of which the language problem is merely symptomatic.

It is easier to identify the beneficiaries of status planning for the Ethiopian mass-literacy campaign. Few would deny that the new rulers were the chief beneficiaries. Their decision to employ vernaculars as media for literacy training helped neutralize the threat of student opposition. Similarly, the establishment of the Académie française appears to have been directed towards the strengthening of an elite, in this case via the centralization of authority and information and via the glorification of the elite dialect and thus of the elite itself.

Did the movement for the restoration of Hebrew as a vernacular in Palestine benefit an elite? Within the Palestinian Jewish community, the promotion of Hebrew helped to legitimize a national movement and to validate the credentials of that movement's leadership, which used Hebrew for public, secular functions. However, from the point of view of the rulers, first the Ottomans and then the British, the Zionist leadership in Palestine represented an antagonistic, revolutionary counterelite, which sought to usurp authority for the sake of Jewish political autonomy. Thus the campaign to vernacularize Hebrew can be viewed as benefiting elites or counterelites, depending on one's point of view. In either case, language planning served the interests of those who would acquire power.

One can argue, in sum, that in all four defining examples, language planning was employed to maintain or strengthen elite power, the power of the influentials, the power of those who get the most of what there is to get, or the power of counterelites. "What there is to get," of course, represents different values, such as the three representative values to which Lasswell refers – income, deference, and safety. Frey (1980) lists eight types of value: power, respect, rectitude, affection, well-being, wealth, skill, and enlightenment, with control over these corresponding to eight types of power: political power, councillorship, mentorship, personal influence, violence, economic power, expertness, and advisory influence. Normally, control over one value is associated with control over others, but the distributions of these values are only imperfectly correlated. An elite of income, for example, may not be an elite of safety, and an elite of enlightenment may not be an elite of income. For some purposes, therefore, it may be useful to speak of "elites" rather than of "the elite," since the latter will vary according to the values used to define it.

One basis for defining elites is the institution through which power is exercised – political, economic, religious, scientific, artistic, educational, and so on. I have argued thus far that political and economic elites or counterelites were beneficiaries, if not the chief beneficiaries, of the language planning carried out in our four defining examples. But other elites may have benefited as well, particularly those elites associated with cultural institutions. Membership in the Académie française, for example, enhances the influence of a literary elite. The feminist campaign enhances the influence of those academics and writers who can show others how to avoid sexist usage. The vernacularization of Hebrew gave employment and honor to language scholars, who helped standardize and elaborate modern Hebrew. And even the Ethiopian mass-literacy campaign may have enhanced, if only momentarily, the influence of university professors or other experts serving as linguistic consultants to the Ministry of Education. One can, of course, argue that in these instances, a cultural elite was coopted by a political or economic elite and that in any event the cultural elite did not initiate the planning. Nonetheless, if the opportunity to benefit from a change does not necessarily induce elites to cooperate, neither does it induce them to resist.

When language planning provides a livelihood for its practitioners, language planning benefits the planner. Editors of new dictionaries, authors of normative grammars, columnists who inveigh against linguistic innovation and decry the decline and decay of the language, authors of books on linguistic etiquette, teacher trainers and teachers who espouse normative forms, and the employees of agencies designed to promote language spread, such as the British Council, all exemplify persons who benefit directly from language planning and who thus have a stake in its continuance. Not all of these persons are members of an elite. To the extent that the implementation of language planning requires the cooperation of non-elite personnel, who themselves may need to make decisions in support of the overall scheme, nonelites must view the operation as beneficial to them, or at least as nonthreatening to their position.

I do not mean to suggest that language planning benefits only elites, counterelites, and their agents. To the extent that the cooperation of the mass is a prerequisite for the maintenance of elites and to the extent that benefits to the mass encourage cooperation with elites, the latter are well-advised to channel benefits to the former or at least to give the appearance of doing so. But just as *cherchez la femme* was a useful guide to motivation in the bad old days of sexist thrillers, so *seek the beneficiary* is a useful guide to our understanding of language planning.

When

Just as time is a dependent variable in the study of diffusion, so is it a dependent variable in the study of power relations. Whereas students of diffusion are interested in the speed with which a given level of acceptance is reached, political scientists are interested in the speed of response to an attempt at influence.

Speed of response to A's attempt to influence B is a function of several determinants, among which are (1) the power relationship between A and B and (2) B's interpretation of what constitutes a speedy response. With respect to the power relationship, the speed of B's response varies with the degree to which power is patterned hierarchically, unilaterally, and directly, and with the degree to which absolute authority is employed, as in military units (Frey 1980).

Though a speedy response need not be a positive one, hierarchical, direct, unilateral, and absolute power is likely to bring about not only a speedy response but a compliant one as well. When Cardinal Richelieu asked the members of an informal club whether they might not like to bring their activities under the patronage of the state, it was an offer they could scarcely refuse. In contrast, proponents of the feminist campaign sought ultimately to influence persons over whom they had no direct authority. But by influencing legislatures, corporations, and professional associations, which *can* impose sanctions on noncompliance, these proponents of language change could exert indirect influence over the targets of their reform.

With respect to interpretations of what constitutes a speedy response, Frey 1980 points out that discrepant interpretations may heighten power conflicts. "University students, for example, who attempt to influence their school's administration, may view four months as an inordinately long response time, probably indicative of stalling. Administrators and faculty, on the other hand, may view such a response lag as extremely rapid – about as fast as the institution can be expected to react – and a clear manifestation of good faith" (698). Thus language planners and students of language planning might do well to consider the time lag which the targets of planning deem reasonable and the possibility of discrepant expectations on the part of the two parties to the power relation. The Hebrew University, for example, permits new immigrant faculty to lecture in English but expects them to switch to Hebrew after three years on the job. Resistance could be expected if this period seemed unreasonable to the lecturers. (By and large, the regulation is observed, although the lecturers' Hebrew often leaves much to be desired, as in my case, not only three years after arrival but also for many years thereafter.)

There is a second aspect of timing which is of interest to political scientists and which is relevant to language planning as well: *power sequencing* (Frey 1980). In power sequencing, A's attempt to influence B may be met by B's refusal to comply or by B's partial compliance or by some kind of evasion on B's part. Then A must try again, an attempt which is followed by another response, and so on, until B complies or until A modifies the original goal or gives up on it. Contingency planning may be employed by both sides in such exchanges. Frey (1980) points out that, for example, when a government passes legislation, it must also indicate the consequences of violating the law, the means whereby violations are to be discovered, and the circumstances whereby appeals may be made. Actors vary in the richness of their repertoires for the promotion or the evasion of compliance. And systems differ in the number of sequences which they are prepared to handle. For example, the tax authorities in some countries view the taxpayer's initial declaration of income as simply the opening gambit in a series of negotiations by which the amount of income subject to tax will be ultimately determined. Other authorities, in contrast, view the initial declaration as bona fide, with the taxpayer subject to criminal penalties should the declaration prove to have been deliberately false.

An example of power sequencing in language planning can be found in the public's response to the Israeli Ministry of Education's attempts to remove English from the curriculum of the first three grades of primary school. In Israel, English instruction is compulsory from the fifth grade, but schools are permitted to introduce it in the fourth grade. The Ministry's reluctance to teach English at lower grades was probably based in part on financial constraints. Most classroom teachers of the early grades are not equipped to teach English. Special teachers would have to be hired, straining an already inadequate budget.

Parents, however, particularly middle-class parents, pressured school principals to introduce English at lower and lower grades. Their demand for earlier English instruction reflects the usefulness of that language in higher education and in the workplace, domains for which parents are eager to prepare their children. Principals often complied with the parents' requests. In the face of this mounting pressure, the Ministry specifically forbade school principals from teaching English in the first three grades. But English did not disappear from those grades. Instead, parents banded together and hired English teachers to give English lessons in the schools, as an "extracurricular activity," although often during regular school hours. All children are expected to participate in these classes. The parents' committee subsidizes those children whose families cannot afford to contribute to the English teachers' fees. (But, of course, the parents' committees of schools which cater mainly to children from poor families tend not to organize such classes at all.) So widespread is the practice that at least one commercial agency exists to match parents' committees with English teachers.

Political scientists' attention to power sequencing reminds us that language planning is seldom a one-shot affair. Implementation of a decision may require repeated efforts by planners to cope with the resistance of those they seek to influence.

How

What are the means whereby elites maintain their power and whereby protoelites seize it from them? The means are essentially four: authority, force, violence, and bribery. Authority refers to the psychological relationship between ruler and ruled whereby the latter views as legitimate the former's right to make and to enforce rules (Ellsworth and Stahnke 1976). Force refers to the ability of rulers to enforce their decisions by punishing violations or evasion of or noncompliance with the rules. Violence refers to the use of physical coercion to maintain or secure authority, as in the state's use of the army and the police and in revolutionaries' use of guerilla forces, assassination, and terrorism. Bribery refers to the use of incentives to induce the ruled to acquiesce in the rulers' power or to help protoelites sieze power. I will confine my discussion here to the acquisition and maintenance of authority.

Authority rests upon *legitimacy*, of which, according to Weber (see Chapter 8), there are three types. *Rational* legitimacy rests upon the perceived lawfulness of the rules. The ruler has the right to make and enforce rules because the ruler's authority is legally constituted. *Charismatic* legitimacy rests upon the perceived sanctity, heroism, nobility, or other valued characteristic of the ruler. The ruler is entitled to make and enforce rules or to empower others to make them in his or her name on the basis of these personal attributes. *Traditional* legitimacy rests on the sanctity, authenticity, or greatness of the tradition which the ruled perceive the ruler upholding and representing. Elites may resort to all three bases to legitimize their rule. For example, the Soviet elite invokes the legal authority of the Party, the charisma of Lenin, and the glorious tradition of Mother

Russia to maintain its legitimacy in the eyes of the masses (O'Dell 1978). Counterelites also invoke these bases in order to claim legitimacy for themselves and to deny the legitimacy of the elites they seek to displace.

Legitimacy must be created and once created defended. Counterelites assert and elites defend their legitimacy "in the name of the symbols of the common destiny" (Lasswell 1936: 29).

> Such symbols are the "ideology" of the established order, the "utopia" of counter-elites. By the use of sanctioned words and gestures the elite elicits blood, work, taxes, applause from the masses. When the political order works smoothly, the masses venerate the symbols; the elite, self-righteous and unafraid, suffers no withering sense of immorality. . . . A well-established ideology perpetuates itself with little planned propaganda by those whom it benefits most. When thought is taken about ways and means of saving conviction, conviction has already languished, the basic outlook of society has decayed, or a new, triumphant outlook has not yet gripped the automatic loyalties of old and young (Lasswell 1936: 29–30).

Language, of course, can not only be fashioned into a supreme symbol of the common destiny, it can be manipulated to help create the *perception* of a common destiny. Counterelites seize or create whatever symbols are available to them to mobilize mass movements and to develop national self-consciousness. Thus language is frequently found as a central symbol in modern national movements, as can be seen in the independence movements of Algerian Arabs, Bengalis, Czechs, Irish, and Jews, to mention only a few.

In the "Language War" of the Palestinian Jews, for instance, we see a clear example of language as a mobilizing symbol in a national struggle. Since the latter part of the nineteenth century, Jewish teachers in Palestine have promoted the use of Hebrew as the sole medium of instruction in Jewish schools. A German–Jewish foundation for the advancement of Jews in technologically underdeveloped countries, the Hilfsverein der Deutschen Juden, planned to set up a technical high school in Haifa. The foundation operated a number of schools in Palestine, all of which used Hebrew as the medium of instruction. Nonetheless, the Hilfsverein felt obliged to promote German in the curriculum of its schools, an effort which aroused resentment. When the Hilfsverein announced in 1913 that its new *Technikum* was to use not Hebrew but German as the language of instruction, on the grounds that Hebrew was insufficiently developed for technical uses, resentment exploded. The teachers left the organization's schools and took their pupils with them. The boycott prevented the implementation of the Hilfsverein's decision. When the institution finally opened after the First World War, it opened not as the *Technikum* but as the *Technion*; its language of instruction was not German but Hebrew. In

Rabin's words (1973: 75): "The Jewish population of Palestine acted on this occasion according to the patterns of national struggle, and we shall hardly go wrong if we consider the Language War episode as the first proof that indeed there had come into being in Palestine a modern Jewish nation, on a predominantly linguistic basis."

When a language serves, or can be made to serve, as a symbol of a glorious past, or of the unique genius of a people, the elites and counterelites who manipulate this symbol can use it to maintain or acquire legitimacy in the name of authenticity and tradition. We will look more closely at such manipulations when we consider corpus planning in a subsequent chapter.

In sum

Lasswell's famous short-hand description, *who gets what, when, how*, provides a useful framework for the study of language planning. For language planners, it yields several useful notions, including those of elite and mass, scarcity, value, power relations, power sequencing, and authority and legitimacy. Additionally it reminds students of language planning that, in Hudson's words (1978: 12), "politics has no values of its own at all ... Nothing is valued in politics unless it is believed to be useful as a means of keeping a stronger group in power or of embarrassing or defeating one's opponents."

Language planning as decision making

Decision making, according to Easton (1968), is a variation on the theme of power as the central focus of political science. Power leads to control over the formulation and implementation of public decisions about the allocation of valued things in short supply. In Easton's influential view, politics is "that behavior or set of interactions through which authoritative allocations (or binding decisions) are made and implemented for a society" (288). Thus the study of public decisions or public policy is frequently seen as the core of political science. A decision-making approach is relevant to an understanding not only of political processes but also of economic and cognitive processes. Economists seek to describe, predict, and explain the economic decisions of consumers, entrepreneurs, and firms. Psychologists seek to describe, predict, and explain information processing whereby people choose among alternatives without certain knowledge as to the outcomes of those alternatives. If decision theory is "an attempt to describe in an orderly way what variables influence choices" (Edwards and Tversky 1967: 7), then it is an interdisciplinary field of study.

There are two traditions of decision analysis, prescriptive and descriptive. The former, normative decision theory, determines how people *should* act in order to attain the best results or at least satisfactory results. In contrast, behavioral decision theory determines what people *actually* do in arriving at their decisions, good or bad. As Bauer (1968) points out, normative proposals must at the least be compatible with what persons and institutions can in fact do. Thus studies of actual decision making serve both normative and descriptive ends.

Within descriptive decision theory, there are at least three foci: the individual, in his or her role as consumer, entrepreneur, gambler, or voter; the organization, particularly the business organization, through which decisions are taken; and the public arena in which public policy is formulated and implemented. With respect to language planning, all three foci are relevant. Language planning is sometimes the product of individuals working largely outside the framework of formal organizations; language planning is sometimes the product of formal institutions – publishing houses, churches, schools, professional associations, and the like; language planning is sometimes the product of governments; and language planning is sometimes the product of all three at once. How then are language-planning decisions made? One accounting scheme is suggested by Dye and Robey's (1980: 3) definition of public-policy analysis, which is "finding out what governments do, why they do it, and what difference it makes." If we do not restrict ourselves to governments, we can expand Dye and Robey's framework as follows: who makes what decisions, why, how, under what conditions, and with what effect?

Who

Who makes policy decisions? Ellsworth and Stahnke (1976) distinguish among *formal elites*, *influentials*, and *authorities*. Formal elites are those who are officially empowered to make policy – presidents, governors, senators, congressional representatives, chief operating executives, school principals, teachers, and so on. Influentials are the privileged sectors of society, those who get the most of what there is to get, as described in the last section. Authorities are those who actually make policy decisions. They are sometimes, but not necessarily, members of the formal elite; they are sometimes influentials; they are sometimes both. Ellsworth and Stahnke point out that the line between influencing and making decisions is clear in theory but not in practice. "The influentials are persons who promise, threaten, advise, beg, or bribe but do not decide. Only when they *order* and obtain compliance are they authorities. Yet influentials sometimes force the decision. When a mugger says, 'Your money or your life!' does the victim 'decide' – does he or she really have a choice?" (40). To the extent to which influentials are fragmented into different groups with competing and contested interests, it is likely that they are influentials and no more. But if only a few individuals or groups put forward recommendations which tend not to be contested, they are likely to be the *de facto* policy makers (Ellsworth and Stahnke 1976).

It is sometimes difficult to identify the authorities, the *de facto* policy makers, if they are not the formal elite. The open exercise of power by a non-official elite lacks legitimacy and is thus likely to arouse the opposition of the ruled. Since the disguise of power may contribute to its exercise, the interested observer may find it difficult to assign roles to players. Of the four defining examples, the identification of *de facto* authority is easiest in the case of the establishment of the Académie française. Cardinal de Richelieu, as the king's chief minister, was an authority officially and *de facto*. In the case of the Ethiopian mass-literacy campaign, the *de jure* authority was the Emperor, in whose name the Derg initially ruled. The Derg exercised *de facto* authority.

When we ask who makes policy decisions, we must specify the level at which the decision is made. What appears as implementation at one level may be policy at another. A municipal school board which institutes a bilingual education program for selected minority groups would not view the choice of textbooks for that program as a policy decision. But from the teacher's point of view, such a choice would be a policy decision. Similarly, a legislature which votes funds for bilingual education would view a school-board's decision as to which minority groups in which schools will benefit from the funding as implementation of the legislation, whereas from the school board's point of view it is a policy decision.

What decisions

Leichter (1975, 1979) identifies five major types of public policy: (1) distributive – policies which allocate goods and services such as health, welfare, and educational benefits, tax and credit subsidies, and loan guarantees; (2) extractive – policies which provide for the payment and collection of taxes; (3) symbolic – policies which allocate status and acknowledge achievement, such as the determination of professional licensing requirements; (4) regulatory – policies which aim to control some aspects of human behavior, such as the regulation of abortion, alcohol consumption; and (5) administrative – policies which concern the organization or administration of government.

Can we fit our defining examples into this framework? To the extent that all language planning aims to influence behavior, we might classify all our defining examples as regulatory policies. But in only two of the examples – the promotion of Hebrew and the feminist campaign – do we find specific behaviors mandated or proscribed. Perhaps the feminist campaign might be considered a symbolic policy, not because of its focus on symbols as means but because of its aim to allocate status. The founding of the Académie française is a clearer example of a symbolic policy, inasmuch as it conferred official recognition on the literary language of an elite. The Ethiopian goal of providing basic literacy in vernacular languages might be viewed as a symbolic policy as well, since it legitimized, if only briefly, the status of those languages and the ethnic groups that speak them. But the policy might also be viewed as distributive, because it aimed to provide educational services to those who did not speak Amharic and thus could not have benefited from an Amharic-only policy.

In addition to these five types of policy, we may describe language planning in terms of Frohock's (1979) substantive-procedural dichotomy. Whereas substantive policies set out *what* is to be accomplished (e.g. language standardization, language renativization, elimination of sexist usage, the eradication of illiteracy), procedural policies state *how* some goal is to be attained (e.g. the use of vernacular languages to promote adult literacy). Substantive policies cannot succeed if the means for their implementation are not specified. Means must be found to promote or enforce policy if the policy is to be more than an expression of good intentions.

Still another classification of policies is provided by Ellsworth and Stahnke (1976), who distinguish between emergency and routine decisions. Almost all political decisions, they assert, are made under some pressure, but some are made under more pressure than others. The Derg's decision to promote vernacular literacy is a good example of an emergency language-planning decision. Legislation mandating that certain types of consumer contract be comprehensible exemplifies less pressured, more routine, decision making. According to Ellsworth and Stahnke, most authoritative decisions are routine in the sense that (1) authorities devote much attention to recurring or persistent problems and (2) routines exist for the consideration of such problems. Routine decision making affords an opportunity to obtain soundings from different interest groups and thus to fashion a policy which will win broad public support.

Why

What motivates decision makers to make policy? If they are an elite, then they make policy in order to maintain or extend their privileges. But decision making is carried out by non-elite as well as by elite personnel. A view of decision making as a reaction to present or potential *stress* can account for decision making by elites and non-elites alike. This view is suggested by Ellsworth and Stahnke (1976), who assert that stress is the primary motivation for the formulation of public policy, i.e. decision making with respect to issues of general importance to society as a whole. Ellsworth and Stahnke define stress as "the impairment of the authorities' ability to govern," (7) which may range from threat to a single authority's tenure in office to threat to a regime, to threat to the entire political order. Thus policy decisions derive largely from authorities' response to, or avoidance of, a threat to loss of power. Because a rise in stress may damage public confidence, authorities try to deal with potential disorder in a routine manner, before disturbances become serious enough to impair the authorities' ability to govern. The Ethiopian literacy campaign can be viewed as an effort to neutralize the threat which the students posed to the new regime.

Ellsworth and Stahnke's explanation of the motivation of public policy is consistent with the incremental nature of much public policy (Lindblom 1959, Wildavsky 1964, Sharkansky 1968). In the United States, the single factor that shows the closest relationship to state-government expenditures in a current year is state-government expenditures the previous year (Dye and Robey 1980). Policy makers reduce their task by considering only *changes* proposed for next year's programs and budgets, which is consistent with the idea that response to, or avoidance of, a threat to loss of power motivates public policy making. By confining policy making chiefly to considerations of incremental change, decision makers promote the routinization of their responses to, and avoidance of, stress, as well as the appearance of consistency. Ellsworth and Stahnke's explanation for public policy is also consistent with the notion, offered earlier, that "nothing is valued in politics unless it is believed to be useful as a means of keeping a stronger group in power or of embarrassing or defeating one's opponents" (Hudson 1978: 12).

Ellsworth and Stahnke's discussion of stress is confined to the formulation of policy affecting the whole society. It is plausible, however, that responses to, and avoidance of, stress motivate decision making also in non-governmental institutions and at all organizational levels.

How

How do authorities arrive at decisions? The rational model of decision making offers the following sequence of activities: (1) identification of the problem, (2) search for information relevant to the problem, (3) production of possible solutions, (4) choice of one solution, (5) implementation of the solution, and (6) a comparison of predicted and actual consequences of action (Brim, Glass, Lavin and Goodman 1962). None of these activities is simple.

"It is no simple task to identify a problem. That something is wrong may be clear to all, but exactly what is wrong is generally not clear"

(Edwards and Sharkansky 1978: 87). Nonetheless, the way one defines the problem influences the policy which is set to deal with the problem. Once the poor attainment of American school children from ethnolinguistic minorities was viewed as an outcome of a mismatch between their verbal resources and the language of instruction, initial instruction via the children's mother tongue appeared as a reasonable solution to the problem. In this view of the matter, the schools were seen both as the locus of the problem and the agent for the problem's solution. Had the poor performance of ethnolinguistic minority children been attributed to inappropriate or inadequate teaching practices, the school would still have been viewed as the locus of the problem and the agent for reform, but solutions other than bilingual education might have appeared as reasonable. On the other hand, if the problem had been viewed as the outcome of economic exploitation, not only would different solutions have been proposed but different agencies of reform would have been selected as well.

Just as different analysts may define a problem differently, different societies may differ in their perception that "something is wrong." The political culture of a society determines what citizens and authorities see as problems, or, at any rate, what they view as within the province of government or other agencies to solve.

The search for information relevant to the problem may be too costly or too time-consuming to be a practical proposition. But even when information is available, decision makers often do not know which information is relevant to the problem. And even when decision makers can distinguish relevant from irrelevant data, much of the data available may be faulty.

Once policy makers have identified a problem, they normally do not have the time or energy to examine all possible alternative solutions (Edwards and Sharkansky 1978). Nor are they willing to consider alternatives which are damaging to their own interests. Further, when examining the limited number of alternatives selected for consideration, they usually cannot arrive at a single best solution because the costs and benefits of any given alternative typically vary from group to group and because the probabilities of any given outcome are usually unknown.

There is general agreement that policy making does not conform to the rational paradigm of decision making. This paradigm assumes a single decision maker or decision-making unit, with a single set of preferred outcomes, knowledge of a reasonably full range of alternatives and of their consequences, the intention of selecting that alternative which maximizes benefits and minimizes costs, and the opportunity, willingness, and ability to make the necessary calculations. "In the process of policy formation every one of these assumptions is violated" (Bauer 1968: 11). Instead, policy makers "rely on *decision rules*, rules of thumb or standard operating procedures that make policymaking manageable and keep decisions within the bounds of political and economic feasibility" (Edwards and Sharkansky 1978: 12).

Case studies of language planning which could describe the policy-making process, the decision rules employed by the relevant decision makers, would make a useful contribution to our knowledge. Such studies need not be confined to grand policy. Studies at the humblest levels would be welcome too, and they would probably be easier to carry out. How does a language teacher determine goals of instruction? How does a school board determine which minority groups will be taught bilingually? How does a publisher decide whether its new dictionary will indicate normative, as distinguished from actual, usage? How does a language academy select among alternatives in an effort to standardize terminology? We need more than descriptions of planners' overt activities, although these too are useful. We need descriptions of their selections of alternatives, their weighing of alternatives, and the outcome of that weighing.

Under what conditions

What are the conditions which influence or determine policy? Leichter (1979) offers an accounting scheme based on the earlier work of Alford (1969), who suggested four broad categories: situational, structural, cultural, and environmental factors.

Situational factors are relatively transient conditions or events, such as wars and riots, which have an immediate impact on policy. As an example Leichter gives the Soweto race riots, mentioned above, which caused the South African regime to drop its insistence on the mandatory use of Afrikaans as a medium of instruction in Black schools. Another example is the momentary change in language policy caused by the Ethiopian revolution. In addition to violent events, Leichter suggests the following categories of situational factors: economic cycles (depression, recession, inflation), natural disasters, political events (e.g. the extension of suffrage, change of government, achievement of independence), technological change, and competition, among the proponents of different issues, for the time, attention, and resources which are available to decision makers.

Structural factors, unlike situational factors, are the relatively unchanging features of a society's political, economic, social, demographic, and ecological structures. Among the political factors which Leichter lists are type of regime (military or civilian, socialist or nonsocialist, competitive or noncompetitive party system), form of government (parliamentary, presidential, nondemocratic), and prior policy commitments. Among the economic factors which he lists are the type of economic system (free market, planned, mixed economy), the economic base (primarily agrarian or industrial, diversified or dependent on a single product), and national wealth and income (size and growth rate of gross national product). Finally, his social, demographic, and ecological factors include population (age structure, birth rate, communal division, geographical distribution, rate of in- and out-migration, level of education), degree of urbanization, natural resources, and geographic location (access to sea or landlocked, tropical or temperate climate, proximity to militarily strong or weak neighbors). Leichter argues that since structural factors are relatively long-lasting, they have a more sustained and thus more predictable impact on policy than do situational factors. As an example of the influence of structural factors on language planning, we may take a country such as Belgium or Canada, where the political and economic competition between two groups constrains government policy concerning the language of each group.

Cultural factors refer to the attitudes and values held by groups within the community or by the community as a whole. Whereas Alford was concerned principally with political values or political culture (e.g. norms regarding the political participation of the individual, norms regarding what it is proper and what it is mandatory for the government to do, political ideology – Marxist, fascist, democratic), Leichter extends cultural factors to institutions and arrangements such as sex roles, marriage, the family, and religion. When Samuel Johnson said that a language academy would be un-English, his view may have been influenced by the *laissez-faire* political norms of his day, which were stronger in England than on the Continent.

Environment factors are events, structures, and attitudes which exist outside the system but which influence decisions within it. According to Leichter, these include the international political environment (cold war, detente), emulation or borrowing of policy ideas from other nations, international agreements, obligations, and pressures (e.g. World Bank loans, treaties), and private international corporations, such as I.T.T. and the Chase Manhattan Bank. As an example of language policy influenced by environmental factors, we can take the influence which American bilingual education programs appear to have had on European educational systems, some of which have subsequently adopted bilingual education as a means of improving the attainment of the children of guestworkers.

Ellsworth and Stahnke (1976) list five factors which influence policy decisions: regime norms, socialization of the authorities, constituencies, need for consistency, and information. The first of these, regime norms, is similar to the political culture which Leichter includes as part of cultural factors. "Taken together, regime norms define the areas of social life in which the authorities may act – they define the mode of official operation – and prescribe relationships between various public officials as well" (Ellsworth and Stahnke 1976: 44). Regime norms are rules of the game.

Socialization of authorities refers to the past experiences, the past associates, and the group affiliations of decision makers, who bring to bear their own histories, expertise, prejudices, and blinkers when formulating policy.

Constituencies refer to those affected by a given policy. No political leader can stay in power without the help of others. "Decision makers must weigh the relative interests of all affected parties, the utility of their continued support, and the probable intensity of their reactions as they make policy" (Ellsworth and Stahnke 1976: 49). Constituencies would appear to be included by Leichter's social, demographic, and ecological structures.

The need for consistency refers to the preference of ordinary citizens and subordinant elites for authorities who are predictable in their decisions. Leaders cannot afford mutually contradictory decisions because these lead to the appearance of erratic behavior. The consequences of any given decision usually foreclose some future options, and because the unintended consequence of one decision may force a second, the need for consistency in conjunction with the consequences of past decisions constrains future decisions.

Finally, the fifth factor, information, refers to the data which are required to make good decisions. Although modern governments and other large organizations devote considerable resources to the gathering and evaluation of information, serious questions are often decided on the basis of relatively little good data. This state of affairs, according to Ellsworth and Stahnke, is a result of time constraints, the difficulty of pulling together information dispersed over several agencies or departments, the difficulty in knowing what data, from the mass collected, are relevant, and difficulty in grasping the full implications of the data.

Ellsworth and Stahnke believe that the most fundamental of these five factors in the shaping of decisions is the regime norms. Leichter, on the other hand, believes that the factors which influence policy have greater or lesser impact according to the policy area. It is probable, he writes, that a polity's population structure has a greater impact on distributive policies than on administrative or symbolic policies. Furthermore, determinants may vary in importance from time to time. It is an open question, he writes, whether the variation in influence from one policy area to another and from one time to another holds constant cross-nationally.

Leichter writes that different analysts stress different factors in accounting for public policy. "For some, political factors account for policy; for others, socioeconomic factors; and for still others, the responsible factor depends upon the area of policy and the historical period. This author is neither surprised nor concerned about the state of the art. It would be extraordinary if a single factor, say political culture, was found responsible for all policies, at all times, in all nations" (9). This is likely to be the case for language planning as well.

With what effect

If policy makers do not conform to the rational paradigm of decision making, it should come as no surprise that they often do not compare the predicted (or hoped for) consequences of a policy with the actual outcome of that policy. There are several reasons. First, the effect of some policies may not be known for many years. Second, data gathering is expensive and time-consuming. Third, policy makers may be more interested in the appearance of purposeful activity than in the consequences of that activity, so long as such consequences do not arouse opposition to their continuance in power. Fourth, policy makers may suspect that their policies have failed (or at least not succeeded very well) and thus they may avoid confirming their suspicions. Fifth, it is often exceedingly difficult to disentangle the effects of a policy from the effects of all other variables which might have influenced the projected or desired outcome. Sixth, as Ackoff (1978: 189) points out, problems rarely stay solved: changing conditions tend to unsolve problems that may once have been solved.

Public policy, in any case, may not be a particularly viable proposition, if Wildavsky's (1979: 8) pessimistic pronouncement is correct: "If planning were judged by results, that is, whether life followed the dictates of the plan, then planning has failed everywhere it has been tried. Nowhere are plans fulfilled. No one, it turns out, has the knowledge to predict sequences of actions and reactions across the realm of public policy, and no one has the power to compel obedience . . . . Why, then, is planning so popular? . . . . Has mankind's desire to control its fate – on paper with a plan, if nowhere else – led to justification not by deeds but by faith? If so, planning is not so much an answer to a question about public policy (what should be done about polluted water or bad health or whatever?) but a question in the form of an answer: provide a plan."

Perhaps language planning is more successful than that, some of the time, at least when directed toward modest goals. But case studies as to the effectiveness of given instances of language planning, aside from surveys of educational attainment involving linguistic goals of instruction, have been relatively rare. Fainberg's work (1983), mentioned above, is a notable exception.

In sum

This brief presentation of an accounting scheme suggested by the study of decision making and public policy has mentioned a great number of variables – particularly those subsumed by the conditions under which planning takes place. Where so many variables might affect the decision-making or policy-making process and where most variables are related to one another, what is the best course of action for language-planning researchers looking for the variables that impinge upon decision making? With respect to public policy, Bauer (1968) suggests that the empirical researcher identify the points of "leverage" in the system and concentrate on those. By point of leverage, Bauer means "a person, institution, issue, or subsystem ... that has the capacity to effect a substantial influence on the output of the system" (21). For language planning the points of leverage are still a matter of conjecture. But an accounting scheme can at least suggest to the researcher what the points of leverage might be.

An accounting scheme for the study of language planning

At the outset of the previous chapter, I suggested that a descriptively-adequate account of any given case of language planning ought to tell us, at a minimum, what actors attempted to influence what behaviors, of which people, for what ends, by what means, and with what results. To these rubrics, it now seems useful to add two more: (1) under what conditions and (2) through what policy-making process. Based on a consideration of the four overlapping frameworks presented in this chapter, I now suggest a more elaborated framework for the study of language planning. Figure 1 presents this framework.

For each rubric, the subrubrics illustrate the range of variables which might usefully be investigated. It is likely that any attempt to employ this framework will reveal useful variables which have been omitted, as well as variables which prove to be unproductive or redundant. I offer the framework as a guide to future investigators in the hope that it will improve our ability to describe, predict, and explain language planning.

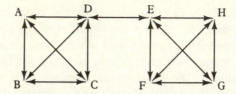

Figure 1. An accounting scheme for the study of language planning

  I What *actors* (e.g. formal elites, influentials, counterelites, non-elite policy
     implementers)

 II attempt to influence what *behaviors*
     A. structural (linguistic) properties of planned behavior (e.g. homogeneity,
        similarity)
     B. purposes/functions for which planned behavior is to be used
     C. desired level of adoption (awareness, evaluation, proficency, usage)

III of which *people*
     A. type of target (e.g. individuals v. organizations, primary v. intermediary)
     B. opportunity of target to learn planned behavior
     C. incentives of target to learn/use planned behavior
     D. incentives of target to reject planned behavior

 IV for what *ends*
     A. overt (language-related behaviors)
     B. latent (non-language-related behaviors, the satisfaction of interests)

  V under what *conditions*
     A. situational (events, transient conditions)
     B. structural
        1. political
        2. economic
        3. social/demographic/ecological
     C. cultural
        1. regime norms
        2. cultural norms
        3. socialization of authorities
     D. environmental (influences from outside the system)
     E. informational (data required for a good decision)

 VI by what *means* (e.g. authority, force, promotion, persuasion)

VII through what *decision-making process* (decision rules)
     A. formulation of problem/goal
     B. formulation of means

VIII with what *effect*

5

Status planning

Just as languages change over time, the functions they serve for particular communities change as well. Familiar examples include the shift in Western Europe from Latin to modern European languages for literary and scholarly purposes, the shift in England from Norman French to English for use in courts of law, and the shift in Indonesia from Dutch to Bahasa Indonesia as the language of government administration. The most spectacular changes of all are shifts in a community's mother tongue, as, for example, the adoption of Arabic as the language of the home throughout most of North African and Middle Eastern territories conquered by the armies of Islam.

Perhaps most of the changes which occur in the functional allocation of a community's languages are spontaneous. Some, however, are the outcomes of planning. For example, the spread of Kiswahili for economic functions in Eastern Africa was the unpremeditated result of expanded trade within a linguistically diverse region. In contrast, the spread of that language for political, educational, and religious functions was the result of deliberate policy (Mazrui and Zirimu 1978). Status planning refers to deliberate efforts to influence the allocation of functions among a community's languages.

Stewart's functions as targets of status planning

What functions serve as targets of status planning? A well-known list of language functions is the one which Stewart (1968) provides in his discussion of national multilingualism. Let us look at each of the functions which he mentions, beginning in each case with his description of the function. Because most of these functions have been targets for the status planning of Hebrew, I refer, when appropriate, to the Hebrew case first.

99

1. "*Official* (symbol: o); function as a legally appropriate language for all politically and culturally representative purposes on a nationwide basis. In many cases, the o function of a language is specified constitutionally." Stewart appears to confine his definition of official language to those languages which a government has specified as official, or declared as appropriate, by law. But it may be useful to distinguish two other types of official language: a language which a government uses as a medium for its day-to-day activities and a language which a government uses as a medium for symbolic purposes, i.e. as a symbol of the state. I refer to these three types as *statutory*, *working*, and *symbolic* official languages respectively. A language may be official in any or all of these senses.

When Britain captured Palestine from the Ottoman Empire in 1918, it found two national communities, one Arab and one Jewish. By that time Hebrew had become the principal language of public discourse among the Jewish population. There was, of course, no rival whatsoever to Arabic as the language of the Arab population. When the British accepted a mandate from the League of Nations in 1922 to administer Palestine, they declared English, Arabic, and Hebrew, in that order, as the official languages of the territory. When Israel emerged as a sovereign state in 1948, all laws in effect under the British remained in force unless specifically repealed or modified. The legal *requirement* to use English was repealed in 1948, thus leaving Hebrew and Arabic in force as official languages.

While Hebrew and Arabic have the same status in law, Hebrew is clearly dominant as the language of day-to-day government activity. Whereas Hebrew and Arabic each symbolize a nationality, only Hebrew symbolizes the Jewish state. Although the official status of English is no longer protected by law, it continues in use for many government functions. For example, paper currency, metal coins, and postage stamps are printed in English as well as in Hebrew and Arabic. When highway and street signs are bilingual, the second language is more likely to be English than Arabic. When government publications, such as reports issued by the Central Statistical Office, are bilingual, the second language is more likely to be English than Arabic. On the other hand, transactions of the Knesset, Israel's parliament, are published fully in Arabic and Hebrew but only the chapter headings are published in English (Fisherman 1972). Thus with respect to the three types of official language in Israel, Hebrew is official in all three senses, Arabic is both a statutory and a working official language but not a symbolic official language, and English is a working official language only.

As a second example, we may take the case of Ireland. When a new constitution formally ended the power of the Crown in 1937, the country changed its name from the Irish Free State to Eire, and the Irish language became the first official language, with English as the second official language. In practice, however, the positions of the two languages are reversed, with English the dominant language. Although all legislation is printed in both languages, almost all parliamentary business is conducted in English. A knowledge of Irish is an employment requirement for certain civil-service jobs, but most of the government's day-to-day transactions are conducted in English. In Ireland, therefore, English is both a statutory and a working official language, whereas Irish is an official language in all three senses, although its use as a working language is far less frequent than is the case with English.

The declaration of a language as official, as in the Irish Constitution, the Proclamation of the King at his Council for Palestine, and the Israeli Knesset's modification of that order, constitute status planning. Why are such declarations made? Certainly they are "unnecessary" from any immediate, "pragmatic" point of view. Many countries, including the United Kingdom and the United States, have no statutory official language. Conversely, statutory official languages are sometimes ignored. When Algeria, Morocco, and Tunisia won their independence from France, they declared Islam as the state religion and Arabic as the state language. Yet a number of years after independence, Gallagher (1968) found French spoken everywhere in the government administration of these three countries "and used as a *de facto* working language, not only at state functions and receptions, but to the point where the Post Office (in Morocco, for example) has refused to accept telegrams written in Arabic and most government offices insist that bilingual forms be filled out in French by preference" (131). Since that time, Arabicization of the Maghrib's government offices has progressed, but even today Arabic is far from universally used. In Tunisia, for example, more than thirty years after independence, only two of sixteen ministries, those of Justice and the Interior, are totally Arabicized, with all documents, reports, and publications in Arabic; some ministries still use French as the language of record, and others run themselves more or less bilingually (Daoud 1987).

Since it is necessary neither to specify an official language nor to observe it once specified, we must look to the symbolic uses of a statutory language rather than to its immediate practical value. Sometimes, as in the case of Arabic in the Maghrib, Hebrew, and Irish, the statutory language symbolizes the common memory and aspirations of the community (or of the majority community), its past and its future. When a community views a language as a symbol of its greatness, specification of that language as official serves to support the legitimacy of governmental authority. When a government recognizes the language of a subordinate minority as a statutory language, as Arabic in Israel, rulers in effect grant symbolic recognition of that group's right to maintain its distinctiveness. Conversely, when a linguistically heterogeneous polity declares one language only as statutory, as the 1986 proposition which made English the official language of the State of California, the declaration in effect denies the legitimacy of diversity.

One can, therefore, argue that in most cases the specification of statutory languages is an exercise in the manipulation of political symbols for the maintenance of ruling elites. If this is true, there are two dangers in such an exercise. First, political rivals may try to win popular support by claiming to be better guardians of the sacred symbols. An unsuccessful move by the Israeli far right, in the early 1980s, to make Hebrew the sole official language of the state, may represent such an attempt. Second, political rivals may try to substitute different symbols for the existing ones in an effort to mobilize mass support.

Whereas a statutory official language is necessarily the outcome of status planning, a government's *use* of given languages for given activities need not be the outcome of deliberate planning. No one had to choose English as the medium for debate in the U.S. Congress, for example. Such usage was taken for granted from the beginning. But the use of working languages is sometimes a matter for conscious attention as was, for example, the replacement of English by Kiswahili in the Tanzanian parliament.

The language of parliamentary debate is peculiarly visible because it occurs in a public setting with immense symbolic significance. Whether or not a parliament has actual power, it symbolizes the state in all its majesty. When the values and traditions associated with the language of debate are consistent with the values and traditions associated with the state, no one pays particular attention. All is as it should be. But when the two sets of values and traditions are discontinuous, as when a newly-independent state uses the language of its former rulers to debate legislation, the gap between the real and the ideal may challenge the legitimacy of governmental authority. What right have you to speak for me if you use an alien tongue? In many cases, newly-independent states have no option but to use the colonial language. If the state is linguistically diverse, the choice of any one indigenous language may be opposed by speakers of all the others. Besides, no indigenous language may be widely known outside the circle of its native speakers. Tanzania was in an exceptional position at independence: most of its population already spoke an indigenous language which was at the same time native to very few: Kiswahili. Thus the promotion of Kiswahili as the language of parliamentary debate favored no substantial group at the expense of any other and symbolized, as English could not, an indigenous African tradition. In short, when government language use is highly visible and occurs in symbolically freighted contexts, a discontinuity between the symbolic value of the language and the symbolic value of its context may exert pressure for change.

Another circumstance which may stimulate status planning regarding governmental language use occurs when the use of a given language for a given government context – election ballots, street signs, or government forms, for example – is viewed as a barrier or a hardship for a given ethnolinguistic minority. A minority leader may be able to attract support over the issue of language discrimination. A mobilized minority may be able to win concessions from a government concerning the latter's language use. Alternatively, a government may seek to pacify an aroused minority by the inexpensive expedient of printing forms in its language. A government continues to use the working languages which have always been used, unless doing so threatens its legitimacy, encourages a counterelite, or otherwise undermines its ability to rule.

If statutory official languages are necessarily the products of status planning, and if working official languages are sometimes the products of status planning, symbolic official languages are never the products of status planning. When the association between a sign and its intended referent is so opaque as to require a decision to fuse them, the sign is not yet a symbol. A sign becomes a symbol after repeated association with its referent. When Ireland and Israel became independent, the Irish and Hebrew languages had become intimately intertwined with their respective national movements. They had become expressions of nationhood. Their extension from national to state symbol was the natural outcome of a successful national movement. With or without legislation, these languages would have served as state symbols. Symbols are created not by legislation but by history. Irish and Kiswahili are not national symbols because the Irish and Tanzanian constitutions proclaim them as national languages. They are national symbols because of their association and identification with their national liberation movements and with their citizens' shared memory.

2. "*Provincial* (symbol: p); function as a provincial or regional official language. In this case, the official function of the language is not nationwide, but is limited to a smaller geographic area." The tripartite division of official languages suggested for countries is appropriate for provincial or regional official languages as well. Indeed, our discussion of status planning for national official languages mentioned California as an example of planning an official language for a subnational entity.

California was the seventh state in the Union to declare English an official language. Dyste (1987) lists California's predecessors as Nebraska (1920), Illinois (1923), Virginia (1981), Indiana (1984), Kentucky (1984), and Tennessee (1984). These declarations by California and its sister states are atypical in that the statutory official language of subnational units is usually not also the majority language of all the other units. None of the states has a majority whose mother tongue is other than English. Quebec, in which French became the only official language in 1974 (Bill 22), is a better example in that a majority of Quebec's population is French speaking, a majority of Canada's Francophones reside in Quebec, and French speakers constitute a minority in all other Canadian provinces.

Provincial boundaries are sometimes drawn or redrawn in such a way as to increase linguistic homogeneity within each province. India is perhaps the most notable example of the creation of administrative units on primarily linguistic grounds. Of India's eighteen states, only two are not fairly homogeneous linguistically. Each of the others has at least half its population speaking the same language (Apte 1976a). Two-thirds of the states have specified their own major language as official, either by itself or as co-official with either Hindi or English. The remainder, including some linguistically quite homogeneous states, have specified English, Hindi, or Urdu as sole official language. Kerala, for example, with about 95 percent of its population speaking Malayalam, specified English as its statutory official language (Apte 1976b). The specification of non-regional languages in some cases as official state language suggests that the linguistic cleavages represented by state boundaries reflect essentially political and economic rather than cultural rivalries.

3. *"Wider communication* (symbol: w); the function of a linguistic system (other than one which already has an o or p function) predominating as a medium of communication across language boundaries within the nation.'' From this and many of the subsequent functions which Stewart lists, he excludes languages which serve an o or p function. This is because official languages at either the national or provincial level usually serve additional functions. Thus it is normally expected that an official language serves, for example, as a medium of communication across language boundaries within a state and is used as a medium of instruction. Of more interest, for Stewart's purposes, are those languages which are *not* official (*o* or *p*) but are nonetheless used for important communicative functions. For purposes of discussing language planning, however, we cannot exclude o and p languages from a consideration of their use in other functions because their use in other functions is often planned. Therefore, even though Stewart's definitions may exclude o and p languages from consideration, I include them in my discussion here.

With respect to the function of wider communication within a state's borders, do we see planning for this function in Israel? In Palestine a lingua franca was indeed necessary among a linguistically diverse Jewish population. The efforts in late nineteenth- and early twentieth-century Palestine on behalf of Hebrew, however, were not to promote Hebrew as a lingua franca among the Jews, although that was a necessary transitional outcome, so much as to restore it to its former status as the language of Palestinian Jewry's everyday life, as it had been two millenia before. Thus it is more appropriate to discuss these efforts under a rubric different from that of "wider communication," which I do below.

Are there cases of status planning for languages of wider communication? If the planned function of communication is vertical integration, a link between ruler and ruled, between center and periphery, then status planning for this function exists. But then, the language is really a working official language, whether or not it is a statutory official language. Thus the Spanish used Quechua in seventeenth- and eighteenth-century multilingual Peru (Heath and Laprade 1982) and the French used Mandingo in their multilingual West African territories (Calvet 1982) to deal with the local populations, if only through interpreters.

Are there instances of status planning for languages of wider communication when the planned function of communication is horizontal integration, a link from periphery to periphery, a bridge over the linguistic gorges that separate worker from worker, peasant from peasant, citizen from citizen, or co-religious adherent from co-religious adherent? Certainly there are instances of status planning which have this effect and the choice of an official language, medium of instruction, or medium of sacred-text literacy, for example, often promotes the spread of lingua francas for horizontal integration. But it is hard to think of deliberate status planning for horizontal integration that is not part of a scheme of vertical integration as well. For example, the framers of India's Constitution hoped that Hindi would not only replace English as the language of vertical integration but that it would also become a link language among the subcontinent's numerous ethnolinguistic groups. Similarly the Soviet Union promotes Russian not only as a language of vertical integration among its huge, heterogeneous non-Russian population but as a link language within this population as well. Just as non-Hindi resistance to Hindi as an official language has retarded its spread as a horizontal link language, so has non-Russian minorities' acceptance of Russian as a national official language facilitated its spread as a horizontal link language.

Can the use of Kiswahili by leaders of the national independence movement in Tanzania to mobilize the multilingual masses be counted as an instance of status planning for a horizontal link language? Probably not. Kiswahili had spread as a horizontal link language before its association with the national liberation movement. There was scarcely an alternative to its use. In any case, counterelites' use of a lingua franca for purposes of mass mobilization, since it links leaders to the masses, as well as the masses to one another, is perhaps as much an instance of vertical as of horizontal integration.

It is plausible that Mazrui and Zirimu's (1978) claim for Kiswahili in

East Africa – that it received the systematic attention of missionaries, educators, and administrators only when it served the purposes of vertical
integration – may be true with respect to languages of wider communication
more generally. A language spreads when potential adopters see a personal
advantage in using it. Elites and counterelites promote languages of wider
communication when they can promote their interests by doing so. There
is a clear advantage for elites and counterelites to promote vertical-link
languages. Unless an advantage can be found in the promotion of horizontal
link languages, their spread is likely to be spontaneous rather than planned.

   Ferguson (1966) points out that Stewart does not distinguish between
indigenous and nonindigenous languages of wider communication within
a country, as for example, between Hindi and English, both of which
are used as media of communication among citizens of India. English,
of course, is also used as a lingua franca between Indians and foreigners.
The use of former colonial languages as both internal and external lingua
franca is a common phenomenon.

4. "*International* (symbol: i); the function of a linguistic system (other
than one which already has an o or p function) as a major medium of
communication which is international in scope, e.g., for diplomatic relations, foreign trade, tourism, etc." Here Stewart refers to international
languages of wider communication which link citizens of one country with
citizens of another. In Israel, the major medium of international communication is English. It is the unmarked language for foreign intercourse –
the language which Israelis think first to use with tourists, foreign cus-
tomers, foreign colleagues, etc. But as in India, English is an official language, even if not a statutory official language. Status planning of
international languages of wider communication takes place in connection
with determining what foreign languages will be taught in the schools.
Typically, those foreign languages which are most useful, or most in
demand as international languages of wider communication, are taught
in school. Indeed, if the language is truly foreign, the school represents
the chief context in which it can be learned. I will return to this topic
in connection with status planning for targets of instruction.

5. "*Capital* (symbol: c); the function of a linguistic system (other than
one which already has an o or p function) as a major medium of communication in the vicinity of the national capital. This function is especially important in countries where political power, social prestige, and economic
activity are centered in the capital." This function is important because
languages often diffuse from the political and economic center to the periphery. Such a location, then, may be an important factor in language
spread. The language to be *spoken* in the vicinity of the capital is not

a focus of status planning, although the *official* language of a capital may be planned. Brussels, for example, has two official languages, Dutch and French. On the other hand, the linguistic composition of a city may be an important issue in the drawing of political boundaries, as, for example, in the dispute about the political organization of the city of Bombay. There the two largest groups where Marathi and Gujarati speakers, with the former outnumbering the latter by a ratio of about 2.5 to 1. Initially, neither group was awarded a linguistic state of its own. Rather, a bilingual state of Bombay was created which included both these groups and the city of Bombay. After considerable controversy, this decision was changed in 1960 whereby the linguistic states of Maharashtra and Gujarat were created, with Bombay city awarded to Maharashtra (Apte 1976a: 232, footnote 1).

6. "*Group* (symbol: g); the function of a linguistic system primarily as the normal medium of communication among the members of a single cultural or ethnic group, such as a tribe, settled group of foreign immigrants, etc. So strong can the association between linguistic behavior and group identity be, that at times a linguistic system with a g function may serve as an informal criterion for ascertaining group membership." Late nineteenth- and early twentieth-century efforts to restore Hebrew and Irish to their status as the ordinary medium of communication for the Irish and the Jews respectively are perhaps the two most celebrated examples of status planning for the group function.

The Irish campaign, when compared to the campaign on behalf of Hebrew, is often considered a "failure." An even smaller proportion of the Irish speak Irish natively now than when the campaign began, and monolingual Irish speakers are in danger of disappearing. On the other hand, a far greater proportion of the population knows Irish today than when the campaign began, largely as a result of the role of Irish in formal education. The restoration movement stimulated an important literary revival; novels, short stories, poetry, and plays continue to be written in Irish. Some radio and television programs are broadcast in Irish.

Still, English, not Irish, remains the language of everyday Irish life, whereas Hebrew has replaced the languages of the Diaspora as the language of everyday life for contemporary Jews in their ancient homeland. Why did the restoration succeed in Palestine but not in Ireland? There are at least three reasons.

First, when the campaign began, the Palestinian Jews were linguistically diverse, whereas the Irish, largely monolingual in English, were linguistically homogeneous. The Jews needed a lingua franca to talk to one another, whereas the Irish did not.

Second, a substantial proportion, perhaps a majority, of Jewish Palestinians were already familiar with Hebrew, at least for liturgical purposes, whereas the majority of the Irish were unfamiliar with Irish. It was an easier task for most Jews to learn to speak Hebrew for secular purposes than for most Irish to learn Irish from scratch.

Third, there were enormous material incentives for the Irish to retain English and relatively few material incentives to learn Irish. To the extent that material incentives favored any of the Jewish languages in Palestine, they favored Hebrew as the language most likely to be known by a Jewish speaker and thus the most practical candidate as a lingua franca. By the end of the First World War, Hebrew had become established as the principal language of public interaction among the linguistically heterogeneous Jewish population in Palestine. This forced most subsequent Jewish immigrants to learn it in order to gain employment. Material incentives clearly promoted the spread of Hebrew once it emerged as the Jews' principal lingua franca. Material incentives were likely to have contributed to its emergence as principal lingua franca as well.

This comparison of the Jewish and Irish efforts to promote ancestral languages as national vernaculars suggests that if planners want a language adopted as a primary language – a language for use inside as well as outside the home – the best place to start is outside the home. As we have seen, Ben Yehuda's use of only Hebrew at home influenced few to follow his example. Similarly, a circle of Dublin families, which banded together to support one another's efforts to use Irish at home, inspired admiration, perhaps, but few converts. English entered Irish homes after economic incentives forced the Irish to learn it and then to conclude that there was little future for Irish. Hebrew entered Jewish homes as a vernacular after a generation had grown up with it in the schools of the new Jewish settlements. Even in the old established settlements such as Jerusalem and Hebron, those children who studied in traditional schools, with Diaspora languages as media of instruction, learned to read the sacred Hebrew texts in school and thus could learn vernacular forms with relative ease. Further, there was both opportunity and incentive to use the language as lingua franca outside the school. Status planning which aims at introducing a language for use at home is probably futile unless there is support for the language outside the home. For Hebrew there was such support. For Irish there was little.

As Rubin (1983) has pointed out, we should not view the campaign for the restoration of Irish as a failure. Inasmuch as the campaign was intended to promote national autonomy, the campaign was won. The campaign was won in 1922 with the establishment of the Irish Free State.

7. "*Educational* (symbol: e); the function of a language (other than one which already has an o or p function) as a medium of primary or secondary

education, either regionally or nationally.'' Ferguson (1966) suggests distinguishing not only between primary and secondary education but also between the lower and upper years of primary school, inasmuch as it is generally in the latter that subject-matter textbooks begin to be used.

Determining media of instruction for school systems is perhaps the status-planning decision most frequently made, the one most commonly subject to strong political pressures, and the one most often considered by educationists and by students of language planning (see, for example, Engle 1975, Fishman 1976, Lambert and Tucker 1972, Macnamara 1966, Spolsky 1977, UNESCO 1953, Fillmore and Valadez 1986).

Thus far we have encountered several examples of educational status planning: the decision to use vernacular languages in the Ethiopian mass-literacy campaign; the decision to permit or encourage the use of vernacular languages as an initial medium of instruction for poor, ethnolinguistic minority children in the United States; the decision to teach some middle-class Anglophone children in Montreal first via French and then via French and English; the decision by nineteenth-century East European immigrants to use Hebrew as an all-purpose medium of instruction in the schools of the new settlements in Palestine; the decision by a German–Jewish foundation in the second decade of the twentieth century to use German as the medium of instruction in its new technical institute in Palestine; and the boycott by the teachers and students of the foundation's schools in Palestine to force the foundation to use Hebrew instead. These examples suggest the range of contexts in which media of instruction are determined.

The Hebrew and Irish cases exemplify the use of language as a focus for nationalist movements. Although Irish was not promoted as medium until political autonomy was attained, the rise of the national movement was accompanied by increased pressure on the educational authorities to teach Irish as a subject. Hebrew, of course, was used as medium for several generations prior to independence. In neither case was the choice of medium determined by a consideration of what medium would most facilitate the children's learning. Rather, the choice was made primarily on political grounds and for political ends.

The degree to which educational considerations influence the choice of medium varies from case to case, but political considerations always play a role. While good arguments can be marshalled to justify vernacular languages as media for initial literacy, the decision to employ them for the Ethiopian campaign had, as we have seen, a strong political motivation. The modern bilingual education movement in the United States was probably motivated more by a concern to improve the educational attainment of poor, minority children than to win the votes of their parents, but the latter motivation cannot have been entirely absent. Similarly, the opposition to bilingual education, which has emerged on the grounds that "bilingual education doesn't work," may be motivated in part by fear of change, particularly the growth of ethnolinguistic minorities as a percentage of the population, the perception that "America doesn't belong to us anymore," and resentment of the economic competition, real or imagined, which these minorities pose to native speakers of English. Concerning Anglophone use of French in Montreal, the parents who initiated the experiment were quite concerned about the educational consequences of the program: they carefully monitored and evaluated the children's attainment before deciding to extend the program. But the impetus for the program was their fear that without a radical educational change, their children would be ill-equipped to compete in an economic world in which knowledge of French was becoming increasingly important.

Political and economic cleavages are often reflected in controversies over the languages to be used as media of instruction. For example, when Pakistan emerged as an independent country, in 1947, there was a bitter controversy between the eastern and western parts of the country, separated by 1,000 miles of Indian territory, as to what medium of instruction should be used. Although a settlement was finally reached whereby Urdu was used in the west and Bengali in the east, the controversy presaged the eventual transformation of East Pakistan to the independent country of Bangladesh. Just as religious conflict led to Pakistan's separation from India, so linguistic conflict led to Bangladesh's separation from Pakistan. Competing economic and political interests were reflected by religious differences in the first case and by linguistic differences in the second. East Pakistan was more populous and poorer than its partner in the west. Bengalis felt exploited economically and dominated politically. Language served as an issue around which their grievances could be mobilized.

The poet Spenser, encapsulating the Tudor policy which aimed at the extirpation of Irish language and culture, observed that "... it hathe bene ever the use of the Conquerour to despise the Language of the Conquered and to force him by all meanes to learne his. ... The speache beinge Irishe, the harte muste nedes be Irishe. ..." (1949 [1596]: 118–119). There are exceptions, however. The brief Italian occupation of Ethiopia, for example, saw the only period in which vernacular languages were used as media of instruction in Ethiopian schools. The motivation was probably that of divide and rule. Turkish was not imposed on the Ottoman Empire's middle-eastern territories, in which Arabic, Islamic language supreme for Turks as well as Arabs, remained the language of commerce, law, religion, and learning. In contrast, the Manchus, who conquered China in the seventeenth-century, present an even more extreme example. In awe of the imposing and ancient Chinese civilization, fearful of being considered barbarians by their subjects, and anxious to win the loyalty of the Chinese scholars, the traditional ruling class, the Manchu rulers devoted themselves

to Confucian tradition and "became more Chinese than the Chinese themselves" (Fitzgerald 1954: 548).

In spite of these examples, there is a kernel of truth in Spenser's remark.
It is common for conquerors to impose their language on the educational
system of the conquered. Such imposition is found even in monolingual
colonies, as in Ireland or Tunisia, although the policy is more justifiable,
from at least an administrative point of view, in the case of linguistically
diverse colonies such as India or Cameroon. The ordinary problems of
teacher training, the preparation of teaching materials and texts, and the
development of curricula and assessment procedures would be com-
pounded if carried out in a multitude of languages, even if the conqueror
wanted to do so. The fewer the languages of instruction, the easier the
administrative task. Life is likely to be easier for the conqueror if at least
some members of the conquered territories learn the conqueror's language.
And usually there will be a demand on the part of the vanquished to
learn this language, which will ordinarily be viewed as a language of economic opportunity.

The decision to use English, French, Spanish, and Portuguese as media
of instruction in linguistically diverse colonies was often based not only
on considerations of efficiency and control but also on a supreme ethnocentric self-confidence. Thomas Arnold, headmaster of Rugby School from
1828 until his death in 1842, wrote while travelling in France and Italy
that "a thorough English gentleman – Christian, manly, and enlightened
– . . . is a finer specimen of human nature than any other country, I believe,
could furnish." Arnold feared that English travelers abroad might imitate
foreign customs, "as in the absurd habit of not eating fish with a knife,
borrowed from the French, who do it because they have no knives fit
for use" (quoted by Strachey 1986 [1918]: 181).

If the English felt superior to the culturally similar French, it is not
surprising that they regarded the peoples of their Asian and African colonies, radically different from them in culture, with contempt. Thomas
Macauley's "Minute on Education," written in 1835 in support of a western system of education in India, in which English would be the medium
of higher education, expressed this extreme Anglocentric confidence: "The
claims of our own language it is hardly necessary to recapitulate. It stands
pre-eminent even among the languages of the West. It abounds with works
of imagination not inferior to the noblest which Greece had bequeathed
to us, – with models of every species of eloquence. . . . Whoever knows
that language has ready access to all the vast intellectual wealth which
all the wisest nations of the earth have created and hoarded in the course
of ninety generations. . . . The question now before us is simply whether,
when it is in our power to teach this language, we shall teach languages
in which, by universal confession, there are no books in any subject which

deserve to be compared to our own . . . and whether, when we can patronize sound philosophy and true history, we shall countenance, at the public expense, medical doctrines which would disgrace an English farrier, astronomy which would move laughter from girls at an English boarding school, history abounding with kings thirty feet high . . . and geography made of seas of treacle and seas of butter" (Nurullah and Naik 1951: 136–7). Durkacz (1983: 205), citing these sentiments, writes that it is no wonder that the English regarded Gaelic, Irish, and Welsh as unworthy of use as media of instruction, a view consistent with colonial contempt for minority languages and cultures.

When colonial territories became independent, the mobilized masses expect greater political and economic participation. These expectations, together with the rhetoric of national liberation movements, which stressed the value of indigenous tradition, authenticity, and uniqueness, may have exerted pressure to replace colonial languages with indigenous languages as media of instruction.

This replacement was sometimes difficult to implement. In the first place, elites were sometimes unwilling to surrender those personal advantages won on the basis of their elite education via a colonial language. If that language were to lose its privileges, they might lose their privileges as well. Second, economic and political rivalry among competing language groups sometimes made each unwilling to see the other's language instituted as a system-wide medium of instruction. They preferred that everyone face the same disadvantage of studying via a colonial language than that some should have the advantage of studying in their own. Third, access to world commerce, science, and technology demands that at least some must learn the imperial languages. An excellent way to impart those languages is to use them as media of instruction.

In short, while most give lip service to the importance of maximizing the educational attainments of pupils, the decision as to what languages will be used to teach them typically depends on political considerations. Since education is, from the state's point of view, a primary means of social control and, from the individual's or family's point of view, a means for social mobility, it is scarcely surprising that the language of instruction should be an important political issue.

8. "*School subject* (symbol: s); the language (other than one which already has an o or p function) is commonly taught as a subject in secondary and/or higher education." Inasmuch as second languages are often taught at primary schools as well, it would be useful to broaden this rubric to include the teaching of a language as a school subject at the lower grades.

Perhaps the first schools in antiquity were the royal colleges of Babylonia and Assyria, language schools for the training of translator-scribes. From antiquity to the present, language teaching has occupied a prominent place in the curriculum. As noted above, Stewart's definition excludes official and provincial languages. Indeed, it is probably safe to assume that, in most cases, when students do not speak such languages natively, they will study them as school subjects. This is reasonable inasmuch as official and provincial languages are normally widely used and thus widely useful, particularly if we do not restrict ourselves to statutory languages but include government working languages as well.

When other than o or p languages are taught as subjects, for what purposes are they taught? Such languages are taught for a number of goals, as for example, to enable worshippers to read sacred texts written in a classical language, to enable students to obtain employment requiring knowledge of a second language, to enable students to benefit from instruction offered via a second language, to link students to an ethnic or national heritage, and to distinguish an elite from the mass.

This last purpose seems to have motivated a centuries-old tradition whereby English grammar schools concentrated on Greek and Latin. Boys learned to construe ancient texts, to translate them into English, and to compose original texts in those languages. When Samuel Johnson was an old man and awoke to find himself with a paralytic stroke, he prayed that his intellect be spared: "I was alarmed, and prayed God, that however he might afflict my body, he would spare my understanding. This prayer, that I might try the integrity of my faculties, I made in Latin verse. The lines were not very good, but I knew them not to be very good" (quoted by Bate 1975: 575). Such skills were of practical use when scholars trained for careers in the church, but by the time Johnson went to school, this was no longer the case.

When Thomas Arnold became headmaster of Rugby School in 1828, Greek and Latin still formed the core curriculum of "a thorough English gentleman," a tradition which Arnold saw no reason to change. He did, however, add an hour's instruction per week in French, although he doubted whether an English boy could ever learn to speak or pronounce it properly (Strachey 1986 [1918]: 171). A watered-down version of this tradition lasted to my own generation, for which Latin (but not Greek) was a required subject for university matriculation. Our Latin teachers told us that studying Latin would "train the mind." But if that was the case, should not the students enrolled in secretarial, commercial, and manual-arts programs have had to read Caesar, Cicero, and Virgil as well? Did their minds deserve to be trained any less than mine?

When students study via a foreign or second language, they must necessarily learn that language if they are to benefit from instruction. It is common in multilingual countries to teach via an official language at the secondary or tertiary levels and to prepare those students who are continuing to these levels by teaching them the official language at the lower levels. When this is the case, success in learning the official language is a prerequisite for secondary or tertiary education.

While it is reasonable that official languages will be taught to those who do not speak them natively, this is not always the case. For example, whereas the study of Hebrew is compulsory in Arab-Israeli primary schools, the study of Arabic is not compulsory in Jewish-Israeli primary schools, although it is widely taught. English is compulsory for both Arab and Jewish children. Thus all Israeli-Arab children and many Israeli-Jewish children must study two languages in addition to their mother tongue. Such a language burden is by no means unusual. The non-Hindi areas of India, for example, follow a "three-language formula" whereby children study the regional language, Hindi, and English as subjects. For many of these children, the regional language is itself an additional language.

The success with which additional languages are learned via their study as school subjects varies widely. It is likely that the chief determinants of variability are the intensity of study, the quality of instruction, and the usefulness of the language outside the school. The chief determinants, in other words, are likely to be opportunity and incentive to learn, a not surprising hypothesis.

Scotton (1972), for example, found that relatively few respondents in Kampala claimed the ability to speak English unless they had been in school long enough to have learned it. Reves' (1983) study of Israeli-Arab secondary-school students provides another example of the importance of opportunity to learn. Her respondents, who lived in Jaffa, now part of Tel Aviv, had many opportunities to learn Hebrew outside school, although they studied it as a school subject. Their opportunities to learn English, on the other hand, were confined chiefly to the classroom. Students at a municipal high school knew Hebrew about as well as the students at a private high school, but the municipal high-school students' knowledge of English was far inferior to that of the private-school pupils, who received instruction of better quality. Reves' study also suggests that differences in incentives may have played a role as well, inasmuch as the municipal-school students were less likely to go to university, where knowledge of English is required, or to take a job requiring knowledge of English, than the private-school pupils.

While political pressure is far less likely to be exerted for or against the teaching of a language as subject, as compared to its use as a medium of instruction, educational policy-makers are often sensitive to the demands of parents and students with respect to which languages should be taught as subjects. Clearly the commercial importance of English has stimulated a widespread demand to learn it. Consequently it is the foreign language most likely to be taught in the schools of non-Anglophone countries. In the last chapter we saw how Israeli parents have circumvented Ministry of Education directives against the teaching of English below the fourth grade. In contrast, the uprising of American university students in the 1960s and their cries for curricular "relevance" resulted in the wholesale abandonment of foreign-language study as a requirement for graduation. For those students, foreign-language proficiency, particularly the limited functional competence they typically attained, seemed as useless as the study of Latin and Greek and almost as anachronistic.

9. "*Literary* (symbol: l); the use of a language primarily for literary or scholarly purposes." The promotion of vernaculars for literary and scholarly purposes is a common feature of nationalist movements, perhaps because such development may serve to raise the national consciousness of the masses or at least of the intellectuals. Also some nationalists may believe that the literary development of a national language buttresses the legitimacy of claims for national autonomy. Nonetheless it is likely that it is not *belles lettres* but the less glamorous non-narrative prose, "the realm of information, not of imagination," that lends prestige to vernacular languages (Kloss 1967: 33).

As Fishman (1982) points out, champions of vernaculars for high-culture functions are unlikely to succeed unless they, or those they represent, control the economic and political apparatus in which the community operates. This is so because people are unlikely to replace an established literary language by a vernacular for high-culture functions unless there are substantial incentives to do so. This is the reason that efforts to promote Yiddish for high-culture functions failed, before the Holocaust cut out the heart of the Yiddish-speaking world. Speakers of Yiddish controlled neither the economic nor the political world in which they lived. In Fishman's words (1982: 311–12): "Ideology, symbolism, and rhetoric are of undeniable significance in language spread – they are consciously motivating, focusing, and activating – but without a tangible and considerable status-power counterpart they become, under conditions of social change, competitively inoperative in the face of languages that do provide such. They may continue to be inspirational but – *particularly in modern times* – they cease to be decisive, i.e., they ultimately fail to safeguard even the intimacy of hearth and home from the turmoil of the econo-political arena" [italics in original].

10. "*Religious* (symbol: r); the use of a language primarily in connection with the ritual of a particular religion." It is useful to broaden this definition to include three overlapping and related subfunctions: (1) exhortation, conversion, and religious instruction, (2) sacred-text literacy, and (3) public

prayer. Some religions, such as Islam and Judaism, confine the recitation of their sacred texts and prayers to one, and only one, sacred language. When the status of a liturgical language is fixed, the language eventually becomes less intelligible to adherents of the religion (unless they study it as a second or foreign language), either because the adherents' language – originally the same or similar to the sacred language – has changed over time, or because the religion has been adopted by speakers of other languages. While the remoteness of liturgical from vernacular language helps to impart an otherworldly aura to the rituals for which it serves as medium, it also may act as a barrier to full religious participation. It may also serve to buttress the power of religious elites who know the sacred languages. When religious reform movements seek either to displace the religious establishment or to encourage the masses to participate more fully in religious life or to make religious ritual more responsive to the needs of the community, a reform of liturgical language policy is sometimes seen. Perhaps the most notable example is the Protestant Reformation, which encouraged Christians to study the scriptures directly, without depending upon the interpretations of priests. Only by making the scriptures available in vernacular languages could this aim be accomplished. Accordingly, the Christian scriptures, formerly available directly in Western Europe only to those who read Latin or Greek, were now translated into vernacular languages throughout Protestant Europe. Another example of a religious reformation inducing a change in liturgical language is Reform Judaism, which promoted the substitution of vernacular languages for Hebrew in public worship. Public reading of the scriptures continued to be carried out in Hebrew, but, unlike Orthodox practice, translations often accompanied or followed reading of the text.

When missionaries seek to convert others to their religious beliefs, they must decide what language to use as the medium for their message. The advantage of using the potential convert's mother tongue is not only that the message is more likely to be understood but also that the message is less likely to appear alien. Ferguson's (1967) account of St. Stefan of Perm, the fourteenth-century Russian Orthodox bishop, illustrates the use of local languages in missionary work. After he was ordained to the priesthood, Stefan returned to his homeland to convert the Komi people. There he found great resistance, in part because of opposition to the Russians, who were beginning to dominate the area politically and economically. Consistent with Stefan's support of Komi resistance to the Russians, he made extensive use of the Komi language in his missionary work. He preached to the Komi in Komi, he translated much of the liturgy into Komi, and he used Komi in public worship and as a medium of instruction in the schools he founded. Stefan was so successful that during his lifetime the majority of the Komi were baptized. His language policy helped to nativize a cultural importation and to win acceptance for it.

Durkacz' (1983) account of the spread of Presbyterianism in Scotland and Methodism in Wales makes clear that the evangelists' use of Gaelic and Welsh to preach was crucial to the spread of those religions. "It has been well said that evangelical religion was bound to the Highlands by grace and Gaelic" (Durkacz 1983: 6). In contrast, the established Anglican churches of Ireland and Wales, which resisted the use of Irish and Welsh as evangelical languages, were relatively unsuccessful in winning converts.

Sometimes missionaries, like St. Stefan, have the same mother tongue as those they seek to convert. More often, they do not. Should they nonetheless learn the languages of the peoples with whom they work? To do so may not be easy. Furthermore, none of the evangelical materials written in the missionary's language can be used without translation. If the mission field is diverse linguistically, missionaries who have learned a local language cannot be transferred to a new area without having to learn another. With such constraints in view, it is perhaps remarkable how often Christian missionaries learn the languages of the populations among whom they work. Indeed this is probably the normal practice. Missionaries have been responsible for reducing to writing hundreds of vernacular languages throughout the world and have been among the first to carry out systematic linguistic analyses of many local languages.

An alternative to using either the language of the missionary or the first language of the local population is to use a widespread lingua franca, as in the use of Quechua and Aymara by sixteenth-century Spanish priests in the Andes (Heath and Laprade 1982) and in the use of Kiswahili by some Christian missionaries in East Africa (Mazrui and Zirimu 1978).

When missionaries use an imperial language for evangelization and that language is also viewed as a requisite for material advancement, a local population's desire to learn that language may actually attract them to the missionaries. Giiz, as mentioned earlier the language of the Aksumite empire, probably spread in the Ethiopian highlands partly as a result of Syrian missionaries' use of that language to teach improved agricultural and handicraft techniques along with the Gospel. Protestant missionaries in India had to resist pressure from local populations to use English as the medium of instruction in the earliest grades. These missionaries preferred to use local languages as media of instruction, viewing these as the best way to convert souls; when English was used, it was generally at higher levels of instruction and for an elite (Durkacz 1983).

The intersection of religion and education as arenas for language planning is strikingly illustrated by Durkacz' account of the eighteenth- and nineteenth-century circulating schools of Wales and the Scottish Highlands. These one-teacher schools, devoted to the inculcation of literacy in the mother tongue, Welsh or Gaelic, moved from one community to the next as soon as their mission of basic literacy instruction was accomplished. The use of the Bible as the basic literacy primer induced religious enthusiasm among the local population, which could then be channeled by the Welsh- and Gaelic-language exhortations of the preachers who followed.

Other functions as targets of status planning

Status planning decisions are made with respect to at least two uses in addition to those identified by Stewart: the mass media and work.

When governments control mass media, they also determine the languages in which the media are conveyed. The Israeli government, for example, determines how many hours of radio and television programming are broadcast in Hebrew, Arabic, and in foreign languages. The pressures which determine the allocation of language to media include demand by various ethnolinguistic groups, willingness to accommodate this demand, desire to promote or to repress given languages, the availability of programs and personnel and the feasibility of producing new programs in given languages.

Perhaps the best-known example of status planning for work is found in the Province of Quebec, which from the mid-1970s has sought to make French rather than English the language of work. Although Francophones comprise about 80 percent of the population, control of economic and financial institutions is concentrated in the hands of the Anglophone minority and foreign Anglophones. Although Francophones have entered middle management in large numbers, Anglophones are overwhelmingly dominant at the top managerial level of large business firms. Francophone workers who aim to enter the ranks of top management have felt obliged to learn English. Material incentives to learn English have inspired non-Anglophone, non-Francophone immigrants (termed "Allophones") to learn English rather than French and to identify themselves with the Anglophones rather than with the Francophone community. The position of French has been further undermined by a falling birth rate among Francophones, who increasingly have felt their relative importance in the Province to be threatened. Accordingly, even before the Quebec nationalist Parti Québécois came to power in 1976, the province adopted legislation to promote French as the language of work.

In 1974, the Liberal Party's Bill 22, the "Official Languages Act," which made French the official language of Quebec, also declared that business personnel must be able to communicate in French, and compelled private businesses to develop a "francization program," leading to the use of French at all levels of employment, in order to receive certain government benefits and to compete for government contracts. In 1977, the provincial government, under the Parti Québécois, adopted Bill 101, the "Charter of the French Language," which broadened the scope of these provisions. The charter stipulated that all businesses employing at least fifty persons must obtain a certificate stating either that the firm is applying a francization program or that no such program is needed (Daoust-Blais 1983). The Charter established a mechanism for implementing these provisions, including coercive measures to ensure compliance. Bill 22 and Bill 101 provide an unusually clear recognition of the importance of commercial incentives for the promotion and defense of language maintenance. They also provide clear recognition that status planning refers ultimately to the status of those who use the language.

Conclusion

In this chapter we have considered the allocation of a community's languages to various functions or uses. On the basis of the examples presented, it is tempting to argue that status planning is most likely to succeed when it is invoked for the pursuit and maintenance of power. It is tempting because the examples are consistent with this hypothesis. But if the hypothesis is correct, it is probably only *partially* correct. Language planning is too complex an activity to be explained by one factor only.

We saw in the last chapter that the most powerful individuals and groups within a community are those which exert the most influence over the distribution of scarce resources or values. Elites attempt to maintain and extend their influence over this process; the mass, to the extent that it is mobilized, seeks a more equitable process; and counterelites, speaking in the name of the mass or in the name of a new ideology, seek to displace the elite and to seize control of the process themselves. The language varieties which comprise a community's linguistic repertoire – all the registers, dialects, or languages in use by the community – can be manipulated by elites and counterelites. These spoken and written varieties are neither equally evaluated nor equally distributed. They are not equally evaluated inasmuch as community members view some varieties as "better" or more "appropriate" than others for particular contexts or purposes. They are not equally distributed inasmuch as no one controls all varieties. Whereas virtually all people may know how to talk to babies, for example, not everyone knows how to talk like a physician examining a patient, a radio announcer broadcasting the news, a marine drill instructor haranguing his troops, or a peasant bargaining at the weekly market.

Elites influence both the evaluation and the distribution of language varieties within the community. They influence evaluation through status planning and distribution through acquisition planning. Status planning influences the evaluation of a language variety by assigning it to the functions from which its evaluation derives. If, for example, higher education is valued, replacement of one language by another as the medium for university instruction is likely to raise speakers' evaluation of the replacement. In other words, status planning is an effort to regulate the *demand* for given verbal resources whereas acquisition planning is an effort to regulate the *distribution* of those resources. Counterelites attack in two ways. They can try to seize control over the distribution of valued verbal resources or they can try to reduce or nullify the value of these resources and elevate others in their place.

Status planning can, in principle, focus upon any communicative function. In practice, it tends to aim at those functions which enable elites to maintain or extend their power, or which give counterelites an opportunity to seize power for themselves. Further, it tends to be involved when changes threaten elites or are desired by counterelites. Even when a function is clearly relevant to the pursuit and maintenance of power, such as the administrative language of a government bureaucracy, status planning is likely not to be invoked if neither elites nor counterelites see any advantage in doing so.

True, ideological engines often drive status planning, and language heroes like Ben Yehuda devote themselves to status planning without any expectation of personal gain. But elites and counterelites are unlikely either to hitch themselves to ideological engines or to exploit the selfless efforts of others if the resulting status planning does not promote the maintenance or pursuit of power. While endorsement or promotion by elites or counterelites does not insure the success of status planning, such planning is unlikely to succeed without it.

Although status planning can, in principle, be devoted to maintaining the functional allocation of a community's languages, maintenance typically becomes a goal only after change is under way. There would be no reason, for example, for foreign governments to set up special afternoon schools for the children of their nationals in Belgium (Segers and van den Broeck 1972) if these children were not in danger of losing their ancestral language or of being illiterate in it. Efforts to *maintain* an allocation, in other words, are really efforts to *return* to an earlier, more desirable state of affairs. Whether efforts are directed to returning to an old allocation or to forwarding a new one, status planning typically works for change.

Status planning, then, is usually invoked when changes in the functional allocation of a community's language is seen as desirable. But elites and counterelites may be slow to alter the *status quo* precisely because they may share, with the community at large, the evaluations which they ultimately seek to change. For example, planners may be slow to propose that Language A replace Language B as a medium of school instruction if Language A is the bearer of an ancient literary tradition and is viewed as an expression of the community's collective memory, whereas Language B is viewed as suitable only for mundane tasks. Planners must change their own evaluations before they can change the public's. If they succeed in changing public evaluation, these new values serve as constraints for future status planning.

6

Corpus planning

Louis Henri Sullivan (1856–1924), an American architect who exerted a considerable influence on skyscraper design, wrote, in connection with the aesthetics of tall office buildings, that "form ever follows function." Sullivan viewed the ideal relationship between form and function as organic rather than mechanical. That is, he did not believe that a design should mechanically reflect utility. Rather, he believed that an authentic style is a natural expression of the civilization in which it is rooted. Thus an architectural design should express the environment from which it evolves as well as the particular functions it is meant to serve (Koeper 1980).

Although the dictum that form follows function was derived from a theory of architectural aesthetics, perhaps it can be applied to corpus planning. Certainly architecture serves as an apt metaphor for the latter. Both the architect and the corpus planner design structures to serve particular functions, rooted in a given social, cultural, political, and historical context. Both the architect and the corpus planner are influenced by this context. Both the architect and the corpus planner operate with an aesthetic theory, implicit or explicit. For example, just as Sullivan believed that a structure should reflect the civilization from which it springs, so some corpus planners believe that the corpus should reflect an indigenous or a classical tradition, or the values of modernity, efficiency, transparency, and the like. Just as an architect's design may or may not please the customer, who may accept or reject the blueprint, build the structure with or without modification, look for a new architect, or abandon the project, so the language planner's design may or may not please the public for whom it is meant. The planner may design, for example, a spelling system which is easy to learn, easy to use, economical to print, inexpensive to implement, and in all technical ways an improvement over the system it is meant to reform. The public may greet the proposed reform with enthusiasm, indifference, scorn, or disgust.

In corpus planning, form follows function in at least two senses. First form follows function in the sense that the corpus planner designs or selects structures on the assumption that a given function, overt or covert, can be served by a modification or treatment of the corpus. With respect to overt functions, implementation of the status-planning decisions encountered in the last chapter frequently demands corpus planning, particularly when a language or language variety is chosen for a communicative function which it has not previously served. For example, when St. Stefan of Perm wanted not only to translate the liturgy into Komi, but also to use Komi as a medium of instruction in his schools, he needed to reduce unwritten Komi to writing. He did so. When late nineteenth- and early twentieth-century Palestinian Jews started to use Hebrew as a medium of instruction in the schools of their new settlements, they had to find or create terms that teachers and pupils could use to discuss the modern subjects taught in school. Accordingly, the Teachers Union in 1904 revived the Hebrew Language Council, which had collapsed six months after its founding by Ben Yehuda in 1890, to serve the needs of the school system. The Council devoted a great deal of attention to devising school and curriculum terminologies and within 50 years had set up standard terminologies for almost all school subjects through high school (Fellman 1977, Rubin 1977). When Irish began to be used for the newly established Irish government and armed services in 1922, the variability found in Irish spelling made the need for a standard orthography more and more obvious, a need which led to the recommendations for a standardized spelling norm (Ó Murchú 1977). Thus form follows function in the sense that the desired communicative function precedes the designed or selected structure.

But what form should the structure take? Should it be closer to or farther from vernacular usage? Should it be indigenous to the language community or should it borrow or adapt a metropolitan or international form? Should it cleave to tradition or should it appear "modern"? If my argument is accepted that language planning is ultimately directed toward non-linguistic ends, it should come as no surprise that such ends influence the form of the desired corpus. When St. Stefan of Perm, for example, reduced Komi to writing, he invented a unique writing system rather than adopting one of the scripts in use by surrounding peoples. He did so to encourage the Komi to view the script as distinctively theirs and, by extension, to view the church as an indigenous institution. It is likely, according to Ferguson (1967), that the saint gave to some of the letters shapes that were reminiscent of the traditional signs which the Komi used as property markers, thus contributing to the script's indigenous appearance. Here, the form of the writing system was influenced by the saint's goal of evangelization.

When confronted by the need for everyday Hebrew vocabulary in turn-of-the-century Palestine, the Hebrew Language Council decided initially to use ancient Hebrew words, but if none was suitable then ancient Aramaic words. Aramaic, in the course of centuries, had become almost as sacred a Jewish language as Hebrew, which came to be written in the Aramaic alphabet. If neither Hebrew nor Aramaic words could be found, the Council decided that words from other Semitic languages would be used. Words from non-Semitic languages were initially thought unsuitable. If terms had to be created *de novo*, the Council wanted to use Hebrew roots, but failing these, the roots from other Semitic languages, particularly those of Arabic were preferred (Fainberg 1983). The use of Hebrew and Aramaic sources emphasized the antiquity of the Jewish presence in Palestine and helped to legitimize Jewish claims of self-determination in the land of their Hebrew-speaking ancestors. It is of interest that, at the beginning of the century, these nationalists saw other Semitic sources, including Arabic, as consistent with the promotion of the Jewish national movement, which had stimulated the use of Hebrew for everyday functions in the first place.

Were latent goals inherent in the standardization of Irish spelling? The largely ceremonial use of Irish for government functions emphasized the legitimacy of the new government's rule. The trappings of majesty enhance the symbols of power. When King George V rode through the streets of London to open Parliament, his coach was resplendent; the horses which pulled it were perfectly matched. When the King read his speech to Parliament, there was no doubt whatsoever as to the form in which the text was spelled. English spelling had been standardized by at least the middle of the eighteenth century. English, of course, was the language which almost all the Irish learned to read first. In contrast to a standard English spelling, did not an Irish spelling in disarray constitute a shabby national symbol?

Indeed, Irish spelling itself had once been standardized. A standard spelling had evolved by the sixteenth century, and remained in use until the turn of the present century, when the classical model began to be abandoned, as writers began to favor a literary language that reflected popular speech (Ó Murchú 1977). Since the spoken language was regionally diverse, considerable variation in spelling resulted. Conflict between traditionalists, who urged a return to the classical spelling, and those who favored regional forms delayed the attainment of a standard norm.

Finally, about twenty-five years after independence, members of the translation section of the Parliament's staff published their recommendations, an essentially traditional norm but which eliminated many of the redundant features of the classical model. Although the compromise was opposed both by traditionalists and by regionalists as well as by those who thought that the reforms were insufficiently radical, the government adopted it immediately for official publications and then for school grammars and texts.

The new spelling spread rapidly (Ó Murchú 1977). The reaction of conservatives was most bitter. Ó Murchú quotes a former Minister for Education, Ó Ceallaigh, who wrote in 1949, "We got ... some unnamed group to mutilate the traditional orthography which we should regard as a sacred heritage, an edifice of the intellect into which has been put the thought and judgement and progressive skill of our sages and evangelists for twelve hundred years." Ó Ceallaigh's impassioned invocation of the orthography's sacred heritage suggests that burnishing of the trappings of majesty and thus the legitimation of the new regime was an important impetus for standardization, which in turn was set in motion by the use of Irish for a new function, that of official language.

Not all corpus planning, however, arises as a consequence of a language's serving a new communicative function. When, for example, in the America of the 1960s, activists began to promote the substitution of *black* for *Negro* and *gay* for *homosexual*, the use of non-androcentric generics, and the use of comprehensible documents, they did so to enhance the power of blacks, gays, women, and consumers, as well as, possibly, the power of their leaders, rather than to enable English to serve new functions. In these cases, just as in the cases of Komi, Hebrew, and Irish, *non-language* goals influenced the desired form of the corpus. Thus in corpus planning, form follows function not only in the sense that a desired communicative function precedes a designed linguistic form but also in the sense that noncommunicative goals (functions) influence the desired form of the corpus.

The cases of corpus planning mentioned thus far exemplify the major types of corpus planning discussed in the literature, as well as an additional category which I suggest here. The traditional primary categories are *graphization*, *standardization*, and *modernization*. Two other categories, *codification* and *elaboration* are often mentioned, but these can be subsumed under the rubrics of standardization and modernization repectively. In addition, I suggest a fourth major category, *renovation*.

Graphization

Ferguson (1968) notes the widespread assumption among linguists that there are no "primitive" languages and that there is no way to rank the overall structural complexity of languages along an evolutionary continuum. He suggests, however, that there are three non-structural dimensions along which the development of languages can be compared: "graphization – reduction to writing; standardization – the development of a norm which overrides regional and social dialects; and, for want of a better terms, modernization – the development of intertranslatability with other languages in a range of topics and forms of discourse characteristic of industrialized, secularized, structurally differentiated, 'modern' societies'' (28).

The provision of writing systems for unwritten languages is an activity which occupies thousands of persons, particularly Christian missionaries, who are probably the most active practitioners of this craft today. Like St. Stefan, modern missionaries must make a fundamental choice between using an existing system and inventing a new one. Each alternative has a long tradition. Ferguson (1968) points out that in the early centuries of the Church's expansion in the East, the usual practice was to employ the Greek alphabet, adding new letters to represent those sounds in the target language which were not found in Greek. But occasionally the planner had a reason to emphasize the distinctiveness of the new writing system. St. Stefan chose this latter course, probably because of Komi opposition to the growing economic and political dominance of the Russians. The fifth-century creation of the Armenian alphabet by St. Mesrop is another example of the creation of a distinct system, different in this case from the Greek and Syriac alphabets found among surrounding peoples (Ferguson 1968).

If the decision to invent a unique script is taken, another fundamental choice presents itself, that between a syllabary, in which each symbol represents a syllable, and an alphabet, in which each letter represents a phoneme. Each of these choices requires still other decisions, such as the degree to which grammatical and derivational information should be preserved, the features of punctuation which are desirable, whether diacritics should be employed, and so forth.

There is a growing literature which offers criteria for judging the adequacy of writing systems (Berry 1958, 1977; Bloomfield 1942; Bolinger 1946; C. Chomsky 1970; N. Chomsky 1970; Fishman 1977; Gudschinsky 1957, 1959; International African Institute 1962; MacCarthy 1964; Nida 1954; Pike 1947; Sjoberg 1964, 1966; Smalley 1964; Venezky 1977). Principles and criteria can be divided into two major categories, (1) psycholinguistic or technical and (2) sociolinguistic.

Psycholinguistic, technical principles and criteria are concerned with the extent to which the writing system is easy to learn, easy to read, easy to write, easy to carry over to another language (transfer of skills), and easy to reproduce by modern printing techniques. As Berry (1958, 1977) has pointed out, these criteria may conflict with one another. What is easy to read is not necessarily easy to write and print. What is easy to learn is not necessarily easy to use. Venezky (1977), for example, suggests that for persons becoming literate an orthography should indicate the sounds of the words, but that for more advanced readers an orthography should indicate meanings rather than sounds.

What is easy to learn may not be easy to transfer. Many writing systems are designed as transitional orthographies. They serve as a bridge from nonliteracy to literacy in a national or official language, which will be the reader's primary written language. Typically, transitional literacy is imparted via the learner's mother tongue. There is, in fact, conflicting evidence as to the efficiency of imparting initial literacy in the mother tongue when the ultimate goal is literacy in a second language (Engle 1975). The use of mother-tongue literacy as a bridge to literacy in a second language is based on two assumptions: (1) that initial literacy skills are typically easier to acquire in the first than in a second language and (2) that it is a relatively easy matter to transfer literacy skills from the first to a second language if the writing systems are similar and if the reader knows the second language. Probably the second assumption, at any rate, is sound, although there is little experimental evidence as to the importance of transfer as a psychological problem (Berry 1977). In any case, if the writing system is designed as a transitional orthography, it will be sensible to use a writing system close to that employed for the second language, the ultimate target of literacy, even if that system is not well-suited to ease of reading the first language.

Not only may goals conflict, but also there may be disagreement as to the means whereby a given goal should be attained. If ease of reading is a goal, how is this goal to be maximized? If one believes that reading entails the matching of written symbols with oral units, then one will design a system which represents each phoneme (if one is using an alphabet) or each syllable (if one is using a syllabary) with a unique symbol. In this way the writing system will represent the phonological realization of each word. Thus, with an alphabetic system, the last symbol in the plural forms of *cat* and *fiddle*, for example, would be different. Similarly, the second vowel in each of the following pairs would be represented differently in the first word than in the second – *mendacious, mendacity*; *narcosis, narcotic*; *serene, serenity*; *seduce, seduction*; *contrite, contrition*. On the other hand, if one believes that a fluent reader recognizes not the correspondence between symbol and sound but rather the correspondence between symbol and meaning, one will design a writing system which reflects underlying grammatical and lexical forms. Thus the last symbol in the plural forms of *cat* and *fiddle* would be the same because it represents the plural morpheme rather than its phonological realization. Similarly the second vowel of each member of the word pairs enumerated above would be spelled the same because such a spelling facilitates identification of meaning.

Berry (1977) points out that if this second view is taken to its limits, one would have to conclude that the alphabetic principle is irrelevant for fluent reading – that fluent readers treat a text as if it were ideographic. Probably few would take such an extreme position. On the other hand, most of those who believe that an ideal writing system should approach a phonemic transcription are ready to modify this approach when it proves impractical. To what extent, then, should a writing system represent the phonological realization of a text and to what extent should it represent abstract underlying grammatical and lexical structures, if one's principal goal is fluent reading? And does it really matter?

Venezky (1977; 47) claims that "when attempts are made to compare reading abilities across cultures, one of the few valid observations which can be made is that *regardless of the phonemic regularity of the orthography*, a significant percentage of children in all countries will be classed as remedial readers, and within this group most will come from lower socio-economic environments" (italics added). An experiment by Rabin and Schlesinger (1974), for example, found no systematic effect of spelling on the speed of reading or on the degree of comprehension, among Israeli seventh-grade pupils presented with Hebrew texts written in three spelling systems that differ in uncertainty (the extent to which they create homographs).

Disagreement about the characteristics which facilitate ease of reading stem principally from disagreement as to the nature of reading. Similarly, differences in opinion as to the nature of learning, writing, and transfer lead to differences in opinion as to the technical desiderata that lead to each of these goals. For example, if we assume that learning to read involves learning to link written symbols to sounds, is it easier to learn the symbols for sounds which are minimally distinct (e.g. /p/ and /b/) when their symbols are also minimally distinct? Or is it easier to learn them when their symbols are maximally distinct? According to Venezky (1977) there is little, if any, controlled investigation to guide us. All in all, one wonders how important it is to cleave to any one technical characteristic in the design of a writing system if the efficacy of that characteristic is debatable and if it must in any event be compromised in order to incorporate other desirable features.

A more pressing reason for a relaxed attitude towards technical considerations is that these seem less important for the acceptance or rejection of a writing system than social considerations. That European Jews wrote Judezmo, a Romance language, and Yiddish, a Germanic language, in Hebrew script had little to do with the technical adequacy of Hebrew to represent those languages. Similarly, that non-Arab Muslim peoples until recently wrote their languages in Arabic script and that Roman Catholic Slavs wrote their languages in Latin script while Orthodox Slavs wrote theirs in Cyrillic script is a function of social not technical constraints. The primacy of social considerations is clearest, perhaps, when we see the same language written in different scripts by different subgroups. Serbo-Croation, for example, is written in Latin script by Catholic Croats and in Cyrillic script by Orthodox Serbs, and it was formerly written in Arabic script by Bosnian Muslims (Billigmeier 1987).

These examples suggest the influence of religious affiliation upon the acceptability of writing systems. Indeed, the scripts associated with sacred texts often spread along with acceptance of the texts themselves. Muslims decorate their mosques with passages from the Quran, written in exquisite Arabic calligraphy, while Roman Catholic bishops trace the letters of the Latin alphabet on church floors during consecration rites (Billigmeier 1987). Supernatural assistance in the invention of writing systems is a common claim, from the ancient Mesopotamians, who believed that the son of their pantheon's king invented writing, and the ancient Egyptians, who credited the god Thoth with the discovery of writing (Billigmeier 1987), to Silas John Edward, founder of a religious movement among the Western Apache. He credited his invention of a writing system, in widespread use among the Western Apache, to "a dream from God" (Basso and Anderson 1973). The other-worldly origin of writing systems helps legitimize the worldly authority which such systems represent. From the Assyrian monarch Hammurabi (c. 1950 BCE) to the present, rulers codify their edicts. Further, without writing, the stable administration of large populations would be difficult if not impossible.

Writing, like other instruments of power, can be wielded by anyone who grasps it. If rulers use writing to maintain power, the ruled use writing to acquire it. Thus subjugated minorities often want their languages to be written in a system that looks as much as possible like the system in use by their rulers, whether or not this system is technically adequate to represent their own languages. If they want to partake of the aura of the rulers' writing system, it is also true that the use of this system will facilitate acquisition of literacy in the rulers' language. When a minority language is reduced to writing primarily to serve as a bridge to literacy in the dominant language, it is reasonable that the writing system of the two languages be similar. To facilitate transfer and to suit the preference of many minorities for a system similar to that of the dominant language, modern Christian missionaries, particularly the Summer Institute of Linguistics, perhaps the largest group employed today in graphization, tend to use the writing system of the national or official language of the country in which the speakers of the unwritten languages are found.

But sometimes minorities want a system different from that of their rulers. They want a system unique to themselves. A fascinating example is provided by the indigenous West African scripts, which include the Vai, Mende, Loma and Kpelle syllabaries and the Bassa alphabet of Liberia and Sierra Leone, the Bamoun syllabary of Cameroon and Eastern Nigeria, and the Bete syllabary of the Ivory Coast, all of which developed after the introduction of the Latin and Arabic scripts (Dalby 1967, 1968). The earliest, the Vai syllabary of Liberia, was invented about 1833. Its invention and acceptance were almost certainly prompted by the Vai's desire to acquire the power and material advantages which belonged to the literates around them: black settlers from America, Europeans, and Mandingo Muslims (Dalby 1967). Africans had come to view their lack of a literate culture as a mark of their subordinate status (Dalby 1968).

Vai is a language with a predominantly consonant-vowel structure, for which a syllabary is well-suited. But it is unlikely that such technical considerations were responsible for the script's acceptance. In fact the syllabary is relatively inflexible (Kotei 1972). Rather, a unique script was consistent with the African tradition of using indigenous symbols for magical purposes, a use which was surrounded by a "high degree of mystery and secrecy" (Dalby 1968). Indeed Dalby suggests that there are "semi-secret applications" of the Vai script. And Scribner and Cole (1981) report that the advantage of Vai literacy which these literates cited most frequently was privacy in keeping track of their own affairs.

In the nineteenth century, the Vai enjoyed an economic status superior to that of neighboring African peoples as well as an enhanced prestige, owing at least partly to their possession of a unique script (Dalby 1967). According to Dalby (1968), the Vai script stimulated competitive feelings among other peoples in the area and consequently a desire for their own unique scripts. Rivalry plus the desire for secrecy led to the creation of different scripts for different vernaculars.

But other motives may also have contributed to the creation and acceptance of these indigenous scripts. Kotei (1972) suggests that while West African peoples may have envied the power and material advantages associated with knowledge of Latin and Arabic scripts, they may also have seen these scripts as a means for their own subjugation. Thus Africans may have viewed the use of African scripts as a means not only for improving their own material conditions but also for resisting the authority of alien others. Another motive, related to that suggested by Kotei, is fear of the cultural innovations associated with the Latin and Arabic scripts. Such a fear seems implicit in the dream which Wido Zobo, inventor of the Loma script, recounted to explain the inspiration for his creation. He dreamed he was face-to-face with God, whom he accused of leaving the Loma in ignorance, without a script. God replied that he feared that the power of writing would lead the Loma away from their traditional beliefs and customs. Wido Zobo promised that the Loma would continue to live as they had in the past and that he would never teach the script to a woman. "God then instructed him how to prepare ink from the leaves of a creeper" (Dalby 1968).

Wido Zobo's revelation implies that an indigenous script can act as a sieve, separating desired from undesired innovations. That is to say, an indigenous script permits its users to benefit from modern technology without sacrificing traditional beliefs and practices. An indigenous script provides an elegant solution to the problem of how to be modern and traditional at one and the same time. In short, the development and spread of West African indigenous scripts provides a useful illustration of the importance of sociolinguistic considerations in the acceptance of writing systems. These considerations typically outweigh technical factors in determining the system's acceptance. To the extent that one seeks technical advice in the creation of a writing system, it might be more useful to talk to anthropologists, political scientists, and sociologists than to linguists and psychologists.

Standardization: "For all people for all time"

In early thirteenth-century England, a royal ordinance prescribed a standard yard, divided into the traditional three feet, each of 12 inches, "neither more nor less" (Chisholm 1980). The ordinance's division of the foot into twelve inches confirmed customary usage. Still, the "neither more nor less" startles those of us who grew up with English linear measurements. To us, the division of the foot into 12 inches seems as inevitable as the number of fingers on a hand. "Neither more nor less" reminds us that the equivalence of an inch to one-twelfth of a foot is arbitrary. It could just as well – in fact far better – be one tenth. If this royal ordinance reminds us of the arbitrary nature of most measurements, it also suggests to us that units of measurement may vary from time to time and from place to place. Indeed, it was variability in the use of such units which prompted the promulgation of the ordinance.

The Roman system of measures, inherited by medieval Europe, had developed into a welter of conflicting national and regional systems (Chisholm 1980) much as the various Romance languages developed from Latin. The residue of these conflicting systems can be seen today. In a world in which the metric system is supreme, the English system of measures is a medieval relic. Even within the English system there are national variations. The United States still uses the medieval value of the gallon and the bushel, inherited from colonial times, whereas these values were changed in Great Britain in 1824. Consequently the U.S. gallon and bushel are today smaller by about 17 percent and 3 percent respectively than their British counterparts (Chisholm 1980). The welter of conflicting systems in medieval Europe, which Charlemagne failed to unify after a strenuous effort to do so, can be contrasted with a high degree of uniformity in the ancient world. The Egyptian cubit, for example, was a widely used unit of linear measurement. Devised about 3,000 BCE, it was based on the length of the lower arm, from elbow to finger tips. This unit was standardized against a master cubit of black granite, against which all cubit sticks in Egypt had to be periodically checked. The accuracy of these cubit sticks is reflected by the Great Pyramid of Gizah, each of whose sides deviates no more than .05 percent from the mean length (Chisholm 1980). The master cubit of black granite is an ancient forerunner of subsequent standards of measurement, such as the platinum-iridium cylinder kept by the International Bureau of Weights and Measures at Paris as the standard kilogram.

While the propagation of the metric system was an important outcome of the French Revolution, the need for a uniform system had been recognized for some time. Gabriel Mouton, vicar of St. Paul's church in Lyon, suggested a linear measure, whose characteristics prefigure those of the modern metric system, about 120 years before the Revolution. So strongly entrenched were customary practices, however, that it took a revolution to make a uniform system possible. Indeed, Chisholm (1980) points out that the metric system has often been adopted during periods of political upheaval, as in Latin America, the Soviet Union, and China. When the metric system was established by law in France in 1799, the motto adopted for the system was "For all people, for all time" (Chisholm 1980), the ultimate standardization.

Rubin (1977), in her discussion of language standardization, points out that all human interaction requires some degree of standardization, i.e. some degree of shared expectations and shared understanding. If each participant in an interaction operates according to different norms, communication breaks down. Indeed, one impetus for the adoption of the metric system was the difficulty in scientific circles of coping with differing national and regional measurements. When communication is largely confined to the local community, in which most people know one another and interact mainly with one another, regional and national variants pose few problems. When networks expand beyond the local community, local variants may impede communication. Just as modern science requires standard measurements and just as mass production requires standard, interchangeable parts, so supra-local communication requires the use of supra-local forms. In many parts of the world, villagers will break off a conversation with one another in the local or regional dialect to address a stranger in the national standard, the supralocal form shared by all. Indeed, one criterion for determining whether two varieties are dialects of the same language or of different languages is whether their speakers share a substantially similar overarching standard variety (Ferguson and Gumperz 1960).

Just as regional and national systems of measurement sometimes proliferate from a common ancestor, so do regional and national language forms sometimes develop from a common linguistic ancestor. Just as standardization in measurement usually procedes from the center to the periphery, so the standardization of language typically radiates outward from metropolitan centers of power. Just as standardization of measurement is often a result of political upheaval and reintegration, so language standardization is often a result of political upheaval and reintegration. The Académie française was founded in such a period. Just as standardization of measurement reveals two types of historical system, a more or less haphazard evolution, like that of the English system of weights and measures, and a planned system, like the metric (Chisholm 1980), so language standardization is sometimes the result of unplanned evolution and sometimes the object of overt planning. Richelieu, the promulgator of a law regulating weights and measures (the Code Michaud of 1629), also founded the Académie française. Finally, just as customary variants in measurement are often difficult to rationalize and unify, so customary variants in language are often difficult to reduce to a universal norm. Johnson (1755), in the preface to his *Dictionary*, quotes Hooker: "Change is not made without inconvenience, even from worse to better" (McAdam and Milne 1963: 7).

But the analogy between standardization in measurement and standardization in language can be stretched only so far. First, precision in language is not always wanted. Artists sometimes seek ambiguity and politicians obfuscation. Humpty Dumpty's view that a word means just what he wants it to mean, "neither more nor less," is sometimes most useful. Second, language is more than a tool. Haugen (1971), commenting on Ray's (1963) and Tauli's (1968) theories of language standardization, argues that their basic postulate, that language is a tool of communication, is faulty. Language, he writes, is such a highly complex cognitive system that it cannot be compared to the tools which men and women have devised to extend their mastery of the environment. Third, when linguistic variants serve as markers of our identity, we may be loath to abandon them, particularly in the name of a soulless efficiency. Finally, it is impossible to freeze the forms of a living language, which transforms itself continuously even as it is itself transformed. No one has put this better than Johnson (1755), in the preface to his *Dictionary* (McAdam and Milne 1963: 24):

> Those who have been persuaded to think well of my design, will require that it should fix our language, and put a stop to those alterations which time and chance have hitherto been suffered to make in it without opposition. With this consequence I will confess that I flattered myself for a while; but now begin to fear that I have indulged expectation which neither reason nor experience can justify. When we see men grow old and die at a certain time one after another, from century to century, we laugh at the elixir that promises to prolong life to a thousand years; and with equal justice may the lexicographer be derided, who being able to produce no example of a nation that has preserved their words and phrases from mutability, shall

imagine that his dictionary can embalm his language, and secure it from corruption and decay, that it is in his power to change sublunary nature, and clear the world at once from folly, vanity, and affectation.

With this hope, however, academies have been instituted, to guard the avenues of their languages, to retain fugitives, and repulse intruders; but their vigilance and activity have hitherto been vain; sounds are too volatile and subtle for legal restraints; to enchain syllables and to lash the wind are equally the undertakings of pride, unwilling to measure its desires by its strength.

Even the metric system, promulgated in 1799 "for all people, for all time," was replaced in 1960 by the Système International, which incorporates and rationalizes the subsystems which proliferated during the twentieth century and which corrects the original eighteenth-century measurements, long known to be not accurate enough for modern science (Chisholm 1980). If even the metric system could not be preserved from change, how much less likely it is that the language planner can "embalm his language and secure it from corruption and decay."

Johnson's strictures refer principally to change over time. Diachronic change, however, is but the outcome of synchronic variation. The variability in language usage which we see all around us, particularly the variability associated with social stratification, is the forerunner of diachronic change. Thus standardization "for all people" is as illusory as standardization for all contexts and "for all time."

Still, if it were possible to find a perfectly standardized language, what would it be like? Ferguson (1962: 10) writes that "ideal standardization refers to a language which has a single, widely accepted norm which is felt to be appropriate with only minor modifications or variations for all purposes for which language is used. Differences between regional variants, social levels, speaking and writing and so on are quite small." Even this ideal of standardization admits of some variability, albeit minor, a reflection of the impossibility of securing perfect uniformity. Note that there are two components to Ferguson's definition, one attitudinal, the other behavioral. Prescription of a norm, whether via published grammars and dictionaries or whether via the pronouncements of editors, teachers, critics, writers, or other language guardians, does not constitute standardization. Codification and pronouncements may be ignored or rejected. The norm must be "widely accepted" and "felt to be appropriate." But this attitudinal condition is also not sufficient for ideal standardization inasmuch as feelings must be translated into action. Actual differences must be "quite small."

In fact, language standardization is more likely to be approached with regard to its attitudinal than to its behavioral component. People, that is, are more likely to agree that an all-purpose model exists than to use it for all the purposes for which they feel it to be appropriate, if in fact they use it at all. Indeed, Labov (1966, 1968) defines a speech community in terms of shared evaluations, not in terms of shared verbal behavior. According to this view, people belong to the same speech community when they evaluate a given instance of language behavior similarly, as "proper," "correct," or "good" or as "improper," "incorrect," or "bad." If language users are more likely to agree that an all-purpose model exists than to use it for all purposes, why is this so?

First, there can be no single-style language users. We move from style to style or from variety to variety to suit our communicative context – oral or written, casual or formal, sacred or secular, and so forth – as well as to suit our communicative intent. Thus, even if we control a standard variety, we modify it or abandon it as the communicative circumstances dictate. Because the style or variety we employ is itself part of the meaning we convey, we cannot restrict ourselves to a single style without restricting our ability to implement our communicative intent. Only computerized voices, oral or written, are restricted to a single style and this is appropriate because they are restricted to a single communicative function. Thus even if we accept a model as correct for all purposes, we do not use it for all purposes.

Second, elites view the symbols of their distinctiveness, linguistic or otherwise, as evidence of their superiority and as justification for their privileged position (Kroch 1978). It is in the interest of elites to promote their own language variety as the single model of correctness, not only to elicit the "veneration of the masses" but also to confer legitimacy upon the pronouncements of the state, the church, and other institutions of control. Can laws and ordinances be legitimate if promulgated in "incorrect" language? Does God speak ungrammatically? Conversely, must not the language of the elite be correct if that is the language of the controlling institutions? The model favored by elites is typically adopted by schools, which in turn promote the public's acceptance of what Milroy and Milroy (1985), in their book on correctness in language, term the "ideology of standardization," the idea that there is a correct way of using the language and that all people *ought* to use it this way.

Those who accept the model or ideal but are unable to use it serve to legitimize their own subordination. By promoting the ideal without imparting to all the ability to use it, the schools help to reproduce the social structure in each generation. On the other hand, if people refuse to accept the ideal, they subvert the existing social order. This, perhaps, explains the consistent linking of language use with morality which Milroy and Milroy discuss. A self-confident elite sees the existing order as moral and the standard as a symbol of that order. A standard language helps maintain a dike against the sea of moral turpitude which threatens to engulf the social, and hence the moral, order. Thus we find that Charlemagne's reform of school and church Latin, a return to what was perceived as the original pronunciation, was carried out "in order that those who aim to please God by living correctly should also not neglect to please him by speaking correctly" (Alcuin, c. 735–804, *De litteris colendis*, cited by Rabin 1985; 81). A modern example of the link between grammar and morality can be found in Eudora Welty's account of the following incident from her childhood (Welty 1985: 30–31):

> The school toilets were in the boys' and girls' respective basements. After Miss Duling [the school principal] had rung to dismiss school, a friend and I were making our plans for Saturday from adjoining cubicles. "Can you come spend the day with me?" I called out, and she called back, "I might could."
>
> "Who-said-MIGHT-COULD?" It sounded like "Fe Fi Fo Fum!"
>
> We both were petrified, for we knew whose deep measured words those were that came from just outside our doors. That was the voice of Mrs. McWillie, who taught the other fourth grade across the hall from ours. She was not even our teacher, but a very heavy, stern lady who dressed entirely in widow's weeds with a pleated black shirtwaist with a high net collar and velvet ribbon, and a black skirt to her ankles, with black circles under her eyes and a mournful, Presbyterian expression. We children took her to be a hundred years old. We held still.
>
> "You might as well tell me," continued Mrs. McWillie. "I'm going to plant myself right here and wait till you come out. Then I'll see who it was I heard saying 'MIGHT-COULD.'"
>
> If Elizabeth wouldn't go out, of course I wouldn't either. We knew her to be a teacher who would not flinch from standing there in the basement all afternoon, perhaps even all day Saturday. So we surrendered and came out. I priggishly hoped Elizabeth would clear it up which child it was – it wasn't me.
>
> "So it's you." She regarded us as a brace, made no distinction: whoever didn't say it was guilty by association. "If I ever catch you down here one more time saying 'MIGHT-COULD,' I'm going to carry it to Miss Duling. You'll be kept in every day for a week! I hope you're both sufficiently ashamed of yourselves?" Saying "might-could" was bad, but saying it in the basement made bad grammar a sin. I knew Presbyterians believed that you could go to Hell.

Johnson's equation of language change with "corruption and decay" is consistent not only with an elite ideology but also with the notion that the standard embodies moral and civic virtue and should thus be maintained. Refusal to accept a reigning ideology is a symptom of civic disaffection and thus moral turpitude. Just as Richelieu viewed heresy – refusal

to accept the ideology of a universal church – as treason, elites more generally view the refusal to accept the ideology of a standard language as subver-
sion. In short, another reason that most people accept the ideology of
a universal standard, at least under conditions of relative political stability,
is that elites promote its acceptance via the institutions under their control.
We associate the power and the glory of those functions for which the
standard is used with the standard itself.

A third reason why we tend to accept the ideology of a universal standard
flows from our attitudes towards writing. We tend to view the spoken
language as ephemeral, an epiphenomenon, a wavering and imperfect
reflection of what we believe to be the true, real, ideal forms embedded
in the written language.

Such an attitude is seen in its most extreme form in classic diglossic
communities, such as in the Arabic-speaking world. A diglossic community, as defined by Ferguson (1959), is characterized by the stable presence of two related languages, which exist side by side in the repertoire
of members of the community for communication within the group. One
language, usually the bearer of an esteemed literary tradition, is standardized and used for literary, scholarly, liturgical, and other formal purposes.
Learned at school, it is never used for ordinary conversation. The other
language, the mother tongue, is used for ordinary, everyday interactions.
Ferguson pointed out that members of such communities view the "high,"
elevated, written variety as the real language. The grammatically and lexically distinct "low" variety, the vernacular used in everyday discourse,
is scarcely viewed as a language at all. In non-diglossic communities, in
which the distance between spoken and written varieties is far smaller,
the veneration of the written variety is less extreme. Still, we tend to
value written varieties more highly than spoken varieties. The association
of the former with sacred texts and with secular power, and the difficulty
involved in learning them contribute to the esteem in which we hold them.
Since written texts are autonomous, their meaning unsupported by material
context, variability in linguistic form is a greater impediment to comprehension than is the case in spoken contexts, where breakdowns in communication can sometimes be observed and repaired, often with the assistance
of nonverbal cues. Variability in written forms also imposes a problem
upon printers and publishers, who seek as broad a market as possible
for their texts. The larger the population that shares a linguistic norm,
the larger the publisher's market.

The problem posed for publishers by competing linguistic forms was
recognized by the first English publisher, William Caxton, who, in the
preface to the first book he published, his translation of *Eneydos* (c. 1490),
wrote:

And that comyn englysshe that is spoken in one shyre varyeth from a nother. In so moche that in my dayes happened that certayn marchauntes were in a shippe in tamyse for to haue sayled ouer the see into zelande/and for lacke of wynde thei taryed atte forlond, and wente to lande for to refreshe them; And one of theym named sheffelde, a mercer, cam in-to an hows and axed for mete; and specyally he axyd after eggys; And the goode wyf answerde, that she coude speke no frenshe. And the marchaunt was angry, for he also coude speke no frenshe, but wolde haue hadde egges/and she vnderstode hym not/And thenne at laste a nother sayd that he wolde haue eyren/then the good wyf sayd that she vnderstod hym wel/Loo, what sholde a man in thyse dayes now wryte, egges or eyren/certaynly it is harde to playse euery man/by cause of dyuersite & chaunge of langage (Culley and Furnivall 1890: 2–3).

Caxton needed a literary standard. His choice, the variety based on the Southeast Midland area, centered on London, was reasonable from the point of view of maximizing his market. The predominance of London as a political and commercial center promoted the variety spoken there.

Standardization of written varieties has typically been more successful than standardization of spoken varieties. This is true for several reasons: the need for a single standard written variety is greater than that of a single standard spoken variety; it is probably easier to impart, via schooling, a standard literary variety, which pupils acquire more or less together from the beginning of their studies, than to impose uniformity on varieties which the pupils already speak when they enter school; and writers can usually exercise more control over their writing than speakers can exert over their speech. There is, for example, essentially one standard written English throughout the Anglophone world, with only a few minor differences in spelling and vocabulary, whereas there are numerous regional and national spoken English standards. Since we tend to glorify the written varieties and since written varieties are likely to be more standardized than the spoken varieties, we tend to accept the written standard as a universal model.

In short, we are likely to accept the ideology of a universal standard because it is in the interests of elites to promote the ideology and because we tend to view the standardized written language as an ideal for all language, confusing the part with the whole. The reason that we do not employ this ideal in all communicative contexts, even when we control the written standard, is that the ideal is only appropriate for some contexts and not others. Use of the ideal in circumstances in which other varieties are called for leads to miscommunication, ridicule, or identification of the language user as foreign, disturbed, disoriented, or otherwise unable to play by the rules of the game, namely the choice of the right variety for the right context.

These are the rules of the game – the language game, so to speak – as it is actually played. We may refer to these rules as descriptive rules, inasmuch as they account for actual behavior. Side by side with these rules is another set of rules. The latter are the "official" rules, rules which most of us believe *ought* to operate, but which in fact operate in a relatively restricted set of contexts. The official rules are prescriptive, telling us what we ought to do. We may accept them as universal in principle but we apply them, if we apply them at all, in only those domains which the descriptive rules tell us are appropriate for the standard.

If it is in the interest of established elites to promote acceptance of a standard, it is in the interest of new and counterelites to promote the acceptance of a new or counter standard. The promotion of counter standards accounts for the existence of many of what Kloss (1967) has termed *Ausbau* languages.

Kloss distinguishes *Ausbausprache*, "language by development," from *Abstandsprache*, "language by distance." An *Abstand* language is a distinct language by virtue of its intrinsic structural differences from all other languages. An *Ausbau* language is a distinct language because it has been deliberately made over and reshaped so that its standardized literary form is distinct from that of other literary standards. Kloss points out that many of the great literary languages of the world such as English, French, and German, are both *Abstand* and *Ausbau* languages. The structure of their spoken language is distinct from that of other languages, and their literary languages have been consciously molded or remolded.

But there are many languages, writes Kloss, which are distinct languages not because they are intrinsically different from other spoken forms but because their literary languages have been deliberately developed. He writes that Faroese and Scots Gaelic, for example, are *Ausbau* languages because their literary standards were developed into distinct forms. But if all speakers of Faroese adopted Icelandic as their literary standard, and all speakers of Scots Gaelic adopted Irish as their literary standard, no one would call Faroese and Scots Gaelic separate languages. Instead Faroese and Scots Gaelic would be viewed as dialects of Icelandic and Irish respectively.

Kloss contrasts *Ausbau* languages not only with *Abstand* languages but also with polycentric standard languages (Stewart 1968), i.e. two variants of the same standard, such as Serbo–Croatian, Moldavian and Rumanian, and Portuguese in Brazil and Portugal. In contrast, pairs such as Czech and Slovak, Bulgarian and Macedonian, and Danish and Swedish, are instances of literary standards based on different dialects which, at a pre-literate stage, would have been regarded by linguists as dialects of the same language.

We can illustrate the development of *Ausbau* languages by describing the emergence of Netherlandic and Afrikaans as standard languages and by comparing the development of those languages with the failure of a standard Flemish to emerge. Netherlandic is the national language of The Netherlands, and, with French, one of the two official languages of Belgium. Although popular usage gives two names to the language, Dutch for the Netherlandic spoken in The Netherlands and Flemish for the Netherlandic spoken in Belgium, it is in fact a single standard language. Although the standard literary language changes sharply at the border separating Germany from The Netherlands and Belgium, local spoken dialects display no such change. Rather, the local dialects spoken in The Netherlands and Belgium are part of a larger dialect area stretching from the North Sea to the Alps, with gradual changes in speech from one village to the next. In the twelfth and thirteenth centuries, the written realizations of these dialects also formed a transitional chain. But by the middle of the sixteenth century, the speech of Brabant, particularly that of its two principal cities, Brussels and Antwerp, the political and commercial centers of the community, was beginning to emerge as a standard for the whole Netherlandic speech community. Then, revolt against Habsburg hegemony caused a political split, with the northern provinces becoming first autonomous, under nominal Habsburg suzerainty, and then independent.

Habsburg hegemony continued over the southern provinces, with rule alternating between Spain and Austria until 1797. After a brief period of French dominance (1797–1814) and a short reunion with the northern provinces (1814–1830), the southern provinces finally achieved independence to become the Kingdom of Belgium. French had become the language of its upper classes. Its lower classes continued to speak Netherlandic, Romance, and Germanic dialects with no supradialectal standard for Belgian Netherlandic emerging.

In contrast, once the northern provinces had become the autonomous United Provinces, a standard literary language rapidly developed, centering on the dialect of Amsterdam. Several factors contributed to this development. The commercial ascendancy of Antwerp passed to Amsterdam, which by the early seventeenth century became an enormously successful shipping, fishing, and banking center for all of Europe. By the middle of the seventeenth century, the United Provinces had become a great commercial and maritime power. The century between the conclusion of the Twelve Years' Truce (1609), when Spain rejected a permanent peace but agreed to treat the United Provinces as sovereign, and the conclusion of the Peace of Utrecht (1713), which marked the subordination of Dutch to English commercial interests, is known in Dutch history as the "Golden Age," the apogee of Dutch commercial and political power. The nation's prosperity during this period, its newly-won independence, and its vigorous and confident sense of purpose generated an extraordinary cultural efflorescence. This was the ground in which standard literary Netherlandic developed and flourished. A legitimating symbol of Dutch political autonomy, it symbolized as well the predominance of the rich, urban merchants and financiers who formed the bulk of the Dutch elite.

In marked contrast to the early hegemony of Netherlandic in the United Provinces, Netherlandic in Belgium did not receive official parity with French until 1938. The numerous efforts to create a standard Flemish, distinct from the standard Netherlandic of the north, have not succeeded. While the latter is accepted as the standard for Belgium as well, fluency in the standard among speakers of local Netherlandic dialects is less widespread in Belgium than in The Netherlands.

While Netherlandic speakers are more numerous than Romance speakers in Belgium, knowledge of standard French has traditionally been more advantageous than knowledge of standard Netherlandic, with Netherlandic speakers more likely to learn standard French than Romance speakers to learn standard Netherlandic. Before the Second World War, the Belgian economy was controlled by French speakers. For Netherlandic speakers above a certain socioeconomic level, acquisition of French was a prerequisite for upward social mobility (Louckx 1978). After the war, the development of the Netherlandic-medium educational network, legislation in support of Netherlandic, and the great expansion of economic opportunities in Flanders have improved the status of standard Netherlandic. Still, the economic and political power of Netherlandic speakers in Belgium had not yet been strong enough to support the emergence of a standard Flemish. Contrast with the powerful Francophone minority remains more salient for Belgian speakers of Netherlandic than with Netherlandic speakers in the country to the north.

Whereas a standard Flemish has not yet emerged, a standard Afrikaans, closely related to standard Netherlandic, has been in use for at least three-quarters of a century, if not longer, in South Africa, whose first European settlers spoke one of the dialects of the United Provinces. From the beginning of Dutch settlement in the seventeenth century, this dialect seems to have been the primary source of what became modern Afrikaans (Moulton 1980). Prolonged geographical separation plus the influence of many non-native speakers, both black and white, on the language led to the gradual divergence of the Netherlandic spoken in South Africa with that spoken in the area from which the first settlers had come. For two hundred years, the developing Afrikaans existed as a spoken dialect, whose written standard was standard Netherlandic.

A movement to make Afrikaans a standard literary language began at about the middle of the nineteenth century. Not coincidentally, this movement originated at about the time of the creation of autonomous republics in the hinterland of the country, established by Afrikaans speakers who had trekked into the interior, in part as a continuation of their eighteenth-century expansion, but more fundamentally as a desire to escape from British rule, with which they were in increasing conflict. The British, in the early part of the nineteenth century, had seized the original area of Dutch settlement and later tried to establish control over the newer Afrikaans-speaking settlements in the interior. However, the unwillingness of the British to expend the funds necessary to control the vast interior led them, in the mid-nineteenth century, to grant independence to the trekker republics.

But recognition of trekker independence did not stop the conflict, as the British subsequently attempted to take control over trekker territory following the discovery there of diamond fields and gold reefs. Efforts to establish British suzerainty over these areas led to the growth of pan-Afrikaner nationalism, increasing clashes between the Afrikaners and the British, and finally the bitter South African War of 1899–1902, resulting in the loss of trekker independence. However, in 1906, the British granted autonomy to the Afrikaner republics, which, in 1910, joined the remainder of British-controlled southern Africa (the Cape Colony and Natal) to form the Union (later Republic) of South Africa, ultimately dominated politically by the Afrikaans-speaking descendants of the seventeenth-century European settlers.

The movement for the creation of a literary standard Afrikaans, then, accompanied the growth of Afrikaner nationalism. Afrikaans was a collective symbol of trekker identity and a legitimating symbol of the Afrikaner presence in Africa. Whereas standard Netherlandic could be seen as a product of Europe and derogated as the mark of an alien presence, standard Afrikaans could be seen as a product of Africa and claimed as the mark of an indigenous people, present in the land for centuries. Efforts to promote literary Afrikaans, beginning in the middle of the nineteenth century, resulted in its gradual adoption by the Afrikaner press, its use in Afrikaner schools (1914) and in the Dutch Reformed Church (1919), and its replacement of Netherlandic as an official language of the Union (1925). Thus one *Ausbau* language came to replace another. While the two literary languages are distinct, one who can read Netherlandic can read Afrikaans with relative ease and one who can speak Netherlandic can, with a little practice, understand spoken Afrikaans (Moulton 1980).

This brief overview of the establishment of standard Netherlandic and standard Afrikaans, in contrast to the failure of a distinct standard Flemish to take root, illustrates Kloss' point that *Abstand* language is a concept derived from the spoken language whereas *Ausbau* language is a concept derived from the written standard. The overview also shows that *Ausbau* languages are the creations of history.

But one can also claim that *all* standard languages, whether *Ausbau* or *Abstand*, are historical creations. Deutsch (1942) describes the historical process whereby speakers of local dialects in Europe accept a standard language. As speakers of local dialect are drawn into wider interactional networks dominated by a political and economic center, they accept the speech of this center, particularly that of the center's elite, as the basis for an overarching standard. As villages are subordinated to towns and towns to states, so dialects are subordinated to standard languages. The standard is usually accepted first for writing and later, with the growth of formal education and of supralocal communication, it becomes accepted for speech between people from different regions and for speech in those communicative contexts which stress supralocal values.

As nationalist or separatist movements arise among speakers of local dialects or among those who accept a standard which, under the pressure of events, seems increasingly alien, and as these people become more and more commercialized, industrialized, and literate, their political and cultural representatives promote a unique, national, overarching standard. A unique standard, a standard that is their own, at one and the same time enhances a sense of common identity among speakers of diverse local dialects, legitimates their claims of separateness and thus their claims for self-determination, and enhances the power and legitimates the authority of those who can control it.

Deutsch (1942), pointing to the phenomenal increase in the number of standard European languages which occurred from the beginning of the nineteenth century to the outbreak of the Second World War, correctly predicted the appearance of more standard languages all over the world. Industrialization, the spread of literacy, and the rise of nationalist movements combine to form national standard languages. Language planning is a typical adjunct of these nationalist movements, as their leaders seek to mold the new standard to mobilize and unify those they hope to lead, to legitimate their claims, and to buttress their authority (Fishman 1972, 1983).

If standardization serves nationalist movements, it also serves colonial and imperial regimes. Ansre (1971) points out that the agents of language standardization in sub-Saharan Africa were mainly western Europeans, who made deliberate efforts to standardize the local languages they used in administration, education, and evangelization. In some cases, they chose one dialect as the basis for the new standard, as in the selection of the Anglo dialect for standard Ewe. In other cases, they promoted a standard based on a composite of the main dialects, as in the creation of standard Shona. In either case, standardization facilitated the governmental administration and the educational and missionary efforts of the colonial regimes.

Although colonial language planners may have viewed their efforts as a service to Africans, they had a vested interest in the standardization they promoted.

The Soviet promotion of standard Turkic languages, for example, has been directed toward keeping these languages as far apart from one another as possible in spelling, grammar, and vocabulary (Henze 1977). This has been done to discourage the emergence of a pan-Turkic lingua franca which could serve as a vehicle for pan-Turkic national consciousness. Similarly, Soviet planners promoted a standard language based on a Persian dialect of the Central Asian Tajiks to separate the Tajiks from Persian speakers outside the U.S.S.R. (Henze 1977). In like manner, *Ausbau* differences between Serbian and Croatian and between Ukrainian and Polish were promoted by church or state authorities who sought to inhibit religious or political unification (Fishman 1983). In sum, the deliberate creation of new standard languages need not be the work of revolutionaries or of leaders of nationalist movements. The retardation of integration is the obverse of the coin which promotes social and political distinctiveness.

The processes leading to linguistic standardization, then, are processes which promote the integration of local networks with a broader interactional network, whose center exerts political, economic, and cultural influence over the periphery. When counterelites seek to detach a periphery from a center and when existing elites try to keep the periphery from falling away, they promote collective symbols of affiliation and attachment as well as incentives for acceptance of the symbols. To the extent that standard languages serve as such a symbol, we can expect elites and counterelites to try to establish them if they do not already exist.

Codification

This discussion thus far has concerned the processes which lead to standardization. What are the processes of standardization itself? Rubin (1977b) separates the standardization process into six interrelated parts, the first three of which are: (1) isolation of a norm, (2) evaluation of the norm by some significant group of people as "correct" or "preferred," and (3) prescription of the norm for specified contexts or functions. The first three components, according to Rubin, always occur together. If the prescription is unnoticed, standardization fails. For standardization to take effect, the prescribed norm must be (4) accepted, (5) used, and (6) remain in effect until another norm replaces it. A common, if not absolutely essential, feature of this process is codification, the explicit statement of a norm.

Codification typically refers to written rules. Indeed, the origin of the term *code* (Latin *codex*) implies a written compilation. Latin *codex* means *the trunk of a tree* as well as *a block of wood split into tablets*, and hence (since the ancient Romans wrote upon wax-coated wooden tablets), *a book*. True, explicit statements of rules can be transmitted orally. Christian catechisms, for example, originally intended for those who cannot read, grew out of an oral tradition of religious instruction. We learn some rules orally to this day. Children transmit the rules of their games to each other orally from one generation to the next. Most of the aphorisms which we use, such as "red sky at morning, sailors take warning," and "rain before seven, shine by eleven," are transmitted orally whether or not they also exist in print. Most of us learn the multiplication table orally. Even rules about writing are sometimes transmitted orally, as in "*i* before *e* except after *c* . . . ." Nonetheless, the codification of standard written languages is typically written. In fact, the existence of written dictionaries, grammars, spellers, and style manuals is usually taken as an essential feature of the standardization of written languages.

While unwritten languages, without written codification, can be standard too, in the sense that speakers accept one variety among several as the best or preferred form of the language, it is reasonable to assume that written codification contributes to the standardization of a language. Written codification can influence speakers separated by time and space and is thus likely to promote the stability of the norm which it encodes. But not all written codifications are accepted even as ideals. Language academies, for example, routinely publish lists of new terms, many of which may be ignored by the public for which they are intended. Benjamin Franklin's proposals for the reform of English spelling, which he published in 1779, were ignored, although he promoted the new spelling among the leaders of the movement for American independence (Weinstein 1982).

To take another example, Leonard's (1929) famous study of the eighteenth-century English grammarians concludes that of the more than 300 grammatical and logical issues raised (among them the use of *they* and its inflected forms as a sex-indefinite generic, discussed in Chapter 1), fewer than a dozen condemned types of construction would be regarded as nonstandard usage today (237). Leonard points out that a better result could have been attained by chance. On the other hand, Leonard concludes that these grammarians did have an effect: (1) they caused a "greater popular appreciation and respect for the mystery or craft of using English" (232), (2) they may have helped to focus writers' attention upon parallelism in sentence structure, thus improving clarity of written expression, and (3) they promoted the diffusion, into the provinces, of a standard already accepted among metropolitan literary persons. It is not true, argued Leonard, that the grammarians standardized metropolitan literary usage. Indeed, he argued that the style of Addison and his contemporaries, in the early eighteenth century, is as close to modern usage as that of a century later.

Alongside that of the grammarians, the other great work of linguistic codification for which eighteenth-century England is known is Samuel Johnson's noble *Dictionary of the English Language*, the first edition of which appeared in 1755 (for analyses of Johnson's dictionary, see particularly Sledd and Kolb 1955, Fussell 1971, Bate 1975). Some of his contemporaries suggested that the *Dictionary* helped standardize the language, particularly English spelling. Lord Chesterfield, for example, in a fulsome puff which he published in the *World*, shortly before the *Dictionary*'s appearance, wrote that "We have at present two very different orthographies, the PEDANTIC and the POLITE: the one founded upon certain dry and crabbed rules of etymology and grammar, the other singly upon the justness and delicacy of the ear. I am thoroughly persuaded that Mr. Johnson will endeavour to establish the former . . . . Spelling, as well as music, is better performed by book than merely by the ear" (quoted by Bloomfield and Newmark 1963: 293).

Boswell spoke of Johnson as "the man who had conferred stability on the language of his country" (quoted by Baugh and Cable 1978: 272). Thomas Sheridan, who by no means idolized Johnson, wrote "If our language should ever be fixed, he must be considered by all posterity as the founder, and his dictionary as the cornerstone" (quoted by McKnight 1929: 376). Johnson himself wrote, in the Preface to the *Dictionary*, that "When I took the first survey of my undertaking, I found our speech copious without order, and energetic without rule: wherever I turned my view, there was perplexity to be disentangled and confusion to be regulated . . . ." and later, in the Preface, he described English orthography as "to this time unsettled and fortuitous" (McAdam and Milne 1963: 4). Nonetheless, Johnson's statement that spelling was unsettled is belied by his statement in the Preface that he generally followed convention, which suggests that a standard spelling had already emerged: "I have attempted few alterations [in spelling] . . . . It has been asserted, that for the law to be *known*, is of more importance than to be *right*" (McAdam and Milne 1963: 7). Chesterfield's reference to frequent misspellings is belied by his own letter, which deviates not a jot from modern orthography. Indeed Wyld (1920: 162) claims that English orthography was uniform by the end of the seventeenth century. Certainly, a cursory comparison of Johnson's orthography with that of earlier eighteenth-century English dictionaries reveals no striking dissimilarity. Sledd and Kolb (1955: 33) believe that Johnson codified "a spelling already pretty well established by the printers." Although they also state that the dictionary "enjoyed high orthographic authority" (33). Thus Leonard's (1929) judgment that Johnson's dictionary, like the works of the eighteenth-century grammarians, helped to diffuse an established metropolitan standard into the provinces seems sound. Similarly,

Sledd and Kolb's judgment that "the English language would be much the same today had Johnson never lived" (134) rings true.

Noah Webster's codifications, on the other hand, his spelling books and dictionaries, helped to spread some of the reforms he advocated for American English (Weinstein 1982). In a textbook example of an *Ausbau* effort, Webster promoted a standard American English which would help to unify Americans and to distinguish them from the English: "Let us then seize the present moment [1789] and establish a *national language*, as well as a national government ... as an independent people, our reputation abroad demands that, in all things we should be federal; be national; for if we do not respect *ourselves* we may be assured that other nations will not respect us" (Webster's emphasis, quoted by Weinstein 1982: 94–95). In the second edition of Webster's *The American Spelling Book* (1790), Weinstein tells us, Webster informed his readers that the strength of tradition had prevented him from including all the reforms he advocated, e.g. *hed, proov, hiz,* and *det* for *head, prove, his,* and *debt.* We also learn that the different editions of Webster's spellers show inconsistent usage: in the 1804 Philadelphia edition, for example, we find *behaviour, savor, favor,* whereas in the Wilmington edition of the same year we find *labor, humour,* and *saviour.* Weinstein proposes a plausible explanation: the printers accepted some innovations but rejected others.

By 1804 Webster had probably sold two million copies of his spelling book, which provided an income that permitted him to work on his dictionary. Between a preliminary dictionary which he published in 1806 and the 1828 edition, which became a basis for American dictionaries down to the present, Webster reduced the number of his innovations. In his 1828 preface he admitted that for many words he was forced to accept the conventional spelling. Weinstein attributes Webster's growing conservatism to several factors: his fear of violence and radical political changes, such as those unleashed by the French Revolution, and a concomitant belief that threats to authority might unleash violence among the masses; his conversion to fundamental Protestantism (1808), which led him to believe that human intervention in a world made by God might be a sin, and his realization that Britain and the British West Indies represented an important market for American agricultural goods (books, too, suggests Weinstein); his circle of friends, as well as the wider network of people with whom he was in contact and whose opinions he respected, disapproved of his most radical changes; New England printers probably resisted radical change; and finally radical change would probably have discouraged sales of the dictionary, an important source of his livelihood. In the end, he did not implement most of his radical proposals, such as substituting *f* for *ph* in *philosophy*, substituting *k* for *ch* in *chorus*, dropping the final *e* in words like *examine*, and the combination of *th* in a single letter. The changes in American spelling which the public finally accepted were, then, quite modest. Weinstein lists them (91):

1 dropping *u* from words like *colour*;
2 using *-ize* endings instead of *-ise* as in *organize*;
3 using *-ice* endings instead of *-ise* as in *practice*;
4. *ct* instead of *x* in *connection*;
5 *er* instead of *re* in *theater* and *center*;
6 dropping double *ll* in words like *traveled* and *labeled*.

While these changes are few, attachment to them may be great, as can be seen by the opposition of some American scientists to changing the spelling of *meter* to *metre* (Haugen 1983). In 1971 the U.S. National Bureau of Standards had proposed the change to secure uniformity in the English spelling of the names of the units for the International System (in return, the British would omit the *-me* in *kilogramme*). An example of the feelings aroused by this proposal is an editorial appearing in 1971 in *Applied Optics*, a journal of the Optical Society of America. It reported that at a meeting of the Publication Board of the American Institute for Physics, "the editors of all the physics journals voted overwhelmingly not to yield the phonetic spelling of meter, liter, diopter in any such compromise with evil" (quoted by Haugen 1983: 278).

Weinstein's description of Webster's work was intended to illustrate the role, in language planning and language change, of "language strategists," nongovernmental innovators who alter language in order to influence society. But Weinstein's description, it seems to me, can also be used to illustrate the constraints which are imposed on language strategists. While Webster was responsible for some changes which have persisted, his codification, like Johnson's, reflected an existing standard far more than it created one.

What then is the role of codification in standardization? Does codification precede or follow standardization? Byron (1976), in her study of the standardization of Albanian, argues that "usage preceded evaluation in Albanian; i.e. the alternates which were subsequently to become standard had already appeared in the pre-1944 literary tradition or in some, or most, of the spoken varieties, but there they competed with other usage [in 1944 Albanian Communists took control of the country and began a campaign to strengthen national autonomy and to modernize the country's economy]. The subsequent activities of language planners formalized the preferred alternates, simultaneously consigning most of their rivals to oblivion" (130). Citing Ferguson (quoted by Rubin and Jernudd 1971b: xx) and Krapp's (1913) contention that usage precedes normalization, she refers to other examples in which language authorities sanction usage which has already widely appeared: Arabic (Altoma 1970), Kiswahili (Ansre 1971), and Hebrew (Fellman 1973). "This phenomenon is not unexpected. Most standardizing languages are simultaneously languages which are in use, and are to that extent already serving the needs of speakers. It is not surprising that many features of pre-standard usage would subsequently find favor with language planners" (130).

Nonetheless, codifications which are nonauthoritative when initially published *can* become, if not themselves authoritative, then at least the basis for a new standard. For example, Vuk Stefanovic Karadzic's grammar of 1814 and his dictionary of 1818 became the foundation of Serbo-Croatian, the major language of Yugoslavia. Similarly, Ivar Aasen's grammar of 1864 and his lexicon of 1873 became the basis of Nynorsk, one of the two official languages of Norway (Haugen 1965). It is probably fair to say that we are not yet able to specify the conditions under which a codification will (1) reflect an already existing standard, (2) promote the diffusion of such a standard, (3) serve as the basis of a new standard, or (4) gain acceptance at all. It is a plausible hypothesis, however, that when the codification represents an innovation, it must serve the economic or political interests of elites or counterelites if the codification is to become authoritative.

Modernization

Modernization, the third and last of Ferguson's criteria of language development, refers to the process whereby a language becomes an appropriate medium of communication for modern topics and forms of discourse. In some respects, the term language modernization is an unfortunate one. As Ferguson points out, there is nothing new or particularly modern about the process. When a language is extended for new functions and topics, its resources expand in order to meet the new demands. Further, the process is not limited to the languages of developing, modernizing societies but occurs in the languages of developed, modern societies as well. Still, the term has merit because it implies an apt analogy with societal modernization.

Among the features which are shared by modern societies are a rapid expansion of knowledge, the application of new knowledge to the production of goods and services, an enhanced specialization of labor, and differentiation of institutions (i.e. functions formerly filled by a few institutions become divided among many), and an increased orientation toward impersonal and utilitarian values, particularly the maximization of efficiency (Germani 1980).

The orientation of modern societies towards knowledge, technology, production, efficiency, and the specialization of labor and institutions

stimulates linguistic elaboration. Indeed, language modernization is sometimes referred to as *elaboration*. New knowledge and technology demand
new terms. The application of new knowledge and technology via specialists and special institutions demands new genres or forms of discourse.
For example, personal-computer technology has spawned not only new
terms (e.g. *disk drive*, *floppy disk*, *hard disk*) but also new genres such
as the reference manual for computer programs and systems ("*Your screen
will look like this: Abort edit (Y/N)?*").

Concern with maximizing the efficiency of production is reflected more by
the standardization of terms and forms of discourse than by modernization.
For example, some American manufacturers may prefer *metre* to *meter* in
order to avoid printing two sets of labels (Haugen 1983). Still, standardization itself is seen as "modern," an attitude which sometimes promotes
standardization of languages in developing countries (Rubin 1977b).

While the development of modern modes of discourse – e.g. news broadcasting, sports broadcasting, television talk shows, computer-driven
instruction – is as much a part of language modernization as the development of new terms, it is the latter which has received the most deliberate
attention by language planners. In fact, deliberate terminological development sometimes represents a staggering amount of work. More than
200,000 Hindi terms, for example, have been approved by the Council
of Scientific and Technological Terminology (Misra 1982); more than
320,000 terms have been approved for Bahasa Indonesia (Alisjahbana 1976
cited by Lowenberg 1983). As an indication of the investment of time
and effort involved, one can refer to Fellman and Fishman's (1977) report
that the Hebrew Language Academy Committee on the Terminology of
Librarianship met about 50 times over a three-year period when translating
the UNESCO terminology for librarianship into Hebrew.

Planners responsible for the elaboration of terminology face several
choices. The first choice is whether to adopt a term already in use or
to coin a new term. Speakers and writers will talk and write about the
stock market, fashion, and football whether or not an approved terminology
exists for those domains. If a consensus has already emerged, i.e. if the
majority of speakers or writers already use a given term to express a given
notion, the path of least resistance is to bestow the planning agency's
approval upon majority usage. This alternative, often chosen, avoids the
necessity of trying to persuade the public to abandon one term in favor
of another. It is probably easier to persuade people to adopt a new term
when it has no well-established competition than to persuade them to
abandon one term in favor of another, although I know of no empirical
test of this proposition. But sometimes it is clear that a consensus has
emerged, either because indeed there is no consensus or because the planners have been unable to determine what it is. Planners must then decide

whether to accept one of the alternatives in use, and if so, which alternative, or to create a new term.

The only circumstance in which there is no possibility of approving prior usage, whether that of the majority or of the minority, is when there is no usage at all, i.e. speakers or writers have not yet needed a term for a particular item. Here, the question is whether to provide a term which will be rarely needed. Fellman and Fishman (1977), who described the working of the Hebrew Language Academy terminological committees for librarianship and inorganic chemistry report that "it was a matter of pride and conviction" (82) that the Hebrew lists be fully intertranslatable with the terminology of international standard languages.

Fellman and Fishman report that, whenever possible, the Librarianship Committee tried to approve established usage among librarians. In a few cases, however, it decided against existing practice, either because these terms were believed to be poor translations of corresponding UNESCO terms or because they were no longer current among younger specialists. Within both the librarianship and the inorganic chemistry committee, the investigators reported that older members were often reluctant to abandon the terms to which they had become accustomed. Presumably, in some of the cases in which accustomed usage was rejected, the planners approved a minority usage. If not, they would have had to coin a term *de novo*.

When language planners choose to coin a new term rather than approve an existing one, they face two alternatives: (1) build the term from indigenous sources, either by (a) giving a new meaning to an existing word, (b) creating a term based on an indigenous root, or (c) translating a foreign term (creating a loan translation) or (2) borrow a word from a foreign language. If the latter is done, a further decision must be made as to how far to indigenize the loan, by modifying its pronunciation, its spelling, or its affixes to suit the structure of the borrowing language.

Jernudd (1977a) points out that the creators of terms face a conflict of goals. On the one hand, they want terms to be readily understood within the target speech community. On the other hand, they want to facilitate communication beyond the borders of their country. The former goal is best pursued by the use of indigenous sources, the latter goal by international borrowing. There is good reason, writes Jernudd, for planners to pursue both ends, even though these ends are basically incompatible. Indigenous terms of course militate against communication between groups whereas international terms are less readily understood within the group which borrows them.

If planners resort to borrowing, they must determine the source language. Lewis (1972, 1983) describes the pervasive influence of Russian terminology on the national languages of the Soviet Union. Soviet language

planners have met the need for new specialized and learned terms in these
languages, with terms of Russian origin or with international terms derived
through Russian. In most of the languages of the USSR, between 70 and
80 percent of the new terms are borrowed from Russian. This uniformity
of technical vocabularies has undoubtedly facilitated the preparation of
educational materials in the many languages of the USSR, just as the
enrichment of these languages' vocabulary has promoted education via
those languages. Nonetheless, elaboration of the national languages via
uniformation with each other and with Russian is likely to strengthen
Russian in the long run by promoting literacy in Russian as a second
language.

Whereas Soviet language planners have imposed Russian terminology
on non-Russian languages, planners for Bahasa Indonesia have not turned
to a single source for borrowing terms. Lowenberg (1983) provides a lively
description of the process. Since independence in 1949, most of the new
terms needed by Bahasa Indonesia's expansion into the domains of industry, commerce, government administration, science and technology, the
mass media, and higher education have been taken from existing words
and morphemes in Bahasa Indonesia and other Indonesian languages or
through loan translations of foreign words. However, there has also been
an influx of foreign terms, stimulating a controversy among Indonesian
language planners.

The controversy concerns the source of loans: European languages, particularly English, or the languages from which Indonesian languages have
traditionally borrowed, particularly Sanskrit. This was the language of
Indonesia's cultural golden age of Hindu influence, a period at which
Indonesian political power in Southeast Asia was at its height, the seventh
through the fourteenth centuries. Lowenberg shows us that both strategies
are currently being applied. Language planners generally turn to Sanskrit
for terminology in the domains of literature, culture, and scholarship.
In contrast, they almost always turn to European languages for terminology
in the domains of modern science and technology.

A similar division, Lowenberg tells us, appears to account for unplanned
or spontaneous borrowings. Indonesia's political and military leaders frequently turn to Sanskrit sources to arouse nationalistic sentiments in support of their policies. Whereas political and military leaders exploit the
traditional authority of Sanskrit, other sectors of society turn to European
languages, particularly English, as symbols of modernity and internationalism. Spontaneous borrowing from European languages tends to be associated with modern, cosmopolitan domains such as fashion, films, science
and technology, national and international politics, and trade.

An interesting borrowing is the English pronoun *you*, increasingly used
by some members of the urban, educated class in personal conversations

"in order to neutralize background distinctions and to express identity with the modern, educated class of Indonesia." *You* contrasts with the pronoun *anda*, which the Indonesian government has been promoting for addressing another person without regard to status distinctions and which has been adopted by the mass media. In Bahasa Indonesia, *you* is restricted to informal conversations between people of the same age, education, and earned status.

In short, Lowenberg tells us, both in planned and unplanned lexical modernization, the source of borrowing is typically determined by the domain and the function of the borrowed term. The Indonesian solution represents a nice compromise between two poles of corpus planning, modernity and authenticity, which, according to Fishman (1983), must both be present for successful modernization.

In spite of the enormous amount of work expanded on lexical elaboration in hundreds of languages around the world, there has been very little empirical research to guide planners with respect to the characteristics of terms which are most likely to be accepted, or with respect to the characteristics of speakers or writers who are most likely to adopt them. A rare example of such research is Fainberg's (1983) study of the acceptance of twenty-five terms approved by the Hebrew Language Academy, referred to in Chapter 4. Rubin's (1971) plea for interim evaluations to provide feedback for language planners has rarely been acted upon. But perhaps we should marvel more at the production of hundreds of thousands of terms than at the fact that the extent of their acceptance is rarely checked.

A Note on Language Planning Terminology

It is ironic that language planning as a field of inquiry has created at least one terminological muddle: what is the difference between *elaboration* and *cultivation* and is either different from *modernization*? In its broadest sense, *modernization* refers to the processes which permit a language to fulfil new communicative functions, either functions new to the community or functions formerly fulfilled in that community by another language. To meet the new demands which are placed upon it, the vocabulary of a modernizing language expands and its users develop new styles, genres, and registers. *Elaboration* and *cultivation* are the two most frequent terms which are applied to these processes.

For Neustupný (1970), *cultivation* refers to the treatment of problems related to matters of correctness, efficiency, register specialization, and style (see Jernudd 1977b). He suggests that a cultivation approach to language planning is typically found in connection with more developed languages. Haugen (1983) finds the term elitist and suggests *elaboration* as a neutral alternative. But Haugen uses *elaboration* to mean the modernization of vocabulary and style. Fishman (1977) views Neustupný's *cultivation* as reiterated elaboration, i.e. planning for more and more specialized communicative functions. The terminological confusion which we find at the core of language-planning terminology reminds us that standardization and modernization are ongoing processes among even the most "developed" of languages.

Renovation

Although graphization, standardization, and modernization are the objects of most corpus planning, there is at least one other object of attention. At the risk of needless elaboration, I propose the term *renovation* for the object of corpus planning. The rapid, successive switches from Arabic to Latin to Cyrillic script imposed by Soviet language planners on the Turkic languages of Soviet Central Asia after the Revolution (Henze 1977), the expungement of Persian and Arabic loanwords from Turkish, as part of the Turkish language reform which began in the 1920s (Heyd 1954, Gallagher 1971), successive efforts at reforming Dutch spelling (Geerts, van den Broeck, and Verdoodt 1977), the plain language movement, and the feminist campaign all represent renovation – an effort to change an already developed code, whether in the name of efficiency, aesthetics, or national or political ideology. Replacement or reform of an existing writing system is not graphization but regraphization. Purification of an already standard language is not standardization but restandardization. The renovated language fulfills no new communicative functions. But if the new forms carry out old communicative functions, they also contribute to the nonlinguistic goals which motivated the linguistic renovation, whether the legitimation of new elites, the discrediting of old ones, the mobilization of political support, or the raising of consciousness. Whereas modernization permits language codes to serve new communicative functions, renovation permits language codes to serve old functions in new ways.

The Good Corpus

Fishman (1983) argues that successful corpus planning "is a delicate balancing act" (117) between the old and the new, traditionalism and rationality. "Everyone wants a chemistry terminology of his own nowadays, at least for lower- and middle-level pursuits, but they generally want it to be *both* 'adequate for chemistry' *and* 'acceptable as their own'" (110). This is no easy task. Nor is it one which can be solved by means of technical considerations alone. Rather, successful corpus planning requires sensitivity to what the target population will "like, learn, and use" (115). Efforts can be made, of course, to lead target populations to like certain models of goodness. Indeed, Fishman writes that the public must be told "why what is being offered to it is desirable, admirable, and exemplary" (112).

Inasmuch as neither untempered traditionalism nor uncompromising rationality are workable solutions to corpus-planning problems, various arguments are forwarded to justify the adoption of loanwords. Fishman mentions several of them. One is to appeal to popular usage by speech networks which are favorably regarded. Another solution is to claim that "theirs is ours." The most extreme example of this approach is the theory which rationalized the importation of English and French loanwords by Turkish language planners who were at the same time expelling Arabic and Persian loanwords. Turkish was declared to be the ultimate source of all European languages. Therefore the use of words from European languages represented not borrowing but repatriation. This has been dubbed the great sun theory. A third approach is to cite the use of a loanword in a positively regarded third language. The term thus becomes an internationalism which belongs to everyone.

Fishman warns us that corpus planners run the risk of defending models of good language which gradually lose public favor as the balance changes between old and new, theirs and ours, modern and traditional. When this happens, younger persons tend to view the planner's products with indifference at best and with ridicule at worst.

Throughout this chapter I have stressed the use of corpus planning by elites and counterelites as a tool for the acquisition and maintenance of power. True, corpus planning may be initiated for purposes other than those of the pursuit and maintenance of power. But, like status planning, the initiative seems most likely to succeed if it can be turned to the advantage of elites or counterelites. If selfless individuals have devoted their lives to a vision of the good corpus, with little hope of material rewards, the success of their product has for the most part depended on its usefulness in forwarding the goals or ambitions of others.

But why should corpus planning advance such goals and ambitions? Why should appeals to values such as authenticity and tradition promote goals such as the centralization of authority, the mobilization of mass support, or the heightening of group consciousness? If elites lead and manipulate the mass, the mass also leads elites, who ignore mass sentiment at their peril. Corpus planning is both a response to, and an exercise in, the creation of mass sentiment. Appeals to values such as tradition and authenticity link the mass to a glorious past, to a supportive network of ethnicity, nationality, religion, or class, and to the elites who espouse these sentiments, and who represent these solidary networks. These links are likely to strengthen the individual's sense of dignity, self-worth, social connectedness, and ultimate meaning as a member of a group linked both to the past and to the future. While corpus planning may be self-serving, it is more than that. If it serves elites, it serves the mass as well.

7

Acquisition planning

Immigrants to Israel benefit from numerous organized efforts to help them learn Hebrew. "Absorption centers," where immigrants live while sorting out their employment and housing arrangements, offer subsidized, on-site, intensive, six-month Hebrew classes. Other classes, intensive and non-intensive, are offered by municipalities for nominal fees. Universities offer special language courses for foreign students and for immigrant faculty and their spouses. When immigrant children go to school, they are offered classes in Hebrew as a second language, if there are enough children to form a class. Otherwise, children may be pulled out of their classes for a few hours of individual instruction per week. A weekly newspaper is published in simplified Hebrew, the news is broadcast daily in simplified (and slower) Hebrew, and Hebrew literature is translated into simplified Hebrew. A television series in simplified Hebrew, produced in the 1970s, is rebroadcast from time to time. All of these programs and devices exemplify acquisition planning, which refers to organized efforts to promote the learning of a language.

Other examples of acquisition planning abound:

To improve the Korean-language skills of Korean–Americans, the University of California at Los Angeles began, in 1987, a program whereby its Korean–American students could travel to Seoul National University for ten weeks of Korean-language study.

To facilitate the acquisition of Russian by non-Russian nationalities in the Soviet Union, Soviet language planners have imposed the Cyrillic script on most of the Soviet minority languages and use Russian models to modernize the vocabularies of these languages.

To promote the study of English, the British Council maintains English-language libraries abroad and sends experts to organize workshops and to advise local personnel about methods of teaching. The Alliance française and the Goethe Institute engage in comparable activities for the promotion of French and German respectively.

To halt the emigration of population from the Gaeltacht, the last remnant of native speakers of Irish for whom Irish is the chief language of everyday life, the Irish government set up state agencies for the economic development of the area. To create urban conditions where new speakers of Irish might transmit their Irish to their children, the government has proposed two new city projects in Dublin which would bring Irish speakers into regular contact with each other and thus promote social support for the language outside the home (Dorian 1987).

When China recovered Taiwan in 1945, Japanese, which had been the sole language of instruction and the dominant language for fifty years, was banned in all mass media. The National-Language policy, the promotion of Mandarin as the national language, begun on the Mainland in the 1920s and 1930s, was introduced to Taiwan. As Berg (1985) points out, the schools were a natural medium for this promotion, inasmuch as the Japanese had left a national network of schools. Local Chinese dialects (Minnan and Hakka) were temporarily permitted for oral communication in the schools. Traditional Chinese reading material was reintroduced and the National-Language reading pronunciation was soon required, although many teachers were unable to implement this rule. Mandarin speakers were imported from the Mainland to help teach via the National Language and to train other teachers to use Mandarin. Gradually the schools have produced more people literate in Mandarin and able to speak at least some Mandarin (Berg 1985). Among the devices employed to promote knowledge of Mandarin have been the early use of radio and newspapers to explain the meaning and purpose of the National-Language policy, a Demonstration Broadcasting Program (1946–1959) which promoted the National-Language pronunciation, and the publication of newspapers in Mandarin printed in transcribed characters (Kwock-Ping Tse 1986).

The *kohunga reo*, or "language nests," set up in the early 1980s to revitalize Maori, provide a final example. In response to a progressive decline in the number of Maori speakers in New Zealand, Maori leaders suggested the establishment of Maori-medium pre-schools, in which older Maoris would serve as caretakers. These caretakers, in fact, would be the generation of the children's grandparents, inasmuch as few of the children's parents could still speak Maori. The new pre-schools received some support from the Department of Maori Affairs, but those local communities who wanted to organize and implement the program had to do most of the work themselves. The number of centers has advanced exponentially: four in 1982, 280 in 1984, and nearly 500 in 1987. "The effect of the kohunga reo cannot be exaggerated; when [in 1981] a bare handful of children came to primary school with any knowledge of the Maori language, now each year between two and three thousand children enter begin-ners' classes having been exposed to daily use of the Maori language and many of them are fluent bilinguals'' (Spolsky 1987). The growing number of children who can speak Maori has encouraged parents, pleased that the children are learning their ancestors' language, to pressure primary schools to establish bilingual programs in English and Maori. When school principals are willing, space is available, and school boards are supportive or at least compliant, such programs have begun, in spite of difficulty in finding staff willing and able to teach via Maori and in spite of lack of curriculum materials, which staff have had to create themselves (Spolsky 1987).

Such examples of acquisition planning can be distinguished from one another on at least two bases: (1) the overt language planning goal and (2) the method employed to attain the goal. With respect to overt goals, we can distinguish at least three: (a) acquisition of the language as a second or foreign language, as in the acquisition of Amharic by non-Amharas in Ethiopia, French by Anglophones in Montreal, spoken Mandarin by Taiwanese; (b) reacquisition of the language by populations for whom it was once either a vernacular – as in the renativization of Hebrew, the attempts to renativize Irish, and the revitalization of Maori – or a language of specialized function, as in the return of written Chinese to Taiwan; and (c) language maintenance, as in the efforts to prevent the further erosion of Irish in the Gaeltacht. It might be said that this last objective represents not language acquisition at all. I include it, however, because maintenance of a language implies its acquisition by the next generation. When a language declines, smaller and smaller percentages of ensuing generations acquire the language. Prevention of decline requires maintenance of acquisition.

With respect to the means employed to attain acquisition goals, we may distinguish three types: those designed primarily to create or to improve the *opportunity* to learn, those designed primarily to create or to improve the *incentive* to learn, and those designed to create or improve both opportunity and incentive simultaneously.

Methods which focus upon the opportunity to learn can in turn be divided into direct and indirect methods. The former include classroom instruction, the provision of materials for self-instruction in the target language, and the production of literature, newspapers, and radio and television programs in simplified versions of the target language. Indirect methods include efforts to shape the learners' mother tongue so that it will be more similar to the target language, which will then presumably be easier to learn. Soviet planning of non-Russian minority languages provides an example.

Examples of methods which focus upon the incentive to learn are the inclusion of English as a compulsory subject in the Israeli secondary-school matriculation examination, a requirement which encourages those pupils who want a matriculation certificate to take their English courses seriously, the setting of language prerequisites for employment, as with Irish for certain civil service jobs in Eire, and Quebec's promotion of French as the language of work, with sanctions for firms which do not comply with Francophonization guidelines.

Methods which enhance simultaneously opportunity and incentive to learn use the target language as the medium of interaction for contexts in which the learner either must enter or wants to enter. Examples are immersion or bilingual educational programs, such as French-medium instruction for Anglophone children in Montreal, the *kohunga reo* in New Zealand, the fourth-century vocational education conducted by missionaries via Giiz, and twentieth-century missionaries' use of Amharic as a medium of instruction in Ethiopia.

Thus a preliminary framework into which acquisition planning can be classified yields nine cells formed by the intersection of two variables: overt goal (acquisition, reacquisition, maintenance) and the chief focus of the method employed to attain the goal (opportunity to learn, incentive to learn, both opportunity and incentive to learn).

As these examples attest, acquisition planning includes far more than the planning of language instruction. Nonetheless, the planning of language instruction accounts for the lion's share of acquisition planning. Further, acquisition planning is a feature of the instructional enterprise at every level of organization, from the Director General of the Ministry of Education to the classroom teacher. Prator, one of the few scholars who regard language teaching as an object of language planning, states this point forcibly: "Language policy is the body of decisions made by interested authorities concerning the desirable form and use of languages by a speech group. It also involves consequent decisions made by educators, media directors, etc., regarding the possible implementation of prior basic decisions. According to this definition, the decision to emphasize in a language class specific skills or linguistic forms – even the choice of a textbook – could become a part of language policy. The latter should thus be one of the primary concerns of language teachers. The entire process of formulating and implementing language policy is best regarded as a spiral process, beginning at the highest level of authority and, ideally, descending in widening circles through the ranks of practitioners who can support or resist putting the policy into effect" (personal communication). Markee (1988), who also considers language teaching as a form of language planning, presents a detailed consideration of the status planning and corpus planning decisions involved in teaching English for specialized purposes.

The role of teachers in carrying out language-planning decisions may be more visible than the role of, say, Israeli disk jockeys, who are constrained to broadcast a minimum number of Hebrew-language songs each day or, say, Hebrew-language supervisors, who edit the grammar of radio scripts according to normative principles. Nonetheless, the role of intermediate and lower-level personnel can no more be ignored in status and corpus planning than in acquisition planning. But acquisition planning, at least that involving direct instruction, heightens our awareness of the role of such personnel.

When planners try to promote second- or foreign-language acquisition they often turn to the school system. Schools are more likely to succeed in this goal if they use the target language as a medium of instruction than if they merely teach the language as a target of instruction. Not only exposure to the language but also incentive to learn it is greater when it serves as medium than when it serves merely as subject of instruction. But no matter how accomplished the schools are in imparting language acquisition, they are unlikely to lead to the language's *use* outside the classroom unless there are practical reasons for such use. This is one of the lessons of the Irish experience. By the time Ireland gained its independence, it had become an Anglophone country. Outside the Gaeltacht, there has been little need for Irish in one's day-to-day life. Government regulations requiring a knowledge of Irish as a condition of employment may have created incentives to learn Irish, but when, as is often the case, there is little need for Irish on the job, there is little reason to continue using Irish once one has been hired. As argued in the first chapter, material incentives outside the school probably operated in the renativization of Hebrew: nationalist fervor may have placed Hebrew in the schools but the linguistic heterogeneity of the Jewish population helped create a vernacular role for it outside the school.

The ultimate impact of the Maori revitalization movement remains to be seen. If it continues there can be little doubt that more Maori children will be proficient in Maori. But will there be great enough incentives to use the language outside the school, so that these children will continue using it when they finish their studies, or will their own children again learn Maori as a second language? That the initiative for the revitalization program has come from the Maoris themselves is an encouraging sign. One reason that efforts to preserve the population size and the regular use of Irish in the Gaeltacht have failed, according to Fennell 1981 (cited by Dorian 1987), is that the governmental promoters of maintenance made no serious attempt to promote the enthusiasm of people of the Gaeltacht themselves. The initiative came from outside. In the Maori case, there *is* local enthusiasm. But it may not be sufficient to create a role for the language outside the school.

In Ireland, the schools have created a large number of bilinguals among persons who would ordinarily be monolingual in English, but schooling has not been sufficient to translate proficiency into active use. Dorian (1987) argues, however, that even if acquisition is not translated into use, there may be considerable value in maintenance efforts. She mentions three: (1) support by community and school of a threatened language can mitigate the negative attitudes towards the language and its speakers, which typically accompany language decline and which have been internalized by speakers and potential speakers of the language; (2) language promotional efforts usually help to transmit the ethnic history and traditional lifeways which are typically threatened along with the language: "the self-awareness and self-confidence which can be gained through the recovery of such information have value in themselves, as the Black community in the United States has found and has forcefully proclaimed" (64); and (3) citing Spolsky (1978), economic benefits accrue to local communities engaged in revitalization or maintenance efforts in the form of jobs for teachers, teacher-aides, teacher-trainers, curriculum and materials developers, and so forth.

When the opportunities to learn a target language are confined chiefly to programs such as classroom instruction, we can evaluate the success of such programs in terms of the number of persons who attain given criteria of proficiency. Often, however, opportunities to learn are not confined to such organized activities. Reves' (1983) study of Arab children's acquisition of Hebrew and English, mentioned in Chapter 5, provides a striking example. As stated above, it is clear that without formal instruction these children would have been unlikely to have learned English, whereas they would probably have learned Hebrew even without the formal instruction they received. But should some weight be assigned to formal instruction as input to these students' acquisition of Hebrew? If so, how much?

The same question can be asked with respect to the Hebrew attainment of immigrants. What is the impact on acquisition that is traceable to planned procedures, in light of the tremendous incentives and opportunities to learn which the immigrant encounters in everyday life? Once Hebrew became established as the principal language of public life, was it not likely that newcomers would have learned it whether or not there were organized efforts to help them to do so? Indeed, Schmelz and Bachi (1974: 769) suggest that the number of adult immigrants who have become Hebrew speakers exceeds any reasonable estimate of the direct output, quantitatively or qualitatively, of public instruction.

But if one wanted to evaluate the effectiveness of these programs, how would one go about it? One could not compare the proficiency of those who had studied in such courses with those who had not, because the two groups would be self-selected and thus not likely to have been equivalent in the first place. If the former were more highly motivated to learn, as is likely, they probably would have attained higher proficiency than the latter even without formal instruction.

Of course these evaluational difficulties are not confined to acquisition planning. Since language planning, whether in respect to form, function, or acquisition, never occurs in a social vacuum, the difficulties for evaluating its effectiveness are considerable. It is rarely simple to determine the degree to which a given planning goal has been met. It is usually far harder to determine what factors contributed to that outcome. It is harder still to determine the relative contribution of each factor to the outcome. Students of language planning, of course, do not face this problem alone. It is common to all who would understand social planning more generally and social change more generally still. It is to social change that our attention now turns.

8

Social change

Each example of language planning which appears in this book arose in the midst of social change. With respect to our defining examples, we see that political centralization along with a growing desire for order accompanied the founding of the Académie française; increased persecution of Russian Jews, a growing Jewish nationalist movement, and rising Jewish immigration to Palestine accompanied the renativization of Hebrew; the growing participation of women in the American work force accompanied the feminist campaign against sex-bias in language usage; and a political and economic revolution accompanied the mass literacy campaign in Ethiopia. That social change accompanies language planning is scarcely surprising, inasmuch as language planning, concerned with the management of change, is itself an instance of social change. In a stable world of complete equilibrium, where each day is much like the one before and the one to come, and where all members of society are satisfied with that condition, language planning would be unlikely. Social change, the appearance of new social and cultural patterns of behavior among specific groups within a society or within the society as a whole, has been implicit throughout this book. This final chapter considers social change explicitly.

Sources of social change

What factors produce social change? The most commonly cited factors include the physical environment, population, discovery and invention, cultural diffusion, ideology, and decision-making.

1. *The physical environment.* According to Huntington (1924), societies change as geographic conditions change. He claimed that shifts in climatic conditions accounted for the successive shifts in power from Crete to Greece to Rome to Constantinople. While the volcanic eruption in the Aegean, about 1,500 BCE., which destroyed the Minoan civilization on Crete, is

a convincing example of environmental determinism, such examples are rare.

Robertson (1981) points out that most environmental factors influence change in interaction with social forces. For example, geographic crossroads such as Asia Minor have always been centers of social change. The bad management which causes soil erosion, leading in turn to economic and political decline, is another example of the interaction between the social and physical environments (LaPiere 1965: 26). Changes in the physical environment in interaction with social behavior were partly responsible for the Ethiopian revolution, which in turn led to the mass-literacy campaign. The inability of the emperor's regime to improve transport, agricultural techniques, and irrigation sufficiently to prevent the crop failure which resulted from drought, combined with the regime's unwillingness to summon international relief once the crop failed, resulted in a disastrous famine, one of the events which helped to leach imperial legitimacy and to remove the emperor from power.

2. *Population.* Substantial increases or decreases in population size, growth rates, or demographic structure influence social life. The results of the Ethiopian crop failure, for example, were exacerbated by the rise in population which had preceded it. The American "baby boom" following the Second World War provides a second example. The rising expectations for material prosperity, the increased number of children per family to support, and inflation increased economic pressure on families and thus on women to work outside the home, even when their children were young. At the same time the rising population, which increased consumer demand, fueled the prosperity which provided needed jobs for women as well as the liberal political climate which supported the feminist movement.

An example of the effects of population decline is the wholesale Irish emigration in the mid-nineteenth century (itself the result of economic exploitation, the failure of the potato crop, and the laissez-faire ideology of the English establishment), which led to the irreversible decline of the Irish language as a vernacular.

3. *Discovery and invention.* Weston (1977) believes that discovery and invention are probably the most important sources of social change. Whether or not they rank first in importance, no one denies their enormous importance as engines of social change. Discovery refers to the perception of an aspect of reality which already exists, such as the circulation of the blood, the principle of the lever, and the principle of steam power. Invention, in contrast, refers to the combination of existing elements to produce

an innovation, either material, like a can opener, or social, like the corporation (Robertson 1981). As Tarde (1903) pointed out, the more numerous the elements in a society, the greater the likelihood that existing elements will be synthesized to produce new elements. Thus inventions tend to accumulate at an accelerated rate. This is why modernization takes less time in the newly modernizing societies of today than it did in the older industrialized societies.

While invention and discovery contribute to social change, it is often difficult to attribute particular social changes to the appearance of particular innovations. The invention of movable type, for instance, and the consequent cheapening of the cost of books probably contributed to the spread of literacy and to the standardization of national languages. But other factors, such as improved transport and communication, the rise of commercial centers, and the centralization of political authority, are also likely contributors. Because innovations never arise in social or technological vacuums, their contribution to social change is usually seen in interaction with other factors.

4. *Cultural diffusion*. The discoveries, inventions, and ideas which arise in one society often spread to others. Today, there are few societies in which the influence of other societies is not present. In no social institution is cultural diffusion more evident than in language. Bilinguals, serving as agents of language change, introduce elements from one of their languages into another, influencing those monolingual speakers of the second language with whom they are in contact. Language purists may rail at the latest importations but be unconscious of elements imported so long ago as to have become nativized. Legislators, for example, who, in the early 1980s unsuccessfully introduced legislation to ban the use of loanwords in Hebrew advertisements, may have been unaware of the foreign origin of hundreds of Hebrew words imported from Greek, Latin, and Persian millennia ago. More obvious are the drastic economic, political, and cultural changes introduced by colonial powers in South America, Africa, Asia, and Oceania. Indeed, the spread of imperial languages, particularly English, as languages of science, administration, and international trade, is one of the most striking legacies of the modern colonial era.

5. *Ideas*. Ideas, beliefs, and ideologies, no less than technology, can diffuse from one society to another. When new ideas or values conflict with old ones, change may result as a consequence of efforts to reconcile them with existing views. While ideologies are a social product, as Marx claimed, there is no doubt that ideologies can themselves contribute to social change,

as Weber and Durkheim argued. Values and ideologies may spread from society to society or from subgroup to subgroup within a society.

In seventeenth-century France, the rising desire for peace, order, and civility helped prepare the ground in which the linguistic ideals promoted by the Académie française could flower. The spread of nationalist ideology, with its romantic association between language and people, promoted the renativization of Hebrew. In twentieth-century America, the spread of values associated with self-realization and individual expression helped promote the feminist campaign. The ideologies of Marxism, nationalism, and modernization helped promote the Ethiopian revolution.

6. *Decision-making.* In a sense, all social change results from decisions. People make some kinds of decision, accept some kinds of alternatives rather than others. The decisions of leaders are often pointed out as decisive determinants of social change. While the "great man" theory of history is adopted by some historians, it is rejected by most sociologists, who point out that it is history which makes individuals rather than individuals who make history: Caesar could not have destroyed the Roman Republic if it had not already been tottering; Hitler could not have come to power without the severe social and economic strains which had preceded his rise (Robertson 1981). Similarly, Richelieu's founding of the Académie française would have had little effect if the cultural and social climate had not been conducive to an ideology of correctness, refinement, and standardization in language. And Betty Friedan's *The Feminine Mystique* would have been as ineffective a catalyst for social change as Mary Wollstonecraft's *Vindication of the Rights of Woman* if the structural changes which preceded publication of Frieden's book had not led readers to accept its message and to act on it. It is the decisions of countless men and women which lead to social change.

The decision-making usually considered a source of social change does not refer, however, to all decision-making. It does not, for example, refer to the diffusion of the mass-produced automobile, which, brought within the means of middle-class consumers, spread as individuals in the hundreds, then thousands, then millions decided to buy one, thus setting in motion a vast transformation of the American cultural and economic landscape. Nor does it refer, for example, to the shift from Irish to English in Ireland, when innumerable Irish parents came to the conclusion that Irish had no future and thus decided to speak English at home (Macnamara 1971). Rather, the decisions which constitute a vital source of social change are those collective behaviors which seek to reform or revolutionize society, and those actions of social agencies and institutions which determine policies in a deliberate effort to effect social change.

Examples of social movements that we have encountered in this book are the feminist movement, the American civil-rights movement, various movements for national liberation or national renaissance, and proselytizing religious movements. Examples of policy-making by social agencies include the land reform implemented by the Ethiopian revolutionary government, the Israeli government's offer of citizenship to all Jewish immigrants, the U.S. government's promotion of its war in Vietnam, as well as many of the language-planning cases described in this book: the bilingual education policies of American federal, state, and municipal governments, the Hilfsverein der Deutschen Juden's desire to open a German-medium technical institute in Palestine before the First World War, the effort by national language academies the world over to standardize, purify, and modernize their languages, the efforts by missionary bodies and by government agencies to reduce minority languages to writing, and so on.

In sum, the forces that promote social change are many and their relationships complex. Each factor operates in a world which contains all the others. Thus theories which rely on one or another of these factors as *the* cause of social change are almost certainly wrong: "No claim that social change is determined by economic interests, ideas, personalities of particular individuals, geographic conditions, and so on, is acceptable. All such single-factor theories belong to the kindergarten stage of a social science's development. Any single factor is always interdependent with several others" (Parsons 1966: 113).

The mechanisms of social change

The discipline of sociology arose in Europe as a response to the cataclysmic changes that followed the French Revolution. The discipline arose in America as a response to the great transformations that followed the Civil War and that accompanied the Industrial Revolution. In each case, there was both an intellectual challenge to understand the mechanisms of change and a practical challenge to control or channel the change (Berger and Berger 1976). This twin challenge remains today in all the social sciences, including language planning.

Numerous theories of social change have been proposed but none is universally accepted. None successfully accounts for all types of social change nor successfully predicts it in all cases. The difficulty in constructing a successful theory of social change is twofold (Robertson 1981). First, in order to understand change, one needs to understand stability, the structure of the *status quo*. Second, the factors that promote change are many, complex, and interrelated. Identifying the relevant factors and their independent and cumulative contribution to change is a formidable task. In what follows, I briefly characterize five theoretical schools that deal with social change and indicate their relevance for language planning: evolutionary, cyclical, functionalist, conflict, and dependency theories.

Evolutionary theories

The early sociologists believed in social evolution, the idea that every society develops through a fixed series of stages, in a predetermined order, from simple origins to increasing complexity until it reaches a final stage of perfection. In the West, the idea of social progress represented a sharp break with medieval notions that social order is divinely ordained and that men and women are wretched as a consequence of humanity's fall from grace. On the contrary, the early sociologists, beginning with Comte, assumed that change means progress.

Comte proposed a three-stage sequence of social development – theological, metaphysical, positive – as a consequence of the development of human intellect through these same stages. All societies will eventually arrive at the positive stage but some will arrive sooner than others.

Spencer, who also held that societies develop through a series of fixed, immutable stages, applied Darwinian notions of evolution to human societies. According to this view, societies change as they compete for scarce resources and adapt in a process of "the survival of the fittest." The fittest, of course, were thought to be western-European societies.

Some early anthropologists, relying on reports from untrained observers in exotic locales, produced theories which claimed that all societies pass through an inevitable sequence of stages, climaxing in western civilization. Such theories were pleasing to western-Europeans in the late nineteenth century, a period of colonial expansion, for the theories justified the unpleasant facts of colonial domination.

Marx also viewed human history as a sequence of fixed stages, as one by one subordinate classes rise to overthrow their oppressors until at last the lowest and most wretched class, the industrial proletariat, will overthrow the whole system, a revolution to be followed by socialism and ultimately communism.

Today, most sociologists and anthropologists reject those determinist theories which view social change as the product of inexorable forces that shape its course in a predetermined direction. Most now hold that human influence can change the course of history through cultural diffusion, including the spread of new norms and values, and collective action.

But evolutionary notions have not entirely died. The functionalist view of social change as the result of increasing specialization, reviewed below, is an evolutionary theory in the sense that complexity is developmentally later than simplicity. In contrast to early evolutionary theories, modern functionalism claims neither that complexity is necessarily better than simplicity nor that there is any inevitability in the process.

There is, however, a modern evolutionary school that does view change as a series of stages. Unlike the early evolutionary theories, however, it is not an all-embracing theory of social change. Rather, it is confined to economic development. This is the so-called modernization school.

The best-known example of modernization theory is Rostow's (1960) "stages of economic growth." He identifies five stages of economic growth through which every society must pass in order to attain "modernity." The key stage, the third, is the "take-off" into self-sustaining growth, during which political and social structures change to permit the institutionalization of the pursuit of economic growth.

Foster-Carter (1985) reviews the chief criticisms of this theory. First, economic historians dispute Rostow's central claim that "take-off" is characterized by a spurt in investment. Second, a number of Latin-American countries whose indigenous communities were either wiped out by conquest or nonexistent in the first place did not start at Rostow's first stage, an agricultural society of pre-modern science and technology and of a rigid social structure in which status is largely fixed at birth. Third, many critics point to Rostow's failure to emphasize connections between the developing society and other societies, particularly those which are far more developed. Finally, if "take-off" can be identified only after the fact, and if development unfolds automatically, it is hard to recommend policy initiatives. Rostow's theory implicitly favors a conservative *laissez-faire* position and ignores the fact that almost all actual take-offs, except that of Britain and arguably that of the U.S.A., have been actively pursued by policies of the central government.

The criticism that Rostow's theory suggests few policy alternatives may be unjustified, inasmuch as Rostow indicates preconditions for development. These preconditions constitute the second stage of development, the stage prior to "take-off." No matter what the origin of the impulse, widespread change begins: trade and services grow, industry, particularly extractive industry, expands, the economy becomes less self-sufficient, and an elite arises that reinvests its profits. "Different groups within the 'modernization' school, as it came to be called, might differ about which particular factor or set of factors was crucial to development – for engineers, it might be harnessing new sources of energy; for educationalists, inculcating scientific attitudes in children; for biologists and medicos raising standards of health and nutrition. But for all of them, western standards and methods were the models to be imitated, and the supply of the needed factors – machinery, seeds, textbooks, medicines – would have to come from the West" (Worsley 1987: 65). Thus another criticism which might be applied to the school is that it is ethnocentric, viewing western development as both a model and a method.

For the social sciences in general and for language planning in particular, the early sociologists' global, unilinear deterministic theories are unconvincing today. Still, these theories are useful, inasmuch as they remind us that changing societies tend to become increasingly complex and that change in one part of the system is likely to involve change in other parts of the system. There are many today who would accept a multilinear, evolutionary approach which posits that societies tend to develop from simple, small-scale communities to large-scale, complex forms, that this change can occur in a number of ways, and that this change is not necessarily progress.

In spite of the criticisms leveled against it, modernization theory may be useful to language planning as both a theoretical and a practical pursuit, inasmuch as it suggests we consider two useful questions with respect to preconditions: (1) To what extent are certain preconditions necessary for successful language planning? (2) To what extent is language planning a precondition for self-sustained economic growth?

With respect to the first question, I have already suggested that corpus planning, prior to changes in the functions for which the language is used, is likely to be ineffective. It is only *after* a language begins to be used for new functions that corpus-planning activities on behalf of those functions are likely to bear fruit. Similarly, acquisition planning is unlikely to be effective if the language in question serves no useful function for the target population.

The answer to the second question, whether language planning can be regarded as an essential pre-requisite for economic development, is not so clear. Language planning is typically involved in the expansion of literacy and in the rise of educational levels in Third World countries. While it is reasonable that a relationship should exist between education and development, it has not been easy to establish the linkage between them (Foster-Carter 1985). Cipolla (1969) points out that the literacy rate was relatively high in Britain when the Industrial Revolution began, but that British literacy rates did not begin to rise thereafter until several generations had elapsed. On the other hand, the first European countries to import the Industrial Revolution from Britain invested some of their new profits immediately in basic education, so that industrialization and literacy rates ran together. Different literacy rates have been suggested as thresholds for development, but, even if one of these is correct, the time-lag between the attainment of a given rate and its effect on the economy may be variable and thus the effect difficult to determine, apart from the difficulty of isolating the effect of one variable when it operates in concert with others. Jobless school leavers are a common phenomenon in the Third World, but it is hard to know whether this results from an inappropriately large investment in education, or from the necessary time-lag which exists between the attainment of a given level of education and its effects on the economy, or because some other necessary condition is absent. "Education may well be a necessary but is certainly not a sufficient condition for development, both economically and socially. In particular, expanding education and hoping for the best is no substitute for direct measures to create jobs" (Foster-Carter 1985: 17).

Cyclical theories

Not all determinist theories of social change are linear. Some propose a cyclical pattern, emphasizing the transitory nature of human societies, which rise and fall, much like the human life cycle. This is a notion forwarded by thinkers from antiquity to the present, including Plato, Heraclitus, Ibn Khaldun, Gibbon, Leibnitz, Spengler, Toynbee, and Sorokin.

Like the early evolutionists, cyclical theorists view social change as inevitable. Unlike them, cyclical theorists believe that the end of social change is not perfection but decay (LaPiere 1965), although some, like Sorokin, posit rebirth and the beginning of the cycle anew. Cyclical theories of social change are today quite out of fashion. "A close reading of the historical record gives an impression not just of great cycles of history, but of innumerable cycles within cycles, within each of which there are still smaller cycles, such as those of the rise and fall of specific arts or ruling families; and the closer the record is read, the more confused the reader becomes, until the order that is imposed upon it by the cyclical interpretation resolves again into the chaos of a multitude of unique events" (LaPierre 1965: 22).

Curiously enough a cyclical theory of birth, growth, and decay was popular in eighteenth-century Europe as an explanation of language change, as witnessed by Johnson's equation of language change with "corruption and decay." This is not surprising in a society which emphasized Greek and Latin in formal education. The great prestige of those languages, coupled with their antiquity, led, perhaps, to the conclusion that modern European languages, not taught in school, were inferior, decadent remnants of a glorious past.

Functionalism

There are two major controversies over the nature of social change. Both date back to the nineteenth century. The first issue, whether social change is a deterministic process, the product of inexorable forces, has more or less been settled. The answer is no.

The second issue is still debated, namely whether social change is a temporary phenomenon, an abnormal condition that leads back to equilibrium, or a permanent phenomenon, a normal condition, the product of ceaseless conflict among competing interests within society (Weston 1977). The view of society as normally in equilibrium is referred to as functionalism. The view of society as a process of ceaseless competition and conflict is referred to as the conflict school.

Durkheim and Weber provided the principal foundations upon which modern functionalism is built. These sociologists turned to theories of smaller scope than those proposed by Comte, Spencer, and Marx, all-embracing theorists who tried not only to explain social change but also to predict its direction.

Durkheim tried to determine the consequences of social phenomena for the society in which they are embedded. Religion, for example, provides a common set of values which strengthen the bonds that hold believers together. Criminality, to take another of Durkheim's examples, strengthens social consensus by arousing collective indignation at the violation of the norm. Durkheim was the direct precursor of the type of analysis which dominated British anthropology under Radcliffe-Brown and Malinowski (Coser 1977).

For Durkheim, a major engine of social change was the increasing division of labor in society, caused by increasing population and accelerated by industrialization. Greater specialization of labor weakens the bonds which bind a community together. When specialization is limited, we interact with our fellows in a variety of roles. One's ties with others are all-embracing. In the idealized country town of the past, for example, the teacher of one's children was likely to be a parishioner in one's church, and it was not at all unlikely that he was also a fellow volunteer in the community's fire brigade and the conductor of the town band, in which one played the trumpet. As the specialization of labor increases, we tend to interact with others in terms of a given role relationship only. One's ties with others tend to be partial, functional, and less secure.

Durkheim called this shift the change from *mechanical* to *organic solidarity*. The latter, marked by limited relationships among most of the people with whom one comes in contact, poses the danger of a lack of secure social ties, a feeling of alienation and rootlessness, what Durkheim called *anomie*. The fragmentation of social relationships leads to the fragmentation of those common meanings which ordinarily provide coherence for an individual's life (Berger and Berger 1976).

Tönnies independently produced a formulation parallel to the shift from mechanical to organic solidarity. The transition to modernity is marked by a shift from the simple, intimate community, *Gemeinschaft*, in which ties among members are all-encompassing, to the complex, urban, impersonal center, *Gesellschaft*, in which ties among people are partial. The transition from *Gemeinschaft* to *Gesellschaft* is a process in which roles become increasingly differentiated from one another, differences among members of society grow, and people feel increasingly estranged from a system of common, overarching values.

A system of common, overarching values which give meaning to life is in essence a religious system. Durkheim's *The Elementary Forms of the Religious Life* showed that religion reflects the society in which it is grounded. Religion is a social phenomenon. Berger and Berger (1976) argue that Durkheim's book demonstrates, even more profoundly, that society is a religious phenomenon: society is based on the ultimate values shared by its members.

Whereas Durkheim viewed the transition from premodern to modern society as the shift from mechanical to organic solidarity, Weber placed the locus of change in individual action. Weber's theories of *charisma* and *rationalization*, through which individual action can transform society, have contributed enormously to our understanding of social change.

He saw charisma, the appeal of leaders who claim authority on the basis of extraordinary personal qualities, as an important revolutionary force throughout history. "Charisma subverts, disrupts, explodes existing institutional structures whether religious, political or anything else" because it denies their legitimacy (Berger and Berger 1976: 336). When charismatic movements succeed, they create new arrangements and transform old ones. Weber pointed out, however, that once a charismatic revolution succeeds, it cannot sustain itself. The informal organization which promoted the dynamic quality of charismatic leadership must be replaced by formal organizations for consolidating the revolution's gains and administering its policies. The second generation accepts as routine what the first generation, the generation of the charismatic leader, saw as new and intensely exciting. Charisma becomes, in Weber's terms, *routinized*: the charismatic leader's descendants create a dynasty or the leader's successors transfer his personal charisma to the office which they now hold. With respect to the language-planning accomplishments of the charismatic generation, the second generation tends to take them for granted.

The second mechanism whereby human action can transform society is via shifts in emphasis from one type of action to another. Modernization in the West, Weber believed, has been marked by increasing emphasis upon goal-oriented, rational action, the rational determination of both ends and means. Rationalization subverts the existing order no less than does charisma, because, like charisma, it denies the legitimacy of tradition. Unlike charisma, it does not destroy itself. "Rationality cannot be routinized. Indeed, rationalization *is* routinization" (Berger and Berger 1976: 346).

For Weber, rationality is the distinctive feature of modern, western society. It is seen especially in the growing importance of bureaucracy, characterized by hierarchical organization, division of labor, and universalistic rules. But the rationality of the West is seen also in the development of its legal systems, its science, and in its religions, particularly that of Protestantism.

The role Weber assigned to Calvinist Protestantism in the development of capitalism was designed to counter the rigid economic determinism of Marx's followers. While not denying that socioeconomic forces are engines of change, Weber held that economic processes are themselves influenced by values and beliefs. He argued that capitalism could not have developed without the Calvinist legitimation of disciplined economic activity, its emphasis on asceticism and deferred gratification, its doctrine that personal salvation is divinely predestined, and its view, developed by Calvin's later followers, that worldly success is evidence of divine favor and thus salvation. This system of beliefs encouraged hard work and the reinvestment of profits, conditions conducive to the development of capitalism. Though this theory cannot be proven, it is persuasive and enormously influential. Few social scientists today would deny the importance of values and beliefs as potential agents of social change.

Parsons was the foremost exemplar of modern functionalism. Like Durkheim, he saw social change accompanying increasing differentiation. Like Durkheim, he emphasized the role of values in regulating society. Like Weber, he argued that to understand a social system, one must examine the motivation of social actors. Unlike Weber, who stressed the reciprocal relationship between social values and social processes, Parsons saw the relationship as unidirectional, with social processes influencing social values.

In his early work (1937, 1951), Parsons stressed the conservative nature of social organization and its resistance to profound change. Society consists of a network of interdependent parts, each of which acts to maintain the system's equilibrium. A change in one part ripples through the network to affect other parts, which adjust so as to absorb disruptive shock and thus keep the whole system in balance. But this early approach did not account for, indeed did not allow, radical change either in common values or in the social system which those values control.

His later work (1961, 1966), however, attempted to reconcile the possibility of revolutionary change with the notion of society as a self-regulating system in equilibrium. According to his later work, social change does not disturb but rather alters social equilibrium. Social change produces a qualitatively new equilibrium (Robertson 1981). Change is evolutionary, producing a society increasingly more complex, as social institutions become ever more differentiated – new institutions arise to perform specialized functions which were formerly performed by a single institution, as, for example, when certain economic and socialization functions were split off from the family and reorganized in separate institutional frameworks.

But what produces differentiation? The answer, according to Parsons, is the imperfect socialization of individuals or subgroups within the system that lead some to be discontented with the allocation of societal resources or with the behavior which others expect of them. Their dissatisfaction produces social movements which, in turn, induce elites to alter those roles or structures which have produced the dissatisfaction. To reduce or remove dissatisfaction, elites differentiate new roles, which are then incorporated into the new system, values are reformulated so as to accommodate the new roles, and the new, more complex system is restored to equilibrium. Parsons believed that this procedure is gradual: it is slowed down by the weight of existing common values, which are slow to change. They change slowly because consensus holds society together. Conflict is abnormal and pathological, even if it leads to a more complex, differentiated society.

To what extent is the functionalist view consistent with what we know about language planning? Perhaps the most compelling aspect of the theory, for language-planning purposes, is the conception of values as a controlling mechanism. If society, in Berger and Berger's (1976) reading of Durkheim's view, is a religious phenomenon, anchored in and controlled by its members' common values, then these values shape planning and constrain the acceptance of planning initiatives. To the late nineteenth-century immigrants to Palestine, for example, Hebrew was an attractive choice as medium of instruction in their new schools. The choice was consistent not only with the immigrants' view of themselves as the heirs of three millennia of tradition, a tradition which justified their choice of Palestine as the site of an autonomous Jewish homeland, but also with the nineteenth-century notion that land and language are the twin foundations of nationhood. Thus the immigrants' values and beliefs led them to found Hebrew-medium schools. Similarly, the belief of the Hilfsverein's directors, that German was a language of high culture, and their desire to promote German as well as Jewish interests, led them to insist on German as the language of Palestine's first modern technical institute. And the Jewish teachers' refusal to accept the directors' decision was promoted by the teachers' nationalist values. In modern Israel, the resistance of Yiddish-speaking religious zealots to the use of Hebrew for secular purposes is consistent not only with their view of Hebrew as a holy tongue, profaned by the mundane, but also by their desire to insulate themselves from the influence of a secular, godless world.

Thus language planners would do well to consider the values of the target populations when deciding among policy alternatives and when promoting a policy once determined. The great sun theory of Turkish, mentioned in chapter six, was not only flattering to the target population's view of itself but also may have mollified Islamic sensibilities, likely to have been ruffled by the attempt to exclude Arabic and Persian loanwords. Compatibility with values and belief systems as a factor promoting the acceptance of an innovation is, of course, not confined to language. It is a consistent finding in studies of the diffusion of innovation (Katz, Levin, and Hamilton 1963; Rogers 1983).

Another aspect of functionalist theory consistent with what we know about language planning is the notion that role differentiation causes social change. New institutions, such as modern education and secular judiciary systems, often bring new languages with them. Just as functions formerly fulfilled by a single institution are now fulfilled by several, so functions fulfilled by a single language are now fulfilled by several. For example, when some of the socialization activities performed by the family were transferred to schools, the local, nonstandard dialect or local language formerly used for these socialization purposes was typically replaced by a standard dialect or by a language of wider communication, usually as a medium for texts but also frequently as a medium of instruction. If local languages continue to be used for the new institution, the language modernization which ensues is essentially a matter of elaboration, lexical, syntactic, and stylistic. And what is linguistic elaboration if not differentiation? Thus we see institutional differentiation leading to linguistic differentiation of function and of form.

The functionalist view of the interrelatedness of all parts of the system, with changes in one part rippling throughout the system to cause changes in other parts, is also consistent with what we know about language planning. A single-factor theory of language planning is no more viable than a single-factor theory of social change more generally. As the four defining examples make clear (and, I hope, most of the others as well), to understand the impetus for any given instance of language planning one must understand the general social context in which it is embedded.

Finally the modern functionalist view of society as a stable, self-regulating system is also consistent with what we know about language planning, but it is consistent only in part. Language, like society, is stable in so far as it continues to be recognizable as itself. No sirens sounded when Old English became Middle English or when Middle English became Modern English. Their transformations were as seamless and continuous as the changes from hue to hue in a rainbow. The language is English still. Speakers of modern Hebrew like to think of themselves as speaking the language that their ancestors spoke in Palestine more than 2,000 years ago. In a sense they are right. But only in a sense. Speakers of Biblical

Hebrew would encounter considerable difficulty understanding the Hebrew of their modern descendants.

Conflict theory

If functionalist theory concentrates on the forces which integrate society and hold it together, conflict theory concentrates on the tensions which disrupt it and pull it apart. Conflict theorists view prolonged equilibrium as an abnormal state of affairs. For them, change is normal. According to conflict theory, change results from the competing interests and values of different subgroups within society as each contends with the others for power. Although Marx was not the first conflict theorist (he was preceded by the seventeenth-century philosopher Thomas Hobbes, who viewed the state as a mechanism for preventing the "war of all against all"), he remains the greatest and most influential of them.

For Marx, conflict is generated by tension between competing economic interests. In the words of the *Communist Manifesto* (1848): "All history is the history of class conflict," i.e. the conflict between the exploited and their exploiters. Conflict arises because the technological means of production change faster than the patterns of class relationships that are organized around the means of production. Feudalism, which bound peasants to the land, was overthrown by capitalism, which requires the free movement of labor. In the current pattern of class relationships, capitalists' ownership of the means of production and their control of government enables owners to exploit the industrial proletariat by retaining surplus value, that portion of production not necessary for the workers' own survival. When the industrial proletariat develops class consciousness and revolts against its oppressors, the existing system will be destroyed. In place of the present government, controlled by capitalists for their own benefit, a government by and for the workers will arise. While Marx viewed this evolution as an inexorable process, he believed that human agency could speed it along. His call for revolution and his justification of revolution explain in part his theory's attraction to revolutionary counterelites.

Dahrendorf (1959), the most influential of modern conflict theorists, believes that conflict is not limited to competition between classes. Conflict can arise between other social groups as well – racial, ethnic, religious, and national. Social change, in his view, can result from tensions between any two groups with conflicting interests. Conflict is so endemic to society that every element is a potential contributor to social change. It is not control over the means of production which causes conflict but rather power itself. Private ownership may be abolished, but power inequalities will always remain. Those in power try to maintain those arrangements, including the dominant value system, which enable them to control the distribution of "what there is to get," both material and nonmaterial. At the same time, those without such power struggle to change those arrangements. He believes that the functionalist assumption of shared common values supposes an unrealistic degree of cultural homogeneity. For Dahrendorf and other modern conflict theorists, it is not common values but coercion which underlies order in society.

Another influential conflict theorist was Mills (1956, 1959), who saw modern society as dominated by a political, military, and economic elite, a "power elite" that creates and maintains, via manipulation, mass acceptance of its rule. Modernization, according to Mills, has concentrated greater power in the hands of this elite and has correspondingly reduced the political power of the mass. This view has been challenged by other theorists who see the conflicting interests of competing elites as a factor which moderates elite power.

The assumption that conflict is endemic to society is consistent with the cases of language planning which appear in this book. Each can be explained, at least in part, as a consequence of power struggles, with the "haves" trying to maintain or fine-tune the existing system and the "have nots" trying to alter the system to increase their own power. The assumption that conflict is so endemic that any element is a potential source of social change is also consistent with our knowledge of language planning. We have seen that women, blacks, homosexuals, and Jews, for example, have taken language-policy initiatives which cannot be wholly explained in economic terms. The assumption of pansocietal conflict is also consistent with Labov's (1972) claim that linguistic change can originate in any sector of society. His data suggest that language change originates with lower, as well as upper, socioeconomic strata and with various ethnic and religious groups. Change often begins within a group as a consequence of its contact with other groups, which stimulates the former to exaggerate features of its own speech as a marker of group solidarity and distinctiveness or to exaggerate, through "overcorrection," the linguistic features of an admired outgroup. The covert prestige of nonstandard linguistic forms, found by Labov (1963, 1966) and Trudgill (1972), is consistent with the assumption that conflict involves the clash of ideologies between the dominated and those who dominate.

In evaluating conflict theory, Robertson (1981) claims that it offers a compelling analysis of significant historical events and contemporary processes such as the overthrow of feudalism by capitalism, the civil rights movement in the U.S.A., and continuing changes in race relations. But, he claims, conflict theory has little to tell us about the dramatic rate of social change brought about by technological development, changes in forms of family organization, or the future direction of social change. It may be that we need functionalist theory as well as conflict theory for an adequate explanation of social change, if indeed a comprehensive theory of social change is possible.

Dependency theory

Dependency theory is a less comprehensive theory of social change. Like modernization theory, described above in connection with evolutionary theories of social change, dependency theory focuses upon the economic development of the Third World. Unlike modernization theory, which views less developed countries as moving along a road to greater development, dependency theory views less developed countries as moving along a dead-end road, a road to nowhere (Foster-Carter 1985). Less developed countries, in this view, are not undeveloped. Rather, they are under-developed, less developed than they would be if they did not exist in a world with the developed, industrial powers.

Dependency theorists maintain that capitalism must be analyzed as a single, world system. The development of the West and the underdevelopment of the Third World can only be understood as consequences of each other. The developed West, in other words, bought its development at the expense of the Third World. Western capitalism developed not only through expropriating the surplus value of its own workers but also by exploiting its colonies, forcing the latter to serve as sources of cheap labor and raw materials and as a captive market for its manufactured goods. Colonization created an international system of stratification, with the metropolitan countries in the role of the ruling class and the colonies in the role of the exploited classes, a system which, in this view, has changed little with the political separation of metropolitan countries from their former colonies.

The best-known representative of the dependency school is Frank (1967), whose key term, "the development of underdevelopment" is the counterpart to Rostow's "take-off" (Foster-Carter 1985). Frank's metaphor of "metropolis–satellite" relations characterizes the world capitalist system, a chain which links dominant to peripheral states via a set of semi-peripheral states. The semi-peripheral states are both exploiters and exploited. They suffer exploitation by the dominant states while simultaneously exploiting the peripheral states as well as the peripheries within their own states, much as the middle class is exploited by the ruling class while benefitting from the exploitation of the workers. Surplus value is expropriated at every level and sent upwards and outwards. The whole chain is a rip-off (Foster-Carter 1985).

According to dependency theory, underdevelopment is the result of the satellites' subordinate position in the world system. The currently developed countries, undeveloped at the outset, never suffered economic exploitation by other powers. They were never underdeveloped.

Dependency theory has been criticized on several grounds. Among those reviewed by Foster-Carter (1985) and Etzioni-Halevy (1981) are the following: There has been real economic growth in at least some Third World countries; colonialism introduced at least some progressive social changes; there may be internal obstacles to growth independent of, or in addition to, the economic distortions imposed by metropolitan powers; a world-system theory does not explain the "upward mobility" of nations like Canada; and a world-system framework in which the communist world and the oil-exporting states have no adequate place is problematic.

Are the insights provided by dependency theory relevant to language planning? Dependency theory suggests at least one question: to what extent is Third-World dependency fostered by the promotion of English and other metropolitan languages as languages of education, science, administration, trade, and intranational communication within Third-World countries? Dependency theorists have criticized modern education in the Third World as fostering cultural dependency and "an isolated and rootless elite infected by individualism, over-identifying with the West, hence ignorant and scornful of (or in any case cut off from) their own societies" (Foster-Carter 1985: 182). The use of metropolitan languages as media for secondary and tertiary education allies Third-World elites to the West and drives another wedge between them and the masses, who have little access to those languages.

Much money and effort are involved in teaching young people enough of a metropolitan language so that they might benefit from instruction via that language. In fact, the average level of attainment in those languages is often so poor that attainment is jeopardized in subject-matter courses in which those languages serve as medium. This in turn may reduce the ability of graduates to contribute to their nations' economic development. Graduates who do master the metropolitan language may be tempted to emigrate to the metropolitan country. In the meantime, the Third-World country provides a market for language-teaching texts and for services provided in the metropolitan language (including those of metropolitan experts in language teaching). It is also possible that the use of the metropolitan language within Third World countries improves the competitive position of metropolitan exporters to those countries.

On the other hand, the use of local languages may be even more unpalatable. In linguistically heterogeneous Third-World countries the use of a metropolitan language for intranational purposes may be perceived locally as placing every ethnolinguistic group at an equal disadvantage (whether true or not) – an alternative usually preferred to giving one group an advantage by using its language only. The use of numerous local languages is usually impractical. Further, at least some people must learn a metropolitan language insofar as one is needed for international communication.

Finally, metropolitan languages are becoming at least marginally indigen-
ized, locally colored by local contexts, the products of the periphery as
well as the center (see Kachru 1986 for a study of non-native Englishes).

Is a theory of language planning possible?

Weston (1977) asserts that there has been a movement away from the
search for a single general theory of social change and that sociologists
have begun to build theories of smaller scope that apply to specific segments
of society. She suggests that this tendency may lead to separate theories
of political change, organizational change, demographic change, and so
on. Is a theory of language planning possible?

A theory of language planning would enable us to explain language-
planning initiatives, the means chosen to effect the goals, and the outcomes
of the implementation. We would understand, in other words, the motivation for setting particular status, corpus, and acquisition goals and for
choosing particular means and the reasons that the means do or do not
effect the goals within a given social context.

Such a theory seems as far from our grasp as the philosopher's stone
and the elixir of youth. It is unattainable, at least at our present level
of competence, not only because language planning is such a complex
activity, influenced by numerous factors – economic, ideological, political,
etc. – and not only because it is directed toward so many different status,
corpus, and acquisition goals, but more fundamentally because it is a tool
in the service of so many different latent goals such as economic modernization, national integration, national liberation, imperial hegemony, racial,
sexual, and economic equality, the maintenance of elites, and their replacement by new elites.

That language planning should serve so many covert goals is not surprising. Language is the fundamental institution of society, not only because
it is the first institution experienced by the individual but also because
all other institutions are built upon its regulatory patterns (Berger and
Berger 1976). To plan language is to plan society. A satisfactory theory
of language planning, therefore, awaits a satisfactory theory of social
change.

9

Summary and conclusions

After offering four defining examples of language planning and discussing various views of the field, I defined language planning as deliberate efforts to influence the behavior of others with respect to the acquisition, structure, or functional allocation of their language codes. I argued that descriptive frameworks can help us to formulate testable propositions about language planning, and I offered frameworks from four academic disciplines. Drawing upon those frameworks, I discussed in turn each of the three primary foci of language planning: status planning, corpus planning, and acquisition planning. Finally, I discussed language planning in terms of various theories of social change.

Based on this tour of language planning as a field of inquiry and as a practical endeavor, I offer the following generalizations:

1. Language planning is a widespread and long-standing practice. It is neither new nor confined principally to developing or under-developed countries.
2. Language planning cannot be understood apart from its social context or apart from the history which produced that context.
3. Language planning is typically motivated by efforts to secure or maintain interests, material or nonmaterial or both. There is nothing peculiar to language planning in this. In the struggle to promote interests one uses whatever ammunition is at hand.
4. Language planning may be initiated at any level of a social hierarchy, but it is unlikely to succeed unless it is embraced and promoted by elites or by counterelites.
5. Neither elites nor counterelites are likely to embrace the language-planning initiatives of others unless they perceive it to be in their own interest to do so.
6. Language planning is not necessarily initiated by persons for whom language is a principal focus. Language planning is initiated not only

183

by writers, poets, linguists, language teachers, lexicographers, and translators, but also by missionaries, soldiers, legislators, and administrators.

7. Elites influence both the evaluation and the distribution of language varieties within a community. They influence evaluation through status planning and distribution through acquisition planning. Status planning influences the evaluation of a language variety by assigning it to the functions from which its evaluation derives. Whereas status planning is an effort to regulate the demand for given verbal resources, acquisition planning is an effort to regulate the distribution of those resources.

8. If language planning serves elites and counterelites, it may also serve the mass, particularly insofar as it strengthens the individual's sense of dignity, self-worth, social connectedness, and ultimate meaning as a member of a group linked both to the past and to the future.

9. Whereas it is in the interest of established elites to promote acceptance of a standard, it is in the interest of counterelites to promote the acceptance of a counterstandard.

10. When counterelites seek to detach a periphery from a center and when existing elites try to keep the periphery from falling away, they promote collective symbols of affiliation. To the extent that standard languages serve as such a symbol, we can expect elites and counterelites to try to establish them if they do not already exist.

11. Language standardization is more likely to be successful with respect to attitude than with respect to behavior. People, that is, are more likely to agree that an all-purpose preferred variety exists than to use it for all the purposes for which they claim it to be correct.

12. Political democratization or increased political participation exerts pressure to increase access to literacy. This may lead either to reducing the gap between spoken and written varieties or to increasing access to formal education, or to both.

13. If language planning is, in some circumstances, a necessary condition for economic development, it is unlikely to be a sufficient condition.

14. Increasing differentiation of social institutions promotes the differentiation of linguistic function and linguistic form.

15. Language policy alternatives which are consistent with the values and belief systems of the target population are more likely to succeed than alternatives which conflict with those values and beliefs.

16. Corpus planning prior to changes in the functions for which a language is used is unlikely to be effective. It is only after a language begins to be used for new functions that corpus planning on behalf of those functions is likely to be effective.

17. Acquisition planning is unlikely to be effective if the language in question serves no useful function for the target population.

18. Language planning, concerned with the management of change, is itself an instance of social change. When established elites seek to extend their influence or to resist the incursions of rivals, when counterelites seek to overthrow the *status quo*, and when new elites seek to consolidate their power, we find pressure for language planning. We also find pressure stemming from ideological and technological changes, which sometimes motivate and sometimes reflect shifts in political and economic arrangements.

19. Language planning contributes both to continuity and change, not only in the target language but also in other social institutions. Language planning contributes to change by promoting new functional allocations of language varieties, structural changes in those varieties, and acquisition of those varieties by new populations. Language planning contributes to stability because it is constrained by the target language's structural requirements and by the values which the language variety represents to its speakers.

20. Language planning is carried out at all levels of organizational hierarchies. The implementation of decisions taken at higher levels of authority requires smaller-scale decisions at lower levels of authority.

21. Successful language planning is seldom a one-shot affair. Implementation of a decision may require repeated efforts by planners to cope with the resistance of those they seek to influence.

22. It is difficult to evaluate the effectiveness of language planning – to determine either the degree to which goals are satisfied or the relative contribution of various factors to the outcome.

23. Language planning rarely conforms to a rational paradigm of decision-making or problem-solving.

24. A theory which enables us to explain the motivation for setting particular status, corpus, and acquisition goals, the reasons for choosing (or avoiding) given means for attaining these goals, and the outcome of the implementation is far from our grasp. It probably awaits a satisfactory theory of social change.

Notes

1 My chief sources for the establishment of the Académie française were Auchincloss (1972); Boulenger (1963); Burckhardt (1940); Church (1972); Elliott (1984); Lough (1954); Maland (1970); Mandrou (1975); O'Connell (1980); Tapié (1974); Treasure (1972); and Wiley (1967).

2 I am grateful to Clifford Prator for suggesting that a language academy be the focus of one of the defining examples.

3 For the feminist case study, my chief sources were Carden (1974); Chafe (1975); Cooper (1984); Friedan (1963); Grossman (1982); Mellor and Stamas (1982); O'Neill (1969); Norwood (1985); and Rytina (1982a, 1982b).

4 The data presented in that study were gathered and analyzed by Patty Daggy, Hilde Dewulf, Elizabeth Kimmel, Margaret Kirk, Sylvia Norris, Rita M. Purcell, Keith Walters, and myself.

5 Ellen Spolsky (personal communication) forcibly made this point to me.

6 My principal sources for the Ethiopian case study were Baissa (1979); Bender, Bowen, Cooper, and Ferguson (1976); Bereket (1980); Erlich (1979); Gilkes (1975); Harbeson (1979); Legum and Lee (1977); Niguse and Bender (1984); Ottaway (1982); Ottaway and Ottaway (1978); and Ullendorf (1965).

7 The countries surveyed were Uganda (Ladefoged, Glick, and Criper 1971), Kenya (Whiteley 1974), Ethiopia (Bender, Bowen, Cooper, and Ferguson 1976), Zambia (Ohannessian and Kashoki 1978), and Tanzania (Polomé and Hill 1980).

References

Abir, Mordechai. 1980. *Ethiopia and the Red Sea: the rise and decline of the Solomonic dynasty and Muslim-European rivalry in the region.* London: Frank Cass.

Ackoff, Russell L. 1978. *The Art of Problem Solving: accompanied by Ackoff's fables.* New York: John Wiley.

Afendras, Evangelos A. 1969. Sociolinguistic history, sociolinguistic geography and bilingualism. In Second International Congress of Social Sciences of the Luigi Sturzo Institute, *International Days of Sociolinguistics*. Rome: Luigi Sturzo Institute, pp. 663–682.

Alford, Robert. 1969. *Bureaucracy and Participation: political culture in four Wisconsin cities.* Chicago: Rand McNally.

Alisjahbana, S. Takdir. 1976. *Language Planning and Modernization: the case of Indonesian and Malaysian.* The Hague: Mouton.

Allen, J. P. B., Bernard Spolsky, and H. G. Widdowson. 1980. Aims. *Applied Linguistics*, 1(1): inside back cover.

Altoma, Salih J. 1970. Language education in Arab countries and the role of the academies. In Thomas A. Sebeok (Ed.), *Current Trends in Linguistics*. The Hague: Mouton. Vol 6, pp. 690–720.

Ansre, Gilbert. 1971. Language standardisation in sub-Saharan Africa. In Thomas A. Sebeok (Ed.), *Current Trends in Linguistics*. The Hague: Mouton. Vol. 7, pp. 680–698.

Apte, Mahadev L. 1976(a). Language controversies in the Indian parliament (Lok Sabha): 1952–1960. In William M. O'Barr and Jean F. O'Barr (Eds.), *Language and Politics*. The Hague: Mouton, pp. 213–234.

1976(b). Multilingualism in India and its sociopolitical implications: an overview. In William M. O'Barr and Jean F. O'Barr (Eds.), *Language and Politics*. The Hague: Mouton, pp. 141–164.

Auchincloss, Louis. 1972. *Richelieu*. London: Michael Joseph.

Bachi, Roberto. 1977. *The Population of Israel*. Jerusalem: Institute of Contemporary Jewry, Hebrew University of Jerusalem, in conjunction with the Demographic Center of the Prime-Minister's Office in Israel.

Baissa, Marilyn Hall. 1979. Civil-military elite interaction in the Ethiopian revolution: the role of students. In Robert L. Hess (Ed.), *Proceedings of the Fifth*

International Conference on Ethiopian Studies: session B, April 13-16, *Chicago, USA*, pp. 771-782.

Basso, Keith H. and Ned Anderson. 1973. A western Apache writing system: the symbols of Silas John. *Science*, 180: 1013-1022.

Bate, Walter Jackson. 1975. Storming the main gate: the *Dictionary. Samuel Johnson*. New York: Harcourt Brace Jovanovich, pp. 240-260.

Bauer, Raymond A. 1968. The study of policy formation: an introduction. In Raymond A. Bauer and Kenneth J. Gergen (Eds.), *The Study of Policy Formation*. New York: The Free Press.

Baugh, Albert C. and Thomas Cable. 1978. *A History of the English Language*. Third edition. Englewood Cliffs: Prentice-Hall.

Beebe, Leslie and Howard Giles. 1984. Speech-accommodation theories: a discussion in terms of second-language acquisition. *International Journal of the Sociology of Language*, 46: 5-32.

Bender, M. Lionel. 1986. Ethiopian language policy 1974-81. *Anthropological Linguistics* 27: 273-279.

Bender, M. Lionel, J. Donald Bowen, Robert L. Cooper, and Charles A. Ferguson (Eds.). 1976. *Language in Ethiopia*. London: Oxford University Press.

Bereket Habte Selassie. 1980. *Conflict and Intervention in the Horn of Africa*. New York: Monthly Review Press.

Berg, Marinus E. van den. 1985. *Language Planning and Language Use in Taiwan: a study of language choice behavior in public settings*. Dordrecht: ICG Printing.

Berger, Peter L. and Brigitte Berger. 1976. *Sociology: a biographical approach*. Revised edition. Harmondsworth: Penguin Books.

Berry, Jack. 1958. The making of alphabets. In Eva Siversten (Ed.), *Proceedings of the Eighth International Congress of Linguists*. Oslo: Oslo University Press, pp. 752-764.

   1977. "The making of alphabets" revisited. In Joshua A. Fishman (Ed.), *Advances in the Creation and Revision of Writing Systems*. The Hague: Mouton, pp. 3-16.

Billigmeier, Jon-Christian. 1987. Alphabets. *The Encyclopedia of Religion*. New York: Macmillan. Vol. 1, pp. 216-222.

Blanc, Haim. 1968. The Israeli koine as an emergent national standard. In Joshua A. Fishman, Charles A. Ferguson, and Jyotirindra Das Gupta (Eds.), *Language Problems of Developing Nations*. New York: Wiley, pp. 237-251.

Bloomfield, Leonard. 1942. Linguistics and reading. *Elementary English Review*, 19(4): 125-130; 19(5): 183-186.

Bloomfield, Morton W. and Leonard Newmark. 1963. *A Linguistic Introduction to the History of English*. New York: Alfred A. Knopf.

Boix, Emili. 1985. The "Norma" campaign in Catalonia: an attempt to influence interethnic language etiquette. Unpublished seminar paper, Linguistic Society of America Summer Institute, Georgetown University.

Bolinger, Dwight L. 1946. Visual morphemes. *Language*, 22: 333-340.

Boone, Lalia P. 1949. Patterns of innovation in the language of the oil field. *American Speech*, 24: 31-37.

Boulenger, Jacques. 1963. *The Seventeenth Century in France*. New York: Capricorn Books.

Brim, O. G. Jr., D. C. Glass, D. E. Lavin, and N. Goodman. 1962. *Personality and Decision Processes*. Stanford: Stanford University Press.

Brosnahan, L. F. 1963. Some historical cases of language imposition. In John Spencer (Ed.), *Language in Africa*. Cambridge: Cambridge University Press, pp. 7–24.

Burckhardt, Carl J. 1940. *Richelieu and His Age: his rise to power*. Translated and abridged by Edwin and Willa Muir. London: George Allen and Unwin. First published in German as *Richelieu: Der Aufsteig zur Macht*, Munich, 1935.

Byron, Janet. 1976. *Selection among Alternates in Language Standardization: the case of Albanian*. The Hague: Mouton.

Calvet, Louis-Jean. 1982. The spread of Mandingo: military, commercial, and colonial influence on a linguistic datum. In Robert L. Cooper (Ed.), *Language Spread: studies in diffusion and social change*. Bloomington: Indiana University Press in cooperation with the Center for Applied Linguistics, Washington, pp. 184–197.

Carden, Maren Lockwood. 1974. *The New Feminist Movement*. New York: Russell Sage Foundation.

Chafe, William H. 1975. The paradox of progress. In James T. Patterson (Ed.), *Paths to the Present*. Minneapolis: Burgess, pp. 8–24.

Chen, Matthew Y. and William S-Y. Wang. 1975. Sound change: actuation and complementation. *Language*, 51: 255–281.

Chisholm, Lawrence James. 1980. Weights and measures. *Encyclopedia Britannica*, Macropedia Vol. 19, pp. 728–735.

Chomsky, Carol. 1970. Reading, writing, and phonology. *Harvard Educational Review*, 40: 287–309.

Chomsky, Noam. 1970. Phonology and reading. In Harry Levin and Joanna P. Williams (Eds.). *Basic Studies on Reading*. New York: Basic Books, pp. 3–18.

Church, William F. 1972. *Richelieu and Reason of State*. Princeton: Princeton University Press.

Cipolla, Carlo M. 1969. *Literacy and Development in the West*. Harmondsworth: Penguin Books.

Cobarrubias, Juan and Joshua A. Fishman (Eds.). 1983. *Progress in Language Planning: international perspectives*. Berlin: Mouton.

Cooper, Robert L. 1979. Language planning, language spread, and language change. In James E. Alatis and G. Richard Tucker (Eds.). *Georgetown University Round Table on Languages and Linguistics 1979*. Washington: Georgetown University Press, pp. 23–50.

1982(a). A framework for the study of language spread. In Robert L. Cooper (Ed.), *Language Spread: studies in diffusion and social change*. Bloomington: Indiana University Press in cooperation with the Center for Applied Linguistics, Washington, pp. 5–36.

(Ed.). 1982(b). *Language Spread: studies in diffusion and social change*. Bloomington: Indiana University Press in cooperation with the Center for Applied Linguistics, Washington.

1984. The avoidance of androcentric generics. *International Journal of the Sociology of Language*, 50: 5–20.

1985. Selling language reform. In Deborah Tannen and James E. Alatis (Eds.), *Georgetown University Round Table on Languages and Linguistics 1985*. Washington: Georgetown University Press, pp. 275–281.

Cooper, Robert L. and Fern Seckbach. 1977. Economic incentives for the learning of a language of wider communication. In Joshua A. Fishman, Robert L. Cooper, and Andrew W. Conrad, *The Spread of English: the sociology of English as an additional language*. Rowley: Newbury House, pp. 212–219.

Coser, Lewis. 1977. *Masters of Sociological Thought: ideas in historical and social context*. Second edition. New York: Harcourt Brace Jovanovich.

Culley, W. T. and F. J. Furnivall (Eds.). 1890. *Caxton's Eneydos 1490: Englisht from the French Liure des Eneydes, 1483*. London: N. Trubner and Co.

Dahrendorf, Ralf. 1959. *Class and Class Conflict in Industrial Society*. London: Routledge and Kegan Paul. Translated, revised, and expanded by the author. First published in German in 1957 as *Soziale Klassen und Klassenkonflikt in der industriellen Gesellschaft*.

Dalby, David. 1967. A survey of the indigenous scripts of Liberia and Sierra Leone: Vai, Mende, Loma, Kpelle and Bassa. *African Language Studies*, 8: 1–51.

1968. The indigenous scripts of West Africa and Surinam: their inspiration and design. *African Language Studies*, 9: 156–197.

Daoud, Mohamed. 1987. Arabization in Tunisia: the tug of war. Unpublished seminar paper, Program in Applied Linguistics, University of California at Los Angeles.

Daoust-Blais, Denise. 1983. Corpus and status language planning in Quebec: a look at linguistic education. In Juan Cobarrubias and Joshua A. Fishman (Eds.), *Progress in Language Planning: international perspectives*. Berlin: Mouton, pp. 207–234.

Das Gupta, Jyotirindra. 1970. *Language Conflict and National Development: group politics and national language policy in India*. Berkeley: University of California Press.

1973. Language planning and public policy: analytical outline of the policy process related to language planning in India. In Roger Shuy (Ed.), *Report of the Twenty-Third Annual Round Table Meeting on Linguistics and Language Studies*. Washington: Georgetown University Press, pp. 157–165.

Davis, Alva L. and Raven I. McDavid. 1949. "Shivaree": an example of cultural diffusion. *American Speech*, 24: 249–255.

Deutsch, Karl W. 1942. The trend of European nationalism – the language aspect. *American Political Science Review*, 36: 533–541.

Dorian, Nancy C. 1987. The value of language-maintenance efforts which are unlikely to succeed. *International Journal of the Sociology of Language*, 68: 57–67.

Durkacz, Victor Edward. 1983. *The Decline of the Celtic Languages: a study of linguistic and cultural conflict in Scotland, Wales and Ireland from the Reformation to the twentieth century.* Edinburgh: John Donald.

Dye, Thomas R. and John S. Robey. 1980. "Politics versus economics": development of the literature on policy determination. In Thomas R. Dye and Virginia Gray (Eds.), *The Determinants of Public Policy.* Lexington: Lexington Books (D. Heath and Co.), pp. 3-17.

Dyste, Connie Diane. 1987. Proposition 63: the California English language amendment. Unpublished masters essay, Department of English (TESL), University of California at Los Angeles.

Easton, David. 1968. Political science. *International Encyclopedia of the Social Sciences,* 12: 282-298.

Edelman, Martin, Robert L. Cooper, and Joshua A. Fishman. 1968. The contextualization of schoolchildren's bilingualism. *Irish Journal of Education,* 2: 106-111.

Edwards, George C. III and Ira Sharkansky. 1978. *The Policy Predicament: making and implementing public policy.* San Francisco: W. H. Freeman.

Edwards, Ward and Amos Tversky. 1967. Introduction. In Ward Edwards and Amos Tversky (Eds.), *Decision Making: selected readings.* Harmondsworth: Penguin Books, pp. 7-10.

Elliott, J. H. 1984. *Richelieu and Olivares.* Cambridge: Cambridge University Press.

Ellsworth, John W. and Arthur A. Stahnke. 1976. *Politics and Political Systems: an introduction to political science.* New York: McGraw-Hill.

Engle, Patricia. 1975. Language medium in early school years for minority language groups. *Review of Educatonal Research,* 45: 283-325.

Erlich, Haggai. 1979. The establishment of the Derg: the turning of a protest movement into a revolution. In Robert L. Hess (Ed.), *Proceedings of the Fifth International Conference on Ethiopian Studies: Session B, April 13-16, Chicago, USA.* Chicago: University of Chicago at Chicago Circle, pp. 761-769.

Etzioni-Halevy, Eva. 1981. *Social Change: the advent and maturation of modern society.* London: Routledge and Kegan Paul.

Fainberg, Yaffa Allony. 1983. Linguistic and sociodemographic factors influencing the acceptance of Hebrew neologisms. *International Journal of the Sociology of Language,* 41: 9-40.

Fellman, Jack. 1973. Concerning the "revival" of the Hebrew language. *Anthropological Linguistics,* 15: 250-257.

1974. *The Revival of a Classical Tongue: Eliezer Ben Yehuda and the Modern Hebrew Language.* The Hague: Mouton.

1977. The Hebrew Academy: orientation and operation. In Joan Rubin, Björn H. Jernudd, Jyotirindra Das Gupta, Joshua A. Fishman, and Charles A. Ferguson (Eds.), *Language Planning Processes.* The Hague: Mouton, pp. 97-109.

Fellman, Jack and Joshua A. Fishman. 1977. Language planning in Israel: solving terminological problems. In Joan Rubin, Björn H. Jernudd, Jyotirindra Das Gupta, Joshua A. Fishman, and Charles A. Ferguson (Eds.), *Language Planning Processes.* The Hague: Mouton, pp. 79-95.

Fennell, D. 1981. Can a shrinking linguistic minority be saved? In E. Haugen,

J. D. McClure, and D. Thompson (Eds.), *Minority Languages Today*. Edinburgh: Edinburgh University Press, pp. 32-39.

Ferguson, Charles A. 1959. Diglossia. *Word*, 15: 325-340.

1962. The language factor in national development. In Frank A. Rice (Ed.), *Study of the Role of Second Languages in Asia, Africa, and Latin America*. Washington: Center for Applied Linguistics of the Modern Language Association of America, pp. 8-14. First published in *Anthropological Linguistics*, 1962, 4(1): 23-27.

1966. National sociolinguistic profile formulas. In William Bright (Ed.), *Sociolinguistics: proceedings of the UCLA Sociolinguistics Conference, 1964*. The Hague: Mouton, pp. 309-324.

1967. St. Stefan of Perm and applied linguistics. In *To Honor Roman Jakobson: essays on the occasion of his seventieth birthday, 11 October 1966*. The Hague: Mouton, Vol. 1, pp. 643-653.

1968. Language development. In Joshua A. Fishman, Charles A. Ferguson, and Jyotirindra Das Gupta (Eds.), *Language Problems of Developing Nations*. New York: John Wiley and Sons, pp. 27-35.

1971. Applied linguistics. *Language Structure and Language Use: essays by Charles A. Ferguson*. Selected and introduced by Anwar S. Dil. Stanford: Stanford University Press, pp. 135-147. First published in Robert G. Mead (Ed.), *Language Teaching: broader contexts*. Menasha: The Northeast Conference on the Teaching of Foreign Languages, 1966, pp. 50-58.

1983. Language planning and language change. In Juan Cobarrubias and Joshua A. Fishman (Eds.), *Progress in Language Planning: international perspectives*. Berlin: Mouton, pp. 29-40.

Ferguson, Charles A. and John J. Gumperz. 1960. Introduction. In Charles A. Ferguson and John J. Gumperz (Eds.), *Linguistic Diversity in South Asia: studies in regional, social and functional variation*. Bloomington: Indiana University Research Center in Anthropology, Folklore, and Linguistics, pp. 1-18.

Fillmore, Lily Wong, Paul Ammon, Barry McLaughlin, and Mary Sue Ammon. 1985. *Final Report for Learning English through Bilingual Instruction*. Submitted to the National Institute of Education. Berkeley and Santa Cruz: University of California.

Fillmore, Lily Wong and Concepción Valadez. 1986. Teaching bilingual learners. In Merlin C. Wittrock (Ed.), *Handbook of Research on Teaching*. Third edition. New York: Macmillan, pp. 648-685.

Fischer, John L. 1958. Social influence in the choice of a linguistic variant. *Word*, 14: 47-56.

Fisherman, Haya. 1972. The "official languages" of Israel: their status in law and police attitudes and knowledge concerning them. *Language Behavior Papers*, 1: 3-23.

Fishman, Joshua A. 1964. Language maintenance and language shift as a field of inquiry. *Linguistics*, 9: 32-70.

1971. The sociology of language: an interdisciplinary social science approach to language in society. In Joshua A. Fishman (Ed.), *Advances in the Sociology of Language*. The Hague: Mouton, Vol. 1, pp. 217-404.

1972(a). Language maintenance and language shift as a field of inquiry: revisited. *Language in Sociocultural Change: essays by Joshua A. Fishman.* Selected and introduced by Anwar S. Dil. Stanford: Stanford University Press, pp. 76–134.

1972(b). *Language and Nationalism: two integrative essays.* Rowley: Newbury House. (Ed.). 1974(a). *Advances in Language Planning.* The Hague: Mouton.

1974(b). Language modernization and planning in comparison with other types of national modernization and planning. In Joshua A. Fishman (Ed.), *Advances in Language Planning.* The Hague: Mouton, pp. 79–102.

1976. *Bilingual Education: an international sociological perspective.* With an appendix by E. Glyn Lewis. Rowley: Newbury House.

1977. Advances in the creation and revision of writing systems. In Joshua A. Fishman (Ed.), *Advances in the Creation and Revision of Writing Systems.* The Hague: Mouton, pp. xi–xxviii.

1982. Attracting a following to high-culture functions for a language of everyday life: the role of the Tshernovits language conference in the "rise of Yiddish". In Robert L. Cooper (Ed.), *Language Spread: studies in diffusion and social change.* Bloomington: Indiana University Press in cooperation with the Center for Applied Linguistics, Washington, pp. 291–320.

1983. Modeling rationales in corpus planning: modernity and tradition in images of the good corpus. In Juan Cobarrubias and Joshua A. Fishman (Eds.), *Progress in Language Planning: international perspectives.* Berlin: Mouton, pp. 107–118.

1985. Macrosociolinguistics and the sociology of language in the early eighties. *Annual Review of Sociology,* 11: 113–127.

Fishman, Joshua A., Robert L. Cooper, and Roxana Ma. 1971. *Bilingualism in the Barrio.* Bloomington: Language Science Monographs, Indiana University.

Fishman, Joshua A., Robert L. Cooper, and Andrew W. Conrad. 1977. *The Spread of English: the sociology of English as an additonal language.* Rowley: Newbury House.

Fishman, Joshua A., Robert L. Cooper, and Yehudit Rosenbaum. 1977. English around the world. In Joshua A. Fishman, Robert L. Cooper, and Andrew W. Conrad. *The Spread of English: the sociology of English as an additional language.* Rowley: Newbury House, pp. 77–107.

Fitzgerald, C. P. 1954. *China: a short cultural history.* Fourth revised edition. New York: Frederick A. Praeger.

Foster, Philip J. 1971. Problems of literacy in sub-Saharan Africa. In Thomas A. Sebeok (Ed.), *Current Trends in Linguistics,* 7: 587–617.

Foster-Carter, Aidan. 1985. The sociology of development. In Michael Haralambos (Ed.), *Sociology: new directions.* Ormskirk: Causeway Press, pp. 1–213.

Frank, Andre Gunder. 1967. *Capitalism and Underdevelopment in Latin America: historical studies of Chile and Brazil.* New York: Monthly Review Press.

1969. *Capitalism and Underdevelopment in Latin America.* New York: Monthly Review Press.

Frey, Frederick Ward. 1980. Political power. *Encyclopedia Britannica.* 15th edition. Macropedia 14: 697–702.

Friedan, Betty. 1963. *The Feminine Mystique.* New York: Norton.

Frohock, Fred M. 1979. *Public Policy: scope and logic*. Englewood Cliffs: Prentice-Hall.

Fuchs, Victor R. 1986. Sex differences in economic well-being. *Science*, 232: 459–464.

Fussell, Paul. 1971. Writing a dictionary. *Samuel Johnson and the Life of Writing*. New York: Norton, pp. 181–215.

Gallagher, Charles F. 1968. North African problems and prospects: language and identity. In Joshua A. Fishman, Charles A. Ferguson, and Jyotirindra Das Gupta (Eds.), *Language Problems of Developing Nations*. New York: John Wiley, pp. 129–150.

    1971. Language reform and social modernization in Turkey. In Joan Rubin and Björn H. Jernudd (Eds.), *Can Language Be Planned? sociolinguistic theory and practice for developing nations*. Honolulu: The University Press of Hawaii, pp. 157–178.

Geerts, G., J. van den Broeck, and A. Verdoodt. 1977. Successes and failures in Dutch spelling reform. In Joshua A. Fishman (Ed.), *Advances in the Creation and Revision of Writing Systems*. The Hague: Mouton, pp. 179–245.

Germani, Gino. 1980. Industrialization and modernization. *Encyclopedia Britannica*, Macropedia 9: 520–527.

Giles, Howard. 1980. Accommodation theory: some new directions. *York Papers in Linguistics*, 9: 105–136.

    (Ed.). 1984. *The Dynamics of Speech Accommodation*. Special issue, *International Journal of the Sociology of Language*, 46.

Giles, Howard, Anthony Mulac, James J. Bradac, and Patricia Johnson. 1987. Speech accommodation theory: the first decade and beyond. In M. L. McLaughlin (Ed.), *Communication Yearbook 10*. Beverly Hills: Sage, pp. 13–48.

Giles, Howard and Philip M. Smith. 1979. Accommodation theory: optimal levels of convergence. In Howard Giles and Robert N. St. Clair (Eds.), *Language and Social Psychology*. Oxford: Blackwell, pp. 45–65.

Gilkes, Patrick. 1975. *The Dying Lion: feudalism and modernization in Ethiopia*. London: Julian Friedmann Publishers.

Gorman, Thomas P. 1973. Language allocation and language planning in a developing nation. In Joan Rubin and Roger Shuy (Eds.), *Language Planning: current issues and research*. Washington: Georgetown University Press, pp. 72–82.

Grossman, Allyson Sherman. 1982. More than half of all children have working mothers. *Monthly Labor Review*, 105.

Gudschinksy, Sarah C. 1957. *Handbook of Literacy*. Revised edition. Norman: Summer Institute of Linguistics.

    1959. Recent trends in primer construction. *Fundamental and Adult Education*, 11: 67–96.

Gumperz, John J. 1958. Dialect differences and social stratification in a north Indian village. *American Anthropologist*, 60: 668–681.

Hall, Robert A. Jr. 1951. American linguistics, 1925–1950. *Archivum Linguisticum*, 4(1): 1–16; (2): 41–43.

Harbeson, James W. 1979. Toward a political theory of the Ethiopian revolution.

In Robert L. Hess (Ed.), *Proceedings of the Fifth International Conference on Ethiopian Studies: Session B, April 13–16, Chicago, USA*, pp. 819–829.

Harding, Edith and Philip Riley. 1987. *The Bilingual Family: a handbook for parents.* Cambridge: Cambridge University Press.

Haugen, Einar. 1959. Planning for a standard language in modern Norway. *Anthropological Linguistics*, 1(3): 8–21.

1961. Language planning in modern Norway. *Scandinavian Studies*, 33: 68–81.

1965. Construction and reconstruction in language planning: Ivar Aasen's grammar. *Word*, 21(2): 188–207.

1966. Linguistics and language planning. In William Bright (Ed.), *Sociolinguistics: proceedings of the UCLA Sociolinguistics Conference, 1964.* The Hague: Mouton, pp. 50–71.

1969. Language planning, theory and practice. In A. Graur (Ed.), *Actes du Xe Congres International des Linguistes: Bucarest, 28 Août – 2 Septembre 1967.* Bucarest: Éditions de L'Académie de la République Socialiste de Roumanie. Vol. 1, pp. 701–711.

1971. Instrumentalism in language planning. In Joan Rubin and Björn H. Jernudd (Eds.), *Can Language Be Planned? sociolinguistic theory and practice for developing nations.* Honolulu: The University Press of Hawaii, pp. 281–289.

1983. The implementation of corpus planning: theory and practice. In Juan Cobarrubias and Joshua A. Fishman (Eds.), *Progress in Language Planning: international perspectives.* Berlin: Mouton, pp. 269–289.

Heath, Shirley Brice and Richard Laprade. 1982. Castilian colonization and indigenous languages: the cases of Quechua and Aymara. In Robert L. Cooper (Ed.), *Language Spread: studies in diffusion and social change.* Bloomington: Indiana University Press in cooperation with the Center for Applied Linguistics, Washington, pp. 118–147.

Henze, Paul B. 1977. Politics and alphabets in inner Asia. In Joshua A. Fishman (Ed.), *Advances in the Creation and Revision of Writing Systems.* The Hague: Mouton, pp. 371–420.

Heyd, Uriel. 1954. *Language Reform in Modern Turkey.* Jerusalem: Israel Oriental Society.

Hofman, John E. 1974(a). The prediction of success in language planning: the case of chemists in Israel. *International Journal of the Sociology of Language*, 1: 39–65.

1974(b). Predicting the use of Hebrew terms among Israeli psychologists. *International Journal of the Sociology of Language*, 3: 53–65.

Hudson, Kenneth. 1978. *The Language of Modern Politics.* London: Macmillan.

Huntington, Ellsworth. 1924. *Climate and Civilization.* Third edition. New Haven: Yale University Press.

International African Institute. 1962. First published in 1930. *Practical Orthography of African Languages.* Memorandum 1. Second edition. Oxford: Oxford University Press.

Irvine, Judith T. 1978. Wolof noun classification: the social setting of divergent change. *Language in Society*, 7: 37–64.

Jernudd, Björn H. 1977(a). Linguistic sources for terminological innovation. In

Joan Rubin, Björn H. Jernudd, Jyotirindra Das Gupta, Joshua A. Fishman, and Charles A. Ferguson (Eds.), *Language Planning Processes*. The Hague: Mouton, pp. 215-236.

1977(b). Prerequisites for a model of language treatment. In Joan Rubin, Björn H. Jernudd, Jyotirindra Das Gupta, Joshua A. Fishman, and Charles A. Ferguson (Eds.), *Language Planning Processes*. The Hague: Mouton, pp. 41-54.

1983. Evaluation of language planning – what has the last decade accomplished? In Juan Cobarrubias and Joshua A. Fishman (Eds.), *Progress in Language Planning: international perspectives*. Berlin: Mouton, pp. 345-378.

Jernudd, Björn H. and Jyotirindra Das Gupta. 1971. Towards a theory of language planning. In Joan Rubin and Björn H. Jernudd (Eds.), *Can Language Be Planned?: sociolinguistic theory and practice for developing nations*. The Hague: Mouton, pp. 195-215.

Jernudd, Björn H. and Jiří V. Neustupný. 1986. Language planning: for whom? Comments presented at the International Colloquium on Language Planning in Ottowa (Canada), May 1986.

Kachru, Braj B. 1986. *The Alchemy of English: the spread, functions and models of non-native Englishes*. Oxford: Pergamon Press.

Kapuściński, Ryszard. 1983. *The Emperor: downfall of an autocrat*. Translated by William R. Brand and Katarzyna Mroczkowska-Brand. New York: Harcourt Brace Jovanovich. First published in Polish as *Cesarz* in 1978.

Karam, Francis X. 1974. Toward a definition of language planning. In Joshua A. Fishman (Ed.), *Advances in Language Planning*. The Hague: Mouton, pp. 103-124.

Katz, Elihu. 1957. The two-step flow of communication: an up-to-date report on an hypothesis. *Public Opinion Quarterly*, 21: 61-78.

Katz, Elihu, Martin L. Levin, and Herbert Hamilton. 1963. Traditions of research on the diffusion of innovation. *American Sociological Review*, 28: 237-252.

Kloss, Heinz. 1967. "Abstand languages" and "ausbau languages". *Anthropological Linguistics*, 9(7): 29-41.

1969. *Research Possibilities on Group Bilingualism: a report*. Quebec: International Center for Research on Bilingualism.

Koeper, H. F. 1980. Sullivan, Louis. *Encyclopedia Britannica*. Macropedia Vol. 17, pp. 794-797.

Kotei, S. I. A. 1972. The West African autochthonous alphabets: an exercise in comparative palaeography. *Ghana Social Science Journal*, 2(1): 98-110.

Kotler, Philip and Sidney J. Levy. 1969. Broadening the concept of marketing. *Journal of Marketing*, 33 (January): 10-15.

Kotler, Philip and Gerald Zaltman. 1971. Social marketing: an approach to planned social change. *Journal of Marketing*, 35 (July): 3-12.

Krapp, George Philip. 1913. Standards of speech and their values. *Modern Philology*, 11: 57-70.

Kroch, Anthony. 1978. Toward a theory of social dialect variation. *Language in Society*, 7: 17-36.

Kwock-Ping Tse, John. 1986. Standardization of Chinese in Taiwan. *International Journal of the Sociology of Language*, 59: 25–32.

Labov, William. 1963. The social motivation of a sound change. *Word*, 19: 273–309.
1966. *The Social Stratification of English in New York City*. Washington: Center for Applied Linguistics.
1968. The reflection of social processes in linguistic structures. In Joshua A. Fishman (Ed.), *Readings in the Sociology of Language*. The Hague: Mouton, pp. 240–251.

Ladefoged, Peter, Ruth Glick, and Clive Criper. 1971. *Language in Uganda*. Nairobi: Oxford University Press.

Lambert, Wallace E. and G. Richard Tucker. 1972. *Bilingual Education of Children: the St. Lambert experiment*. Rowley: Newbury House.

LaPiere, Richard T. 1965. *Social Change*. New York: McGraw-Hill.

Lasswell, Harold D. 1936. *Politics: who gets what, when, how*. New York: McGraw-Hill.

Latham, Earl. 1980. Political science. *Encyclopedia Britannica*. Macropedia. Vol. 14, pp. 702–707.

Lazarsfeld, Paul F. and Robert K. Merton. 1949. Mass communication, popular taste, and organized social action. In William Schramm (Ed.), *Mass Communications*. Urbana: University of Illinois Press, pp. 459–480.

Legum, Colin and Bill Lee. 1977. *Conflict in the Horn of Africa*. New York: Africana Publishing Company.

Leichter, Howard. 1975. *Political Regime and Public Policy in the Philippines*. DeKalb: Center for Southeast Asian Studies.
1979. *A Comparative Approach to Policy Analysis: health care policy in four nations*. Cambridge: Cambridge University Press.

Leonard, Sterling Andrus. 1929. *The Doctrine of Correctness in English Usage 1700–1800*. Madison: University of Wisconsin Studies in Language and Literature. No. 25.

Lévi-Strauss, Claude. 1969. A writing lesson. *Tristes Tropiques*. Translated by John Russell. New York: Atheneum, pp. 286–297. First published in French by Librairie Plon, 1955.

Lewis, E. Glyn. 1972. *Multilingualism in the Soviet Union: aspects of language policy and its implementation*. The Hague: Mouton.
1982. Movements and agencies of language spread: Wales and the Soviet Union compared. In Robert L. Cooper (Ed.), *Language Spread: studies in diffusion and social change*. Bloomington: Indiana University Press in cooperation with the Center for Applied Linguistics, Washington, pp. 214–259.
1983. Implementation of language planning in the Soviet Union. In Juan Cobarrubias and Joshua A. Fishman (Eds.), *Progress in Language Planning: international perspectives*. Berlin: Mouton, pp. 309–326.

Lieberson, Stanley. 1970. *Language and Ethnic Relations in Canada*. New York: John Wiley and Sons.
1982. Forces affecting language spread: some basic propositions. In Robert L. Cooper (Ed.), *Language Spread: studies in diffusion and social change*. Bloom-

ington: Indiana University Press in cooperation with the Center for Applied Linguistics, Washington, pp. 37–62.

Lindblom, Charles. 1959. The science of muddling through. *Public Administration Review*, 19: 9–88.

Louckx, Freddy. 1978. Linguistic ambivalence of the Brussels indigenous population. *International Journal of the Sociology of Language*, 15: 53–60.

Lough, John. 1954. *An Introduction to Seventeenth Century France*. London: Longmans, Green.

Lowenberg, Peter H. 1983. Lexical modernization in Bahasa Indonesia: functional allocation and variation in borrowing. Studies in the Linguistic Sciences, 13(2): 73–86.

MacCarthy, P. A. D. 1964. Criteria for a new orthography for English. In David Abercrombie, D. B. Fry, P. A. D. MacCarthy, N. C. Scott, and J. L. Trim (Eds.), *In Honour of Daniel Jones: papers contributed on the occasion of his eightieth birthday 12 September 1961*. London: Longmans, Green and Co.

Mackey, William F. 1983. Language status policy and the Canadian experience. In Juan Cobarrubias and Joshua A. Fishman (Eds.), *Progress in Language Planning: international perspectives*. Berlin: Mouton, pp. 173–206.

Macnamara, John. 1966. *Bilingualism and Primary Education: a study of Irish experience*. Edinburgh: Edinburgh University Press.

  1971. Successes and failures in the movement for the restoration of Irish. In Joan Rubin and Björn H. Jernudd (Eds.), *Can Language Be Planned? sociolinguistic theory and practice for developing nations*. Honolulu: The University Press of Hawaii, pp. 65–94.

Maland, David. 1970. *Culture and Society in Seventeenth-Century France*. New York: Charles Scribner's Sons.

Mandrou, Robert. 1975. *Introduction to Modern France 1500–1640: an essay in historical psychology*. London: Edward Arnold.

Markee, Numa Piers Philip. 1986. Unpublished prospectus for a dissertation in applied linguistics: an appropriate technology model of communicative course design. Submitted to the Applied Linguistics Program, University of California at Los Angeles.

  1988. An appropriate technology model of communicative course design. Unpublished doctoral dissertation submitted to the Program in Applied Linguistics, University of California at Los Angeles.

Mazrui, Ali A. 1975. *The Political Sociology of the English Language: an African perspective*. The Hague: Mouton.

Mazrui, Ali A. and Pio Zirimu. 1978. Church, state and marketplace in the spread of Kiswahili: comparative educational implications. In Bernard Spolsky and Robert L. Cooper (Eds.), *Case Studies in Bilingual Education*. Rowley: Newbury House, pp. 427–453.

McAdam, E. L. Jr. and George Milne. 1963. *Johnson's Dictionary: a modern selection*. New York: Pantheon Books.

McCarthy, E. Jerome. 1968. *Basic Marketing: a managerial approach*. Third edition. Homewood: Richard D. Irwin.

McGuire, William J. 1969. The nature of attitudes and attitude change. In Gardner

Lindzey and Elliot Aronson (Eds.), *The Handbook of Social Psychology*. Second edition. Reading: Addison-Wesley. Vol. 3, pp. 136–314.

McKnight, George H. 1929. *Modern English in the Making*. New York: D. Appleton.

Mellor, Earl F. and George D. Stamas. 1982. Usual weekly earnings: another look at intergroup differences and basic trends. *Monthly Labor Review*, 105(4): 15–24.

Miller, George A. 1950. Language engineering. *Journal of the Acoustical Society of America*, 22(6): 720–725.

Mills, C. Wright. 1956. *The Power Elite*. New York: Oxford University Press.

1959. *The Sociological Imagination*. New York: Oxford University Press.

Milroy, James and Lesley Milroy. 1985. *Authority in Language: investigating language prescription and standardisation*. London: Routledge and Kegan Paul.

Misra, Bal Govind. 1982. Language spread in a multilingual setting: the spread of Hindi as a case study. In Robert L. Cooper (Ed.), *Language Spread: studies in diffusion and social change*. Bloomington: Indiana University Press in cooperation with the Center for Applied Linguistics, Washington, pp. 148–157.

Moulton, William G. 1980. Germanic languages. *Encyclopedia Britannica*. Macropedia Vol. 8, pp. 15–25.

Neustupný, Jiří V. 1970. Basic types of treatment of language problems. *Linguistic Communications*, 1: 77–98.

1983. Towards a paradigm for language planning. *Language Planning Newsletter*, 9(4): 1–4.

Nida, Eugene A. 1954. Practical limitations to a phonemic alphabet. *The Bible Translator*, 15 (January–April): 35–39, 58–62.

Niguse Abbebe and M. Lionel Bender. 1984. The Ethiopian Language Academy: 1943–1974. *Northeast African Studies*, 6(3): 1–7.

Norwood, Janet L. 1985. Perspectives on comparable worth: an introduction to the numbers. *Monthly Labor Review*, 108(12): 3–4.

Noss, Richard. 1967. *Language Policy and Higher Education*. Vol. 3, part 2 of *Higher Education and Development in Southeast Asia*. Paris: UNESCO and the International Association of Universities.

Nurullah, Syed and J. P. Naik. 1951. *A History of Education in India (during the British Period.)* With a foreword by Zakir Husain. Second edition. Bombay: Macmillan.

O'Barr, William M. and Jean F. O'Barr (Eds.). 1976. *Language and Politics*. The Hague: Mouton.

O'Connell, Daniel Patrick. 1980. Richelieu, Cardinal de. *Encyclopedia Brittanica*. Fifteenth edition. Macropedia Vol. 15, pp. 830–834.

O'Dell, Felicity Ann. 1978. *Socialization through Children's Literature: the Soviet example*. Cambridge: Cambridge University Press.

Ohannessian, Sirarpi and Mubanga E. Kashoki (Eds.). 1978. *Language in Zambia*. London: International African Institute.

Ó Murchú, Máirtín. 1977. Successes and failures in the modernization of Irish spelling. In Joshua A. Fishman (Ed.), *Advances in the Creation and Revision of Writing Systems*. The Hague: Mouton, pp. 267–289.

O'Neill, William L. 1969. *The Woman Movement: feminism in the United States and England*. London: George Allen and Unwin.

Ottaway, Marina. 1982. *Soviet and American Influence in the Horn of Africa*. New York: Praeger.

Ottaway, Marina and David Ottaway. 1978. *Ethiopia: empire in revolution*. New York: Africana Publishing Company.

Parsons, Talcott. 1937. *The Structure of Social Action: a study in social theory with special reference to a group of recent European writers*. New York: McGraw-Hill.

   1951. *The Social System*. Glencoe: The Free Press.

   1961. Some considerations on the theory of social change. *Rural Sociology*, 26: 219–239.

   1966. *Societies: evolutionary and comparative perspectives*. Englewood Cliffs: Prentice-Hall.

Pike, Kenneth L. 1947. *Phonemics: a technique for reducing language to writing*. Ann Arbor: University of Michigan Press.

Polomé, Edgar C. and Clifford P. Hill (Eds.). 1980. *Language in Tanzania*. London: Oxford University Press.

Pool, Ithiel de Sola. 1973. Communication systems. In Ithiel de Sola Pool, F. W. Frey, W. Schramm, N. Maccoby, and E. B. Parker (Eds.), *Handbook of Communication*. Chicago: Rand McNally, pp. 3–26.

Rabin, Chaim. 1973. *A Short History of the Hebrew Language*, Jerusalem: The Jewish Agency.

   1983. The sociology of Hebrew neologisms. *International Journal of the Sociology of Language*, 41: 41–56.

   1985. Massorah and "ad litteras". *Hebrew Studies*, 26(1): 81–91.

Rabin, Chaim and I. M. Schlesinger. 1974. The influence of different systems of Hebrew orthography on reading efficiency. In Joshua A. Fishman (Ed.), *Advances in Language Planning*. The Hague: Mouton, pp. 555–571.

Rao, L. J. 1971. Generalizations about the diffusion of innovations. In Everett M. Rogers and F. Floyd Shoemaker, *Communication of Innovations: a cross-cultural approach*. Second edition. New York: Free Press. Appendix A.

Ray, Punya Sloka. 1963. *Language Standardization: studies in prescriptive linguistics*. The Hague: Mouton.

Regev, Zina. 1983. Language cultivation in the field of registers: a case study in language planning within the school system. Unpublished doctoral dissertation presented to the Hebrew University of Jerusalem. (In Hebrew)

Reskin, Barbara F. (Ed.). 1984. *Sex Segregation in the Workplace: trends, explanations, remedies*. Washington: National Academy Press.

Reves, Thea. 1983. What makes a good language learner? Personal characteristics contributing to successful language acquisition. Unpublished doctoral dissertation submitted to The Hebrew University of Jerusalem. (In Hebrew)

Ring, J. A. 1985. When the Buem worked together for the written word. Unpublished seminar paper, Linguistic Society of America Summer Institute, Georgetown University.

Robertson, Ian. 1981. *Sociology.* Second edition. New York: Worth.

Rogers, Everett M. 1983. *Diffusion of Innovations.* Third edition. New York: Free Press.

Rogers, Everett M. and F. Floyd Shoemaker. 1971. *Communication of Innovations: a cross-cultural approach.* Second edition. New York: Free Press.

Rogers, Everett M., Linda Williams, and Rhonda B. West. 1977. *Bibliography of the Diffusion of Innovations.* Council of Planning Librarians Exchange Bibliography 1420, 1421, and 1422. Monticello: Council of Planning Librarians.

Rostow, Walt W. 1960. *The Stages of Economic Growth: a non-communist manifesto.* Cambridge: Cambridge University Press.

Rubin, Joan. 1971. Evaluation and language planning. In Joan Rubin and Björn H. Jernudd (Eds.), *Can Language Be Planned? sociolinguistic theory and practice for developing nations.* Honolulu: The University Press of Hawaii, pp. 217–252.

1977(a). Indonesian language planning and education. In Joan Rubin, Björn H. Jernudd, Jyotirindra Das Gupta, Joshua A. Fishman, and Charles A. Ferguson (Eds.), *Language Planning Processes.* The Hague: Mouton, pp. 111–129.

1977(b). Language standardization in Indonesia. In Joan Rubin, Björn H. Jernudd, Jyotirindra Das Gupta, Joshua A. Fishman, and Charles A. Ferguson (Eds.), *Language Planning Processes.* The Hague: Mouton, pp. 157–179.

1983. Evaluating status planning: what has the past decade accomplished? In Juan Cobarrubias and Joshua A. Fishman (Eds.), *Progress in Language Planning: international perspectives.* Berlin: Mouton, pp. 329–343.

1985. Review of Carol M. Eastman, Language Planning: an introduction. *Language in Society,* 14: 137–141.

Rubin, Joan and Björn H. Jernudd (Eds.). 1971(a). *Can Language Be Planned? sociolinguistic theory and practice for developing nations.* Honolulu: The University Press of Hawaii.

1971(b). Introduction: language planning as an element in modernization. In Joan Rubin and Björn H. Jernudd (Eds.), *Can Language Be Planned? sociolinguistic theory and practice for developing nations.* Honolulu: The University Press of Hawaii, pp. xiii–xxiv.

1977. *References for Students of Language Planning.* Honolulu: East–West Culture Learning Institute.

Rubin, Joan, Björn H. Jernudd, Jyotirindra Das Gupta, Joshua A. Fishman, and Charles A. Ferguson (Eds.). 1977. *Language Planning Processes.* The Hague: Mouton.

Rubin, Joan and Roger Shuy (Eds.). 1973. *Language Planning: current issues and research.* Washington: Georgetown University Press.

Rytina, Nancy F. 1982(a). Earnings of men and women: a look at specific occupations. *Monthly Labor Review,* 105(4): 25–31.

1982(b). Tenure as a factor in the male–female earnings gap. *Monthly Labor Review,* 105(4): 32–34.

Sanborn, Henry. 1964. Pay differences between men and women. *Industrial and Labor Relations Review,* 17: 534–550.

Schmelz, Uziel O. and Roberto Bachi. 1974. Hebrew as everyday language of the Jews in Israel – statistical appraisal. In American Academy for Jewish Research, *Salo Wittmayer Baron Jubilee Volume: on the occasion of his eightieth birthday*. New York: Columbia University Press. English section. Vol. 2, pp. 745–785.

Scotton, Carol Myers. 1972. *Choosing a Lingua Franca in an African Capital*. Edmonton and Champaign: Linguistic Research, Inc.

Scribner, Sylvia and Michael Cole. 1981. *The Psychology of Literacy*. Cambridge: Cambridge University Press.

Segers, Jan and Jef van den Broeck. 1972. Bilingual education programs in the Belgian province of Limburg. *Sociolinguistics Newsletter*, 3(2): 15–16.

Sharkansky, Ira. 1968. *Spending in the American States*. Chicago: Rand McNally.

Sjoberg, Andrée F. 1964. Writing, speech, and society. In Horace Lunt (Ed.), *Proceedings of the Ninth International Congress of Linguists*. The Hague: Mouton, pp. 892–897.

   1966. Socio-cultural and linguistic factors in the development of writing systems for preliterate peoples. In William Bright (Ed.), *Sociolinguistics: proceedings of the UCLA Sociolinguistics Conference, 1964*. The Hague: Mouton, pp. 260–276.

Sledd, James H. and Gwin J. Kolb. 1955. *Dr. Johnson's Dictionary: essays in the biography of a book*. Chicago: The University of Chicago Press.

Smalley, William A. and others. 1964. *Orthography Studies: articles on new writing systems*. London: United Bible Societies in cooperation with the North-Holland Publishing Co., Amsterdam.

Spenser, Edmund. 1949 [1596]. A vewe of the present state of Irelande, discoursed by way of a dialogue betweene Eudoxos and Irenius. In Rudolf Gottfried (Ed.), *Spenser's Prose Works*. Volume 9 of Edwin Greenlaw, Charles Grosvenor Osgood, Frederick Morgan Padelford, and Ray Heffner (Eds.), *The Works of Edmund Spenser: a variorum edition*. Baltimore: The John Hopkins Press, pp. 39–231.

Spolsky, Bernard. 1977. The establishment of language education policy in multilingual societies. In Bernard Spolsky and Robert L. Cooper (Eds.), *Frontiers of Bilingual Education*. Rowley: Newbury House, pp. 1–21.

   1978. American Indian bilingual education. In Bernard Spolsky and Robert L. Cooper (Eds.), *Case Studies in Bilingual Education*. Rowley: Newbury House, pp. 332–361.

   1987. Maori bilingual education and language revitalization. Ramat-Gan: Bar-Ilan University. Unpublished paper.

Stewart, William. 1968. A sociolinguistic typology for describing national multilingualism. In Joshua A. Fishman (Ed.), *Readings in the Sociology of Language*. The Hague: Mouton, pp. 531–545. Revised version of An outline of linguistic typology for describing multilingualism. In Frank A. Rice (Ed.), *Study of the Role of Second Languages in Asia, Africa, and Latin America*. Washington: Center for Applied Linguistics of the Modern Language Association of America, 1962, pp. 15–25.

Strachey, Lytton. 1986. *Eminent Victorians*. Harmondsworth: Penguin Books. First published in 1918 by Chatto and Windus.

Tapié, Victor-L. 1974. *France in the Age of Louis XIII and Richelieu.* Translated and edited by D. McN. Lockie. London: Macmillan. First published in French as *La France de Louis XIII et de Richelieu.* Paris: Flammarion, 1967.

Tarde, Gabriel de. 1903. *The Laws of Imitation.* New York: Holt.

Tauli, Valter. 1968. *Introduction to a Theory of Language Planning.* Uppsala: Almqvist and Wiksell.

    1974. The theory of language planning. In Joshua A. Fishman (Ed.), *Advances in Language Planning.* The Hague: Mouton, pp. 49–67.

Thorburn, Thomas. 1971. Cost-benefit analysis in language planning. In Joan Rubin and Björn H. Jernudd (Eds.), *Can Language Be Planned? sociolinguistic theory and practice for developing nations.* Honolulu: The University Press of Hawaii, pp. 251–262.

Treasure, Geoffrey R. R. 1972. *Cardinal Richelieu and the Development of Absolutism.* New York: St. Martin's Press.

Trudgill, Peter. 1972. Sex, covert prestige and linguistic change in the urban British English of Norwich. *Language in Society,* 1: 179–195.

Ullendorff, Edward. 1965. *The Ethiopians: an introduction to country and people.* Second edition. London: Oxford University Press.

UNESCO. 1953. *The Use of Vernacular Languages in Education: the report of the UNESCO meeting of specialists, 1951.* Paris: UNESCO.

U.S. Bureau of the Census. 1974. *Statistical Abstract of the United States: 1974.* Washington: U.S. Government Printing Office.

    1982. *Statistical Abstract of the United States: 1982–83.* Washington: U.S. Government Printing Office.

    1984. *Statistical Abstract of the United States: 1985.* Washington: U.S. Government Printing Office.

Venezky, Richard L. 1977. Principles for the design of practical writing systems. In Joshua A. Fishman (Ed.), *Advances in the Creation and Revision of Writing Systems.* The Hague: Mouton, pp. 37–54. First published in *Anthropological Linguistics,* 1970, 12(7): 256–270.

Warner, Kenneth E. 1974. The need for some innovative concepts of innovation: an examination of research on the diffusion of innovation. *Policy Sciences,* 5: 433–451.

Weinreich, Uriel. 1963. *Languages in Contact: findings and problems.* With a preface by André Martinet. The Hague: Mouton. Originally printed as Number 1 in the series Publications of the Linguistic Circle of New York. New York, 1953.

Weinstein, Brian. 1980. Language planning in Francophone Africa. *Language Problems and Language Planning,* 4(1): 55–77.

    1982. Noah Webster and the diffusion of linguistic innovations for political purposes. *International Journal of the Sociology of Language,* 38: 85–108.

    1983. *The Civic Tongue: political consequences of language choices.* New York: Longman.

Welty, Eudora. 1985. *One Writer's Beginnings: the William E. Massey Sr. lectures in the history of civilization 1983.* New York: Warner Books.

Weston, Louise. 1977. *The Study of Society*. Second edition. Guilford: The Dushkin Publishing Group.

Whiteley, Wilfred H. (Ed.). 1974. *Language in Kenya*. Nairobi: Oxford University Press.

Wildavsky, Aaron. 1964. *Politics of the Budgetary Process*. Boston: Little Brown.
   1979. *Speaking Truth to Power: the art and craft of policy analysis*. Boston: Little Brown.

Wiley, W. L. 1967. The French Academy. *The Formal French*. Cambridge: Harvard University Press, pp. 84–107.

Wollstonecraft, Mary. 1792. *A Vindication of the Rights of Woman*. London: Joseph Johnson. Republished: Carol H. Poston (Ed.). 1976. New York: Norton.

Worsley, Peter. 1987. Development. In Peter Worsley (Ed.), *Sociology*. Third edition. Harmondsworth: Penguin Books, pp. 48–83.

Wyld, Henry Cecil. 1920. *A History of Modern Colloquial English*. Oxford: Basil Blackwell.

Index

Wiley, W. L., 186, 204
Williams, Linda, 59, 201
Wilmington, 147
Wollstonecraft, Mary, 15, 167, 204
women's liberation movement, *see* feminist
   movement
workplace, 118-19
World, 146
World Bank, 94
World War II, 143
Worsley, Peter, 170, 204
writing: function, 143; skill, 128

writing systems, 33, 60, 125-31, 154
Wyld, Henry Cecil, 146, 204

Yiddish, 11, 14, 115, 128, 176
you, 152-3
Yugoslavia, 149

Zaltman, Gerald, 72, 196
Zambia, 186
Zirimu, Pio, 99, 105-6, 117, 198
Zobo, Wido, 130-1